Anthology of Non-Fiction

Barbara Bleiman, Sabrina Broadbent
and Michael Simons

Edited by Barbara Bleiman, Sabrina Broadbent and Michael Simons

Activities by Barbara Bleiman and Sabrina Broadbent
Additional material by Jenny Grahame and Michael Simons

Designed by Liz Elwin
Cover by Dave Bradshaw, Push Design
Printed by Redwood Books, Trowbridge Wiltshire

© The English and Media Centre 1995
136 Chalton Street, London NW1 1RX
ISBN 0 907016 12 X

Acknowledgements

We wish to thank the following who have kindly given permission for the use of copyright material:

Victor Gollancz for *Fever Pitch* by Nick Hornby; *Private Eye* for 'Madonna's Diary' by Craig Brown in *Rear Columns Collected Diaries of the Famous*; William Hodge & Co Ltd, for 'The Day of Execution', an extract from *Trial of Craig and Bentley* (1954) ed Montgomery Hyde in *Notable British Trials* series; extract from *The Great Railway Bazaar* by Paul Theroux (1975) reproduced by permission of the publishers Hamish Hamilton Ltd; material from *I Know Why the Caged Bird Sings* by Maya Angelou is reproduced by kind permission of the publishers, Virago Press; *The Guardian Source Book* for 'Drugs', *The Guardian* ©; extract from *The Bog People* by P V Glob and 'The Tollund Man' from *Wintering Out* both published by Faber and Faber Ltd; Phil Redmond Enterprises Ltd for 'The Brutal Truth' by Phil Redmond; Random House UK Ltd for extract from *An Evil Cradling* by Brian Keenan; David Higham Associates for extract from *Distant Voices* by John Pilger, published by Vintage; Reed Consumer Books for extract from *The Lost Continent* by Bill Bryson published by William Heinemann Ltd; *The Guardian* for 'A Response to Germaine Greer' by David Belton; Random House UK Ltd. for extract from *If This is A Man* by Primo Levi; *The Independent* for 'Klondyke Kate' by Liza Cody.

We have made every effort to obtain copyright permission. We would be grateful to hear from anyone we have been unable to contact.

Contents

Style and Culture

Travel

Argument

Autobiography

Reportage

Information

Political and Legal Documents

Letters

Introduction

The National Curriculum requires that pupils should be introduced to a wide variety of non-fiction texts that 'show quality in language use and portray information, issues and events relating to contemporary life or past experience in ways that are interesting and challenging'.

Most teachers of English would accept the importance of pupils' entitlement to experience a range of significant non-fiction texts during their time in school. However, finding such texts and making them accessible and interesting to their students can be rather more daunting. The shared story is a daily experience in most primary classrooms and, by the time they reach secondary school, most children have developed a familiarity with the codes and conventions of narrative and many will have become confident readers of narrative and writers of their own narratives. By contrast, many children can go through their primary and early secondary education with little direct or explicit study of non-fiction texts and genres. Whilst they encounter non-fiction texts in their daily lives and in their content-based school subjects, studying how they work *as texts*, through explorations of genre, language, voice, audience and purpose, has traditionally had a much lower profile in the English classroom than literary study. In this anthology we have attempted to give non-fiction texts an accessible and prominent place in the English curriculum. The selection here represents a variety of genres, voices, times, cultures, attitudes and issues. The writing is vigorous, powerful and sustained and should be read aloud, just as one might a short story or a class novel. The activities at the end of each section aim to enhance pupils' ability to discuss, read and write about non-fiction as well as develop their own non-fiction writing repertoire. The underlying thinking behind both the selection of texts and the activities has been to make challenging texts accessible and enjoyable and to offer detailed suggestions for classroom work that will allow pupils to engage with the texts.

Most texts in this anthology are suitable for GCSE, GCSE 17 and A Level courses. However there are some texts which most Year 9 classes could tackle with some teacher adaptation of the activities.

Using the Anthology

The texts themselves appear without contextualising material as one would find in a short story collection. Where it is considered useful to provide background information about texts, this appears in the Classroom Activities at the end of each section.

It is important that teachers look at the Classroom Activities section before embarking on work on individual texts, to see whether there are activities for pupils which are to be done before reading or at a specified point during the reading.

It is essential that teachers read the texts thoroughly before using them with a class in order to be aware of the level of difficulty and of the suitability of the subject matter and language for their pupils. Some of the texts contain strong language and teachers should use their discretion when selecting texts for reading aloud.

Klondyke Kate

The first time I saw Klondyke Kate in person was one dark rainy night at the Bath Pavilion. The MC introduced her as 'the official British Ladies Wrestling Champion', but she didn't come out. The crowd howled. She was balking because the management had got her music wrong. Someone in the back row yelled, 'Play 'Roll Out the Barrel'. She'll come out to that.' Everyone laughed, but eventually she appeared. The first thing I heard her say was, 'Shut yer mouth. Shut yer *dirty* mouth.' This was before she reached the ring. She snarled her way through an unruly mob of hissing, spitting people, already winding them up, already threatening and playing dirty. The Ladies Champion was *not* a lady.

Wrestling is basic entertainment, rude in the old sense of the word, and a wrestling crowd is not an opera crowd. The people who go to the fights are not there for subtlety or aesthetics. They want stories. They are a panto audience thirty years on, and they want to be part of the act. They need heroes and villains. In the ring, Klondyke Kate is a villain, but she is a heroine to me.

She breaks all the rules. She is fat and she shows it off in a black leotard, under bright lights, in front of hundreds of jeering, sneering men and women. Most overweight women hide. Klondyke Kate leans over the ropes and shouts, 'What are you looking at? Eh? Eh?'

She talks back. By no stretch of the imagination could she be called deferential. If you insult her, she insults you in return. 'My arse is prettier than your face,' a man screams. 'Come up and show us,' Kate screams back.

'Ignore them,' my mother used to say to me when I came home bleeding internally from some playground slight. 'Show them you're above it all.' I couldn't. I wasn't. I always made matters worse by fighting back. But like most little girls I wanted to be loved and approved of. So when I grew up I learned to control my temper. I taught myself to be nice. Most of the time. Women are supposed to look good, to behave well, to court love and approval.

Klondyke Kate doesn't. She glares across the ring at her little, perky opponent and shows no sympathy for her knee bandage. She will work mercilessly on that hurt knee later. She is not in the ring to show that women are the nurturing, caring sex. She is there to win by fair means or foul –

1

preferably foul. A villain is supposed to play dirty, and Kate takes the job seriously.

One thing that Channel 4's coverage of sumo has taught us is that fat people can be athletic. They can be very fast and very strong. Klondyke Kate is a fast, strong wrestler. She need not bite, choke, pull hair, stomp or gouge. She could win fairly, if she wanted to. She does not because it is her job to be the villain, and she is forced to be the villain because she is big and does not look pretty in a leotard. She does not look like what our culture demands of a heroine. She is not large-eyed, long-legged, glossy-haired, neat or petite.

Not many women have enough courage to be unpopular. It goes against our conditioning. We try hard to be acceptable. We try to look acceptable. If we are fat, we diet. If we're hairy, we depilate. If we are not pretty, we compensate with make-up and humour. If we are angry or ambitious, we hide it as far as we can. Kate does none of this. I don't know if she would rather be the popular heroine. If she would, it doesn't show, and in any case nature didn't give her much choice. She makes the best of a bad job by becoming a beautiful villain.

So there she is in the middle of the ring, a barrel in black tights. She smashes, mashes and crushes her opponent. The game little thing, pretty in pink, fights back. Kate becomes quite evil. She cheats blatantly. The crowd goes berserk. 'Dirty slag!' they scream.

A little old man is so furious that he bounds out of his seat and runs down the aisle to the ringside. The bouncers are waiting for him, but he stops short. He is beside himself with rage and probably hasn't moved this fast for forty years.

'You ...' he screams, 'you ...' Spittle flies from his mouth glittering like diamonds in the spotlights. He cannot think of anything bad enough to say. Finally it comes out: 'You ... you *bucket nut!*' he screeches.

'Come up here,' Kate sneers at the hysterical old man. 'We'll see who's got a bucket nut!' Kate's face – her bucket nut – says it all. It isn't a face to look at over the teacups.

Afterwards, when it was all over, I went to talk to Kate. She had been disqualified – there was no way her opponent could have won if she hadn't – and I was a little nervous. But the outrageous villain was calmly signing autographs at the back of the hall. She was watching the time, she said, because she had to get home to her little boy.

'What's your weak point?' I asked. 'As a fighter, I mean.' 'These,' she said, and she held out her hands. 'I keep breaking my fingers.' Her hands were tiny. 'I have to wear children's rings and gloves.'

Up there, behind the ropes, she had been so big and mean I'd never even noticed.

Liza Cody
Heroes & Villains, *The Independent*, 25 July 1992

Boring, Boring Arsenal

Arsenal v Newcastle 27.12.69

'All those terrible nil-nil draws against Newcastle,' my father would complain in years to come. 'All those freezing, boring Saturday afternoons.' In fact, there were only two terrible nil-nil draws against Newcastle, but they occurred in my first two seasons at Highbury, so I knew what he meant, and I felt personally responsible for them.

By now I felt guilty about what I had got my father into. He had developed no real affection for the club, and would rather, I think, have taken me to any other First Division ground. I was acutely aware of this, and so a new source of discomfort emerged: as Arsenal huffed and puffed their way towards 1-0 wins and nil-nil draws I wriggled with embarrassment, waiting for Dad to articulate his dissatisfaction. I had discovered after the Swindon game that loyalty, at least in football terms, was not a moral choice like bravery or kindness; it was more like a wart or a hump, something you were stuck with. Marriages are nowhere near as rigid – you won't catch any Arsenal fans slipping off to Tottenham for a bit of extra-marital slap and tickle, and though divorce is a possibility (you can just stop going if things get too bad), getting hitched again is out of the question. There have been many times over the last twenty-three years when I have pored over the small print of my contract looking for a way out, but there isn't one. Each humiliating defeat (Swindon, Tranmere, York, Walsall, Rotherham, Wrexham) must be borne with patience, fortitude and forbearance; there is simply nothing that can be done, and that is a realisation that can make you simply squirm with frustration.

Of course I hated the fact that Arsenal were boring (I had by now conceded that their reputation, particularly at this stage in their history, was largely deserved). Of course I wanted them to score zillions of goals and play with the verve and thrill of eleven George Bests, but it wasn't going to happen, certainly not in the foreseeable future. I was unable to defend my team's inadequacies to my father – I could see them for myself, and I hated them – and after each feeble attempt at goal and every misplaced pass I would brace myself for the sighs and groans from the seat next to me. I was chained to Arsenal and my dad was chained to me, and there was no way out for any of us.

Life after football
Arsenal v Valencia 14.5.80

Football teams are extraordinarily inventive in the ways they find to cause their supporters sorrow. They lead at Wembley and then throw it away; they go to the top of the First Division and then stop dead; they draw the difficult away game and lose the home replay; they beat Liverpool one week and lose to Scunthorpe the next; they seduce you, half-way through the season, into believing that they are promotion candidates and then go the other way ... always, when you think you have anticipated the worst that can happen, they come up with something new.

Four days after losing one cup final, Arsenal lost another, to Valencia in the European Cup-Winners Cup, and the seventy-game season came to nothing. We outplayed the Spanish team, but couldn't score, and the game went to penalties; Brady and Rix missed theirs (some say that Rix was never the same again after the trauma of that night, and certainly he never recaptured his form of the late seventies, even though he went on to play for England), and that was that.

As far as I am aware, there isn't another English club that has lost two finals in a week, although in the years to come, when losing in a final was the most that Arsenal supporters dared to hope, I wondered why I felt quite so stricken. But that week also had a beneficially purgative side effect: after six solid weeks of semi-finals and finals, of listening to the radio and looking for Wembley tickets, the football clutter was gone and there was nothing with which to replace it. Finally I had to think about what I was going to do, rather than what the Arsenal manager was going to do. So I applied for teacher training college back in London, and vowed, not for the last time, that I would never allow football to replace life completely, no matter how many games Arsenal played in a year.

Seats
Arsenal v Coventry 22.8.89

These are some of the things that have happened to me in my thirties: I have become a mortgage holder; I have stopped buying *New Musical Express* and *The Face*, and, inexplicably, I have started keeping back copies of Q Magazine under a shelf in my living room; I have become an uncle; I have bought a CD player; I have registered with an accountant; I have noticed that certain types of music – hip-hop, indie guitar pop, thrash metal – all sound the same, and have no tune; I have come to prefer restaurants to clubs, and dinners with friends to parties; I have developed an aversion to the feeling that a bellyful of beer gives you, even though I still enjoy a pint; I have started to covet items of furniture; I have bought one of those cork boards you put up in the kitchen; I have started to develop certain views – on the squatters who live in my street, for example, and about unreasonably loud parties – which are not altogether consistent with the attitudes I held when I was younger. And, in 1989, I bought a season-ticket for the seats, after standing on the North Bank for over fifteen years. These details do not tell the whole story of how I got old, but they tell some of it.

You just get tired. I got tired of the queues, and the squash, and tumbling half-way down the terrace every time Arsenal scored, and the fact that my view of the near goal was always partially obscured at big games, and it seemed to me that being able to arrive at the ground two minutes before kick-off without being disadvantaged in any way had much to recommend it. I didn't miss the terraces, really, and in fact I enjoyed them, the backdrop they provided, their noise and colour, more than I ever had when I stood on them. This Coventry game was our first in the seats, and Thomas and Marwood scored directly in front of us, at our end, and from our side.

There are five of us: Pete, of course, and my brother, and my girlfriend, although her place is usually taken by someone else nowadays, and me, and Andy, who used to be Rat when we were kids in the Schoolboys' Enclosure – I bumped into him on the North Bank in George's second season, a decade or so after I had lost touch with him, and he too was ready to leave the terraces behind.

What you're really doing, when you buy a seat season-ticket, is upping the belonging a notch. I'd had my own spot on the terraces, but I had no proprietorial rights over it and if some bloody big-game casual fan stood in it, all I could do was raise my eyebrows. Now I really do have my own home in the stadium, complete with flatmates, and neighbours with whom I am on cordial terms, and with whom I converse on topics of shared interest, namely the need for a new midfielder/striker/ way of playing. So I correspond to the stereotype of the ageing football fan, but I don't regret it. After a while, you stop wanting to live from hand to mouth, day to day, game to game, and you begin wanting to ensure that the remainder of your days are secure.

Nick Hornby
Fever Pitch, 1992

Sole Mate Strides On

In step with youth fashion for three decades, the Dr Martens boot is set to stamp its image on a range of men's clothing.
SIMON CAULKIN reports.

On the second floor of Shellys Shoes on the corner of Oxford Street and Regent Street, one of London's most distinctive cult meetings is taking place. A scowling black-clad youth with a fearsome haircut and clothes made of safety pins is stamping around in a pair of big black boots. Nearby, a neat Japanese couple are discussing styles, while two young Dutch women in shorts and backpacks, and several teenagers of both sexes browse the shelves. A businessman is admiring his newly shod feet in the mirror.

Shellys is a shrine to the footwear which, once you've noticed, seems to be everywhere this summer; it is the year of the boot, black with leggings is classic, but the ankle-watcher can also spot feet in brown, red, green and blue. Some legs end in floral boots, green or purple velvet boots, denim, corduroy, and tartan boots. There are boots with suits, boots with micro skirts, boots with shorts. Even children's boots.

But only the terminally unhip would imagine that any boot will do. For Shellys customers, tourist or native, the one brand that counts carries a black and yellow tag at the heel, a chunky sole and (usually) a row of tell-tale yellow stitching round the welting.

This is the notorious Dr Martens, DMs: Britain's contribution to the world youth look of the nineties and one of the strangest business success stories of recent decades.

A pair of DMs can be and is made to signify practically anything. National Front or Socialist Worker, high style or no style, hetero or gay, Harrods or Hoxton. Ted Polhemus, co-curator of the V&A's street-style exhibition, to be held next year, says: 'What's interesting is the way DMs have become an essential adjective of modern culture, combining a lot of very different meanings.'

Aficionados accept no substitute. Claire Beadle, aged 23, an artist, wore her three and a half year-old 'steelies' every day for two years as a student. Her size 3s are dwarfed by the .2s of her partner George – 'big enough for the cat to play in'. DMs, Claire explains, 'were first and they're still the best. There are lots of fakes, but they don't last. Mine are part of every outfit I have.'

Even parents love DMs. They note that despite the brand's success, long-lasting DMs still cost just half the price of more suave Timberlands, for example. For those who can't afford the £30- £70 for a basic pair, Ms Beadle recommends the thriving market in secondfoot DMs: 'Some pairs get passed around several times before they find the right home'.

In financial terms, DMs are equally heavy duty – a patch of British dominance in a footwear industry which has been losing ground to imports for 30 years. They support nearly one tenth of the entire UK footwear industry and all of the village of Wollaston, Northamptonshire, a centre of British shoemaking since the 17th Century.

In all, 20 companies, 40 manufacturing units and 2,400 people turn out parts of the DM range, which now stretches to brogues, sandals and Junior Docs. The companies' combined turnover was nearly £130 million in 1992, and is heading for £190 million this year.

The company at the centre of the Dr Martens enterprise is R Griggs and Co., a Wollaston family firm founded in 1901. Its export division has just won a Queen's Award for Export. The DM-wearing managing director, Stephen Griggs, the fifth generation of the shoemaking family, notes that the weekly output of Doc Martens would shoe a full house at Wembley Stadium twice over – 'a bit frightening, really'.

Nicholas Calvert, director general of the British Footwear Manufacturers' Federation, is less bashful: 'Griggs is a wonder story!'

The original Dr Martens was Dr Klaus Maertens, a German physician who, while recovering from a skiing accident in wartime Munich, with the help of an engineer friend devised a shoe with an air-cushioned sole. The prototype was made of old tyre. Dr Maertens' shoes, soon selling all over Europe, were blameless comfort shoes, designed to make walking easier for the elderly.

The transition to the altogether different Dr Martens came in 1959 when the inventors advertised in *Shoe and Leather News* for a partner to produce the shoes under licence in Britain.

The advertisement was answered by Bill Griggs, Stephen's grandfather. Griggs' traditional product – heavy screwed and stitched miners' and army boots – was coming under increasing pressure from a new moulded sole boot called Tuf, lighter and more flexible. To combat the threat, Griggs had organised a joint venture with several local firms, called Wollaston Vulcanizing.

The Maertens sole – man-made, resistant to chemicals and shock absorbent – seemed just the thing the joint venture needed to kick hell out of Tuf. Anglicised as Dr Martens and branded as Air Wair, the first pair of British DMs rolled off the production line on April 1 1960. To commemorate the date, the style was named 1460, a solid, value-for-money work boot which sold well to heavy walkers such as police and postmen through the sixties.

It might have remained there but for the intervention of an unknown young man in the sixties. 'Sometime, somewhere, there must have been a skinhead who first pulled on a pair of 1460s,' Mr Griggs muses. Embarrassing as it was to have your main product turn overnight into the uniform of the urban dispossessed, Mr Griggs admits: 'It did put DMs on the map'.

They have never been off it since. After the initial 'bovver boot' era, it seemed that 'as every new youth movement came along and faded, there was a DM which fitted', Mr Griggs says: 'punks, glam, New Romantics, anti-fashion, grunge. A surge of demand for boys' sizes turned out to come from women, so a women's range was launched. Cult shoe stores such as Shellys and Schuh, and Red or Dead, the avant-garde clothing firm, began customising the boots, decorating them with safety pins, bright laces and beading. Later, they worked with the manufacturer to extend the range to fashion items such as denim or patent leather DMs. (*Guardian* readers can now buy vegan Dr Martens, certified free of all animal materials.)

Students took up DMs, and from the late eighties even increased output could not keep up with demand. Latterly, exports have taken up the running, first to Europe and Australasia, then Canada and the US. 'We didn't have to introduce the product to North America. It came to us. Because it is such a cult shoe in the UK, its fame preceded it and people throughout the world are beating a path to our door,' the managing director of the export company told the magazine *Overseas Trade*. DM exports jumped from £7 million in 1990 to £18 million in 1992.

On the production side, say industry observers, DMs are 'a shoe-man's dream', combining seemingly unlimited demand for a shoe with little specialist work in the upper, a basic style which barely changes, and standard production technology. Seventy per cent of output is still composed of the original eight-eyelet boot and three-eyelet shoe.

On the back of this, Mr Griggs' firm has been able to fund steady expansion. As sole licensee, it long since bought out its partners in Wollaston Vulcanizing and all the erstwhile rivals in Wollaston. The Griggs family, Stephen says, has no interest or need to go public – and he has two children, not yet of DM-wearing age, who might want to follow in his footsteps.

For now, Mr Griggs has no plans to increase output beyond 220,000 pairs a week, which will probably be reached by Christmas. 'Then it's time for a breather', he says, 'to keep the market hungry.' In the longer term, if the Chinese or Russians began walking around in DMs – a prospect of almost unimaginable size – he would consider setting up a joint venture to make boots in the Far East. But only for the Far East, he insists: 'The 'Made in Britain' aspect is essential for Europe'.

Does he ever worry about DMs going out of fashion? 'We used to, but we're not the height of fashion – we're more like the blue jeans of shoes.' He adds that although the company is best known for the boot, the key to the brand as well as the subject of the licence is actually the sole, which can be used 'as a platform for almost anything'.

The secret of the consistent demand is that this is also true in a cultural sense. Again like jeans, anyone can take a pair of DMs and adapt them for his or her own identity purposes. So 'although they say tough, working-class punk, you see them in outfits with African beads or hippy turbans,' says Mr Polhemus.

Equally extraordinary, he points out, is the way Doc Martens has survived this multiple appropriation with its meaning and energy intact: 'Dr Martens is all about giving people an edge. In terms of weightiness, Timberlands would probably serve just as well for kicking heads in. But semiologically other brands just don't pack the same punch.'

King of the boot, Dr Martens is now gearing itself up for a different test: the launch of a range of men's clothes in the autumn. This is the product of a new venture, Dr Martens Clothing, combining Mr Griggs and Red or Dead.

DM Clothing is run by Red or Dead's founders, Wayne and Geraldine Hemingway, from a spartan building in Wembley. A British Triumph Tiger motorbike stands assertively outside the front door; the sole adornment in reception is a flight of three winged DMs – small, medium and large – on the wall. To work, the new label will need to incorporate some of the same witty forthrightness of the flying Docs – or, as Wayne Hemingway puts it, 'the lasting style, affordability and durability', which have made the footwear a cult.

It won't, he insists, be a fashion brand. 'Men have favourite clothes, things that they hang on to and come back to. We're looking for classic styles, things that a man could wear at any stage'. The press release speaks of clothes aimed at 'real men'. 'Manly but basic', Mr Griggs suggests. 'It's a difficult brief, but it will be wonderful if the clothes can conjure up a similar image to the footwear'.

Mr Griggs, who has invested £3 million in DM Clothing, denies that the venture smacks of opportunism. It is the result of market pull rather than promotion push, he says. Around the world people were already stealing the logo to stamp on T-shirts and jackets – in some cases whole ranges.

It is an indication of the distance Dr Martens has travelled that the clothing range will make its debut not at Milletts or Camden Market but at Selfridges and Harrods, which have bought the entire first collection. The only question now is: could Doc Martens survive the granting of a Royal Warrant?

Simon Caulkin
The Guardian, 1993

Alone Again, Naturally

Material girl, material world... although she now rejects the tag, life goes on as Madonna shops at Jean Paul Gaultier's Paris shop.

On the upper floor of Madonna's New York apartment is a hallway she jokingly calls the 'boxing hall of fame'. Its walls hold framed black-and-white photographs of fighters: Joe Louis, Sugar Ray Robinson and more than one Muhammad Ali. Madonna proudly points out that the largest Ali photo is autographed; it reads 'Madonna – We are the greatest!' 'I love boxing,' the singer says, surveying the sweaty torsos along the walls. Is it the skill, the strength, a sense of kinship with fellow arena performers? She turns and fixes her visitor with a level gaze. 'I love the brutality,' she says.

There's no brutality today. For the moment, Madonna is a hostess, graciously promoting *Bedtime Stories*, her first album in two years. She is wearing tight, flared black pants and a sheer, low-cut, black Ann Demeulemeester shirt over a black brassiere; the shirt is knotted at the midriff, showing off the famous navel, now pierced with a gold ring that holds a diamond horseshoe – 'for luck', Madonna says. A half-dozen gold chains and a crucifix hang around her neck; she has a small gold ring in her nose. Her hair is flashy yellow with dark roots; her eyebrows are blonde, her red fingernails slightly chipped.

She sits across a stainless steel counter in her kitchen. 'I thought this would be a good place,' Madonna says, in a nasal business-like tone. 'People find some of the bigger rooms intimidating.'

Later she will show her Picasso and the video clip for her new single, 'Secret', from *Bedtime Stories*. The song turns away from the sexual fantasies of her 1992 album, *Erotica*, and leaves behind Madonna's usual come-ons to declare, 'Happiness lies in your own hand'.

Madonna thrived in the 1980s on being sensational and suggestive against a tame mainstream backdrop. In the early 1990s she became vulgar instead of shocking. But in a career whose only constant has been constant change, she is trying on a mantle of something like innocence.

The lyrics on her new album are rarely profound. Madonna has recast herself as a crooner but without the melodrama of songs like 'Live To Tell.'

Many of the songs have pentatonic melodies, making them both concise and seemingly unresolved, with a melancholy undertow; the tone is subdued, with touches of lushness. Still, she can't resist a few digs at naysayers. In 'Human Nature', for instance, she sarcastically sings, 'Oops, I didn't know I couldn't talk about sex', after which the chorus lilts, 'I'm not sorry'.

But for the rest of the album, Madonna takes her antagonists' advice: she sings not about sex but about yearning and often, loneliness. In 'Sanctuary' pygmy-like hoots and throbbing low bass notes frame Madonna's declaration 'It's here in your heart I want to be carried'. In 'Inside Of Me' a wailing saxophone breaks the surface of a smooth ballad that avows 'Even though you're gone/Love still carries on'. In most songs she's simply alone.

Reflecting on her success the singer says: 'I've been famous for a decade now, and famous in a really all-encompassing way and a really unforgiving way. I started out very idealistic, a rosy-cheeked, wide-eyed girl from the Midwest. When I see people with that desperate need to have public attention, and with a really naive idea about what it takes and what is required I laugh and think, 'If you could only imagine'.'

Naive, Madonna is not – and she clearly knows what is required. She has had a startlingly long run. Few performers built lasting careers in the 1980s, yet through instinct or planning Madonna has gauged audience demand with impressive precision. She has garnered outsize reactions through small gestures – performing with a bare navel, putting extra bumps and grinds into a Las Vegas-like show, and shown in the process just how little leeway had been granted to female pop performers until she came along.

In songs and videos she has played the disco cheerleader and the street flirt, the elegant diva and the woman in the gingham dress, the gum-chewing home girl and the untouchable icon. Some observers have considered Madonna's transformations to be marketing tactics, like fluctuating hemlines. She denies it. 'Everything I'm doing is my own catharsis,' she says. 'My work is a kind of self-portrait. The whole delving into erotica and dealing with my sexual fantasies was my own inner struggle with the way I was raised, the Catholicism that is deep in my bones, and my own sense of guilt and sin. It's about my own inner struggle with repression.'

On *Bedtime Stories* Madonna has remade herself again. Her album *Erotica*, she says, 'was one side of me, and this is another side of me. It's not to say I'm not interested in exploring that avenue any more. I think everybody else thinks I went as far as I could go, but we won't get into what everybody else thinks.'

Ah, but that's inevitable. Over the last decade Madonna Louise Ciccone, now 36 years old, has made herself the most famous woman in the world. She doesn't just write songs, sing, dance and make video clips; she entertains the universe as an icon, as the subject of gossip, theory, praise and defamation. She has provided total-immersion entertainment: enough sounds, images, actions and apparitions to fill everything from radio air-time to tabloid front pages.

Indeed for fans and detractors Madonna has been the ultimate workaholic bad girl, sexy and ambitious, staying on top through ceaseless, meticulous change. 'I can never relax,' she says. 'People have always concentrated on my sex life and completely negated the fact that there's an awful lot of work involved in all of the things I've done. If I was actually doing all the things people accuse me of, I don't think I could be anywhere near as productive as I've been.'

Her production hasn't stopped with *Bedtime Stories*. There are television appearances and an eventual tour to go with the album. She is also continuing to run her entertainment company, Maverick, backed with $60 million from Time Warner; one project is a film to star Madonna based on Arlyne Brickman's life as a Mafia book-keeper (described in Teresa Carpenter's book *Mob Girl*). Since 1985 and *Desperately Seeking Susan*, Madonna has not found another effective film role playing someone other than herself.

What do the professional students say about Madonna? 'I look at her as a barometer of culture,' says Cathy Schwichtenberg, the editor of *The Madonna Connection*, a 1993 collection of academic essays exploring the performer's influence on contemporary culture. 'I also see her as waging semiotic warfare, working with certain strategies to upend stable categories of sexuality and gender. In popular culture Madonna serves as a vehicle to open up issues of gay sexuality, of race, of power and desire.'

Madonna's reaction to the Madonna-studies industry? 'I laugh. It's amusing,' she says. 'It's flattering because obviously I'm on a lot of people's minds. Everyone's got this obsession about me being really calculating and manipulative, and I think it's just because the stuff that I do pushes so many buttons. People think that it didn't just come off in a spontaneous way but it did, believe me.'

By itself most of Madonna's music has been catchy and innocuous with many early songs offering incentives to dance and the true-blue promises of girl-group pop. She wore lingerie and crucifixes, but her sentiments could have been found in a 1950s high school yearbook. The exception was her 1985 hit 'Material Girl', which Madonna now disowns. After pointing out that she didn't write it, she adds: 'I'll never sing it again as long as I live.'

Yet 'Material Girl' helped make Madonna the perfect symbol for Reagan-era America: materialistic blonde as a Hollywood fantasy, adept at creating a career through photo opportunities. She was a virtuoso of the superficial, and it took some time for pop critics – distracted by her unexceptional musical skills – to realise that mastery of surfaces is a gift all its own.

Riding the new medium of MTV in the early eighties, Madonna quickly added images to her music. She was a punky dancer, the knowing object of desire: a model, a movie star, a bride. One step ahead of the mass audience's attention span, she also riffled at high speed through old movie images: Monroe, Jean Harlow, Louise Brooks, Marlene Dietrich, Giulietta Masina.

For most of the 1980s, however, Madonna's songs were simply promises of fidelity and fun. The images were of a girl who had been around but who with the right guy would feel 'like a virgin' again. Yet while songs seemed to cater to male desire, Madonna's audiences were full of young girls, the 'wannabes' who saw in her a woman determined to get what she wanted, at home in multiple identities. Her message was murkier than it seemed at first: not simply 'take me, I'm yours,' but 'take me, and you're mine'.

Madonna's popularity didn't really embolden her until the middle of that decade, when she came out with the song 'Papa Don't Preach'. It took on a controversial topic – an unwed mother-to-be decides to keep her baby – but with a safety net: the baby's father wants to marry her. Later, with the 1989 album *Like A Prayer* Madonna's songs suddenly acquired depth: the lyrics interweave faith and family, abuse and redemption, along with fluffy pop.

But the last vestiges of sweetness or inhibition were dropped in the nineties. It was as if the performer had decided to live up to the worst nightmares of her detractors. If they thought she was too racy singing Borderline, showing her navel in 1984, then she'd really express herself.

The single 'Vogue' (1990), while unveiling a black drag-queen subculture, carried a Madonna manifesto: 'Strike a pose; there's nothing to it'. Her *Blond Ambition* tour included a simulated-masturbation scene, and in the widely discussed 1991 documentary *Truth Or Dare*, Madonna invited the camera to witness everything except business meetings.

With her album *Erotica* she would turn away from tame lyrics altogether, conjuring a murky, late night atmosphere of sex and sado-masochism as she whispered, 'There's a certain satisfaction in a little bit of pain.' The album would appear concurrently with the nude photographs and polymorphous tableaux of Madonna's book, *Sex*. Her 1993 tour production, *The Girlie Show*, included a topless dancer and an on-stage group grope.

More recently, Madonna startled the audience of US talk show host David Letterman by repeatedly dropping a favourite four letter word into a combative interview. And after she and Letterman publicly reconciled on the *MTV Video Music Awards* show – 'Watch your language,' he scolded – she traded raunchy banter on stage with Aerosmith. But by then *Bedtime Stories* had already been recorded, and Madonna knew her next public statement would be one of tenderness and loneliness rather than bravado.

'To go through life with that ridiculous caricature of myself preceding me, to constantly have to break it down, made me feel that kind of loneliness,' she says, 'not just in terms of relationships but with friendships and people in general – it gets very exhausting.'

Nevertheless, Madonna seems resigned to incessant criticism. 'People that are intimidated or threatened by my point of view are always trying to diminish me or erase me or negate me,' she says. 'They've been saying the same thing all through my career. It's like saying I'm a disco tart that's going to go away, and then it was that I'm materialistic.

'I stand for the eighties, and the eighties are over, so I'm over. I don't think about the eighties part of me and the nineties part of me, I am just doing what I want to do. And it just happens to be the nineties. How have I survived? Read the lyrics.'

Jon Pareles
New York Times, reprinted in *The Guardian*, 1st November 1994

Madonna's Diary

I'm at present devoting my emotional and artistic resources towards creating an ambient stage environment for my next World Tour. Like, I'm obsessed with black at the moment, like it means night and death and mystery and pepsi, right? So we're gonna start off with just this black curtain, and the black curtain will rise to reveal a stage totally black, okay? And then I'll be carried on by these six black guys, right? And I'll be dressed all in black with black hair and a black mask, and the thing is no one in the audience will know I'm even on stage for over forty minutes so it'll be like church or something and then I'll sing my new number, 'Spank My Butt (All Day Long)' and it'll be like Picasso and Dali and Bosch and the Pope and Sigmund Freud all rolled into one, just incredibly powerful and traumatic.

People are always wanting to know about my art collection. It's a very private collection, very personal. I mean it means a lot to me so I don't want to open it up to the world, know what I mean?, but I have a Dali, and I have a Daily too, she helps me clean up, and I have a Picasso of a cup of tea, from his Brew Period I suppose, and I have a really beautiful Frida Kahlo of a nostril with a spider in it and another outasight one by Frida Kahlo of a woman's hand with its fingers chopped off and ants all over it which is like a really positive image for all women and gays. I guess Frida was just too beautiful for this world.

My real favourite artist at the moment is a guy from years back, Italian like me, called René Sonce, like he painted lots of Jesuses on the Cross and Jesuses as a baby and angels and blah blah and he painted literally hundreds of the other Madonna, the one before me, in fact it was he who made the other Madonna into a big deal, like before he discovered her she couldn't sing and you never see pictures of her even dancing, like I guess her career had a setback what with that baby, but René saw through all that bullshit and he made her into a really big star, like you see his pictures of her in every gallery in the world and she's not even dressed that great, like maybe she had a weight problem. The pressures on her from fans must have been amazing, and she most likely had to learn to come to terms with herself, so I identify with her one helluva lot, though as far as I know she never produced a video, lousy marketing department I guess.

I was giving a rare interview the other day and I said to the interviewer, I can only spare another ten minutes, you know, I've got three more rare interviews to give before I have my shredded carrot for lunch, then I got my two-hour workout, then there's another four rare interviews before I become an essentially very private person all over again for a photographer from *People* magazine. So he says, 'Tell me about the hidden Madonna, the Madonna nobody knows, the very private and reclusive Madonna, the Madonna who's alone in her apartment with her fears and obsessions,' and I say, 'Jeez, that's the side of Madonna I keep from the world, the side that was totally wrecked by my marriage to Sean Penn, the side that is coming to terms with Catholic guilt, the side that can't seem to hold down a conventional relationship because she feels so open to misunderstanding, the side whose whole private life is in a constant state of disarray, the side that couldn't handle Warren Beatty looking at other women, the side that feels the need for reassurance from the public yet is always at the same time in retreat, you wanna know about that side?' And the interviewer, he says, yeah, tell us about that side of Madonna, and I say, 'Sorry, I never talk to anyone about that side, it's totally, totally, *totally* private.' Like, otherwise, your whole life becomes public property, you know?

I've been designing my own costume for my next video to accompany my new single, 'Pump Your Stuff; Big Boy'. I've gone for a complete change of image to reflect a whole new outlook in my emotional and spiritual development.

When I recorded my massive worldwide hit, 'Let My Fingers Feel Your Body (Krishna Krishna)', I was really into Zen Buddhism, and my stage costume – a leather G-string with spiked brassiere and fishnet tights – seemed to draw on this very Eastern approach to my religious fears and obsessions.

Then I was seriously into feminist studies and the role of oppressed woman in the 20th century when my next big hit, 'Find Me a Guy (Who Wants Me Bad'), came out, so I changed my costume to present a positive image for women everywhere – a rubber bondage-style body-stocking with high heels.

Finally, I was reading up a helluva lot on vegetarianism in the 1990s, and I wanted to make a strong pro-vegetarian statement, so I recorded my biggest hit yet, 'Suck! Suck! Suck! (You' re Mine Tonite)', wearing a specially designed costume of lurex brassiere and suede thong.

'Pump Your Stuff; Big Boy' is basically about the insanity of celebrity and the urban nightmare of 21st century society, and to express this in costume I have had Gaultier make me something totally different, like a real break with the past. It's an all-black PVC clingshirt with leather straps, and it exposes a sexual side of my art and my personality which I have previously been too insecure to portray before. It's an entirely new me obsessive, reclusive, concerned and very, very private.

Craig Brown
Private Eye Rear Columns Collected Diaries of the Famous, 1992

Style and Culture Activities

Klondyke Kate

1. The writer

This piece comes from the *The Independent Magazine* which runs a column called 'Heroes and Villains' in which well known people are invited to write about someone they admire or detest.

The editor of the column says that the choice of Hero or Villain should tell the readers as much about the writer as about the object of his or her attention. How much does this piece tell you about the writer Liza Cody?

● In pairs, look through 'Klondyke Kate' again and note down where and what information we get about the writer from the text on a chart like this one:

Quote or reference	What this tells us about Liza Cody
Not many women have enough courage to be unpopular	*She admires women who break society's rules about female behaviour*

2. My hero or heroine

Working in small groups, draw up a list of people that you are interested in and think would be suitable as subjects for the 'Heroes and Villains' column in the magazine. Here are some suggestions to help you get started:

Cleopatra
Lenny Henry
Postman Pat
Courtney Love
Ryan Giggs

● Working in pairs or alone, choose one person that you want to write about. Draft a piece of writing about them called 'My Hero' or 'My Heroine'.
● When you are happy with what you have written, try writing about the same person but as if you hate and detest them calling it 'My Villain'.

Boring, Boring Arsenal

● Listen to the extracts being read aloud.

1. Years later, they talk – 'Boring, Boring Arsenal'
● Role-play the conversation between Nick Hornby and his father years later when they are remembering their times at Arsenal matches. You could begin like this:

Father: Arsenal though. They were always terrible.
Nick: They did win sometimes Dad.

2. Writing in the same style – 'Life after football'
The second extract ends with Nick Hornby vowing to end his obsession with Arsenal but the next section, 'Arsenal v Southampton' begins:
'The first match of the season, so you're always that bit keener to get along.'
● Have a go at continuing this extract in the Nick Hornby style. After you've drafted part of it, read it aloud to a partner and hear theirs.
● Now read Nick Hornby's version. Help each other to think about Hornby's writing style by answering the following questions about the extract:

Is this written using a lot of specialist football language that excludes non-football fans or does he manage to avoid that?
Is this written in very formal language which makes the reader feel distanced or in a conversational style that draws the reader in (by using personal pronouns for example, like 'they', 'I' and 'you')?
Does this writer take himself and his subject very seriously?
Is this just about football?

3. Fans and fanatics – 'Seats'
How accurate is Nick Hornby's description of the obsessed fan? Does such behaviour apply only to football?
● Talk for a few minutes about obsessions that you have had yourself.
● In small groups draw up a list of 10 symptoms of the obsessive fan. It doesn't have to be about football, it could be about a singer, cheese and onion crisps or some other obsession.

4. Getting older
Look again at the final section where Nick Hornby writes about getting older and describes some of the tell-tale signs.
● Write your own short piece about becoming a teenager in which you point out all the little changes in habits, attitudes, lifestyle, behaviour and possessions. You could begin like this:
'These are some of the things that have happened to me in my teens. I stopped collecting lollipop sticks...'

Sole Mate Strides On

1. Getting the reading done
- In groups of five, brainstorm onto a large piece of paper everything you know or associate with Dr Martens boots.
- Read the article in small groups taking it in turns. When you have finished use a photocopy of the article and add some subheadings throughout the article to make it easier for another reader to follow.
- Make a poster listing Five Facts or 'Did You Knows?' about DMs.

2. Sole Mate Strides On at GCSE
- Working in groups, imagine that this text has been chosen by a GCSE Examinations Board for one of their English exam papers next year. You work for the Board and have been asked to come up with a choice of three tasks for the exam paper which the candidate has one hour to work on. Your tasks can be in several parts and should offer helpful guidance to the candidate.

Here are some of the syllabus aims and assessment criteria that your will need to bear in mind:

In Paper 2 candidates will be offered a choice of tasks based on the content of a non-literary text requiring them to understand, order and present facts, ideas and opinions.

Candidates must demonstrate that they can:
a) understand and evaluate facts, ideas and opinions which they encounter in their reading;
b) recognise different levels of explicit and implicit meanings and attitudes in texts which vary in style and complexity;
c) understand and appreciate choices which writers, including themselves, may make in language structure and form to achieve the effects which they want.

- When you have written out your choice of three tasks, swap them with those of another group and evaluate the tasks they have set. Talk about the following:

Do they meet the aims and criteria above?

Do they help candidates to show what they have understood about the text?

Do they provide guidance to help candidates structure their response?

Does the task suit the time allowed?
- Feed back together to share comments and ideas about suitable tasks or questions.

3. Selling DMs
You are going to make an advertisement to help sell DMs. In small groups, read through the following stages of the activity, talking and making notes about your ideas and plans as you do so.

Select your target audience
Decide who you are intending your ad for. It should be for:

A young middle-aged group between the ages of 25 – 35

or

A youth audience aged between 13 and 18.

You may want to target an even smaller group within these audiences, for example, the parents of toddlers and small children for a new range of Tiny DMs or just boys or just girls in the youth age group.

Choose your advertising medium
Think about where your ad is going to appear. You should choose between:
A 30 second radio ad
or
A print ad in a magazine or newspaper
or
A poster on a bus.

The content of the ad
Talk first about what you know and like about the advertising medium you have selected. How will the medium affect the content? Make a list of what it will have to have in it. Here are some reminders to help you:

Print ads should include:
An eyecatching image
A memorable slogan or catchphrase or joke or play on words to draw the reader in to the ad, fix the meaning of the image and say something instant about the product
Copy – a few additional lines that help to define the audience and sell the product

Radio ads should include:
A scripted voice over
A jingle
Music or sound track

Remember that what you decide to put in your ad will be affected not only by your choice of medium but also by which audience you have selected.
● Finally, produce your ad or plan to present your ideas to the rest of the class.

4. Research and write your own style article
● Talk about examples of other style items that have stood the test of time. For example:

The Leather Jacket
The T Shirt
Levis
The Little Black Dress
Flip Flops
The Trainer

● Decide on an item of clothing and then research it getting several different sorts of people to talk about what that item means to them. Draw up your list of questions first, for example:

When do you wear it?

Why?

What does it make you feel about yourself?

Where and when did you buy it?

What do you think it says about you to others?

- After you have done your research, look again at the 'Sole Mate Strides On' article to help you structure your article. You could write your piece around five main paragraphs: Description, History, Style, Production and The Future. Include quotes from the people you have researched and some illustrations if possible.
- You could try writing a poem or song using the voice of a particular style item in which it speaks for itself. For example, 'The Grey Suit Rap' or 'The Ballad of the Slingback'.

Alone again, naturally

1. Re-reading the text

There are two main voices in this article: the journalist's and Madonna's.

- Try reading it in pairs paragraph by paragraph with one of you being Madonna and the other being the journalist. You will find that quite often one of you will have to improvise questions and responses.
- Role play the beginning or end of the interview using the text to help you get started and to give you clues about what was said between them.

2. Giving an interview

Like all famous people, Madonna stage-manages her public image very carefully. Giving interviews is part of the publicity that every star needs to remain in the public eye.

- Talk about other forms of publicity that you can think of that someone like Madonna might use.
- Look back through the article and list five things about herself that Madonna wants the public to know. Back up everything on your list with a quote from the text. Share your findings with the rest of the class.

3. Interview technique

This piece of writing started off as an interview between the journalist and Madonna. He would have recorded their conversation on tape.

- Try writing up part of the interview as a script.

Where the journalist has included direct quotations you know you can include those as things Madonna actually said. Often though, you will have to 'read between the lines' to work out the questions he probably asked or other things she said which he has not quoted.

Include stage directions to show what they are doing or where they are. Your script should remain true to the article so that you should be able to show where in the text you got your clues and ideas. You could start like this:

(John Pareles is waiting in the hall on the upper floor of Madonna's New York apartment. The door opens and Madonna appears.)

M: So you like my boxing hall of fame huh?

JP: (Shakes her hand) John Paroles, New York Times. I'm so glad you could make this interview. Yeah, these photos, they're terrific. So...physical...

M: I love boxing. I love the brutality.

3. Viewpoint and audience

● Find the following quotes from the article and look at their context i.e. the words that come before and after which help fix its meaning.

> '...performing with a bare navel, putting extra bumps and grinds into a Las Vegas-like show...'

> '...Madonna's music has been catchy and innocuous...'

> '...She wore lingerie and crucifixes...'

> '...repeatedly dropping a favourite four-letter word...'

● Experiment with viewpoint and audience by writing each quote into the following different contexts:

an article by a writer who is shocked by Madonna

an article by a writer who finds her ridiculous

Madonna's Diary

1. What is this text?

● Read the first page aloud and then stop. What can you deduce about this text? Make some suggestions to answer the following:

Why was it written?

Who was it written for?

What is it trying to do?

Where might it appear?

What attitudes to Madonna are readers of this likely to have?

● Finish reading the piece and share initial impressions with other groups. Does this seem like a diary to you or is the idea of a diary simply a way of doing something else?

21

2. Parodies

This piece comes from a satirical magazine called *Private Eye* which ridicules and exposes the rich, the powerful and the famous.

> **A definition of parody**: Parody is mimicry of someone's style in a humorous or satirical way.

• Look through the diary again and pick out two or three examples of parody which you could use as an example to show what parody is and how it is working in the case of *Private Eye* and Madonna. You will need to think about the following:
Which aspect of Madonna or Madonna's style are they attacking? e.g. her way of speaking, the things she talks about, the lyrics of her songs, her publicity strategies?
How do they ridicule it? e.g. through exaggeration, repetition, some other way?

3. Diaries of the rich and famous

• Write your own parody in the form of a famous person's diary. Your aim is to ridicule the main aspects of that person's style but write in a voice that is recognisably theirs.

Dr Johnson's Journey to the Western Isles

N ear the way, by the water-side, we espied a cottage. This was the first Highland hut that I had seen; and as our business was with life and manners, we were willing to visit it. To enter a habitation without leave, seems to be not considered here as rudeness or intrusion. The old laws of hospitality still give this licence to a stranger.

A hut is constructed with loose stones, ranged for the most part with some tendency to circularity. It must be placed where the wind cannot act upon it with violence, because it has no cement; and where the water will run easily away, because it has no floor but the naked ground. The wall, which is commonly about six feet high, declines from the perpendicular a little inward. Such rafters as can be procured are then raised for a roof, and covered with heath, which makes a strong and warm thatch, kept from flying off by ropes of twisted heath, of which the ends, reaching from the centre of the thatch to the top of the wall, are held firm by the weight of a large stone. No light is admitted but at the entrance, and through a hole in the thatch, which gives vent to the smoke. This hole is not directly over the fire, lest the rain should extinguish it; and the smoke therefore naturally fills the place before it escapes. Such is the general structure of the houses in which one of the nations of this opulent and powerful island has been hitherto content to live. Huts however are not more uniform than palaces; and this which we were inspecting was very far from one of the meanest, for it was divided into several apartments; and its inhabitants possessed such property as a pastoral poet might exalt into riches.

When we entered, we found an old woman boiling goat's-flesh in a kettle. She spoke little English, but we had interpreters at hand; and she was willing enough to display her whole system of economy. She has five children, of which none are yet gone from her. The eldest, a boy of thirteen, and her husband, who is eighty years old, were at work in the wood. Her next two sons were gone to Inverness to buy meal, by which oatmeal is always meant. Meal she considered as expensive food, and told us, that in Spring, when the goats gave milk, the children could live without it. She is mistress of sixty goats, and I saw many kids in an enclosure at the end of her house. She had also some poultry. By the lake we saw a potato-garden, and a small spot of ground on which stood four shucks [stooks] containing each twelve sheaves of barley. She has all this from the labour of their own hands, and for what is necessary to be bought, her kids and her chickens are sent to market.

With the true pastoral hospitality, she asked us to sit down and drink whisky. She is religious, and though the kirk is four miles off, probably eight English miles, she goes thither every Sunday. We gave her a shilling, and she begged snuff; for snuff is the luxury of a Highland cottage.

Samuel Johnson
A Journey to the Western Islands of Scotland, 1775

Boswell's Journey to the Western Isles

When we had advanced a good way by the side of Loch Ness, I perceived a little hut, with an old-looking woman at the door of it. I thought here might be a scene that would amuse Dr Johnson; so I mentioned it to him. 'Let's go in,' said he. We dismounted, and we and our guides entered the hut. It was a wretched little hovel of earth only, I think, and for a window had only a small hole, which was stopped with a piece of turf, that was taken out occasionally to let in light. In the middle of the room or space which we entered, was a fire of peat, the smoke going out at a hole in the roof. She had a pot upon it, with goat's flesh, boiling. There was at one end under the same roof, but divided by a kind of partition made of wattles, a pen or fold in which we saw a good many kids.

Dr Johnson was curious to know where she slept. I asked one of the guides, who questioned her in Erse. She answered with a tone of emotion, saying (as he told us) she was afraid we wanted to go to bed to her. This *coquetry*, or whatever it may be called, of so wretched a being, was truly ludicrous. Dr Johnson and I afterwards were merry upon it. I said, it was he who alarmed the poor woman's virtue. 'No, sir,' said he, 'she'll say, 'There came a wicked young fellow, a wild dog, who I believe would have ravished me, had there not been with him a grave old gentleman, who repressed him: but when he gets out of the sight of his tutor, I'll warrant you he'll spare no woman he meets, young or old.'' 'No, sir,' I replied, 'she'll say, 'There was a terrible ruffian who would have forced me, had it not been for a civil decent young man who, I take it, was an angel sent from heaven to protect me.''

Dr Johnson would not hurt her delicacy, by insisting on 'seeing her bedchamber', like Archer in *The Beaux' Stratagem*. But my curiosity was more ardent; I lighted a piece of paper, and went into the place where the bed was. There was a little partition of wicker, rather more neatly done than that for the fold, and close by the wall was a kind of bedstead of wood with heath upon it by way of bed; at the foot of which I saw some sort of blankets or covering rolled up in a heap. The woman's name was Fraser; so was her husband's. He was a man of eighty. Mr Fraser of Balnain allows him to live in this hut, and keep sixty goats, for taking care of his woods, where he then was. They had five children, the eldest only thirteen. Two were gone to Inverness to buy meal; the rest were looking after the goats. This contented family had four stacks of barley, twenty-four sheaves in each. They had a few fowls. We were informed that they lived all the spring without meal, upon milk and curds and whey alone. What they get for their goats, kids, and fowls, maintains them during the rest of the year.

She asked us to sit down and take a dram. I saw one chair. She said she was as happy as any woman in Scotland. She could hardly speak any English except a few detached words. Dr Johnson was pleased at seeing, for the first time, such a state of human life. She asked for snuff. It is her luxury, and she uses a great deal. We had none; but gave her sixpence apiece. She then brought out her whisky bottle. I tasted it; as did Joseph and our guides: so I gave her sixpence more. She sent us away with many prayers in Erse.

James Boswell
The Journal of a Tour to the Hebrides, 1785

Des Moines

I come from Des Moines. Somebody had to.

When you come from Des Moines you either accept the fact without question and settle down with a local girl named Bobbi and get a job at the Firestone factory and live there for ever and ever, or you spend your adolescence moaning at length about what a dump it is and how you can't wait to get out, and then you settle down with a local girl named Bobbi and get a job at the Firestone factory and live there for ever and ever.

Hardly anyone ever leaves. This is because Des Moines is the most powerful hypnotic known to man. Outside town there is a big sign that says WELCOME TO DES MOINES. THIS IS WHAT DEATH IS LIKE. There isn't really. I just made that up. But the place does get a grip on you. People who have nothing to do with Des Moines drive in off the interstate, looking for gas or hamburgers, and stay for ever. There's a New Jersey couple up the street from my parents' house whom you see wandering around from time to time looking faintly puzzled but strangely serene. Everybody in Des Moines is strangely serene.

The only person I ever knew in Des Moines who wasn't serene was Mr Piper. Mr Piper was my parents' neighbour, a leering cherry-faced idiot who was forever getting drunk and crashing his car into telephone poles. Everywhere you went you encountered telephone poles and road signs leaning dangerously in testimony to Mr Piper's driving habits. He distributed them all over the west side of town, rather in the way dogs mark trees. Mr Piper was the nearest possible human equivalent to Fred Flintstone, but less charming. He was a Shriner and a Republican – a Nixon Republican – and he appeared to feel he had a mission in life to spread offence. His favourite pastime, apart from getting drunk and crashing his car, was to get drunk and insult the neighbours, particularly us because we were Democrats, though he was prepared to insult Republicans when we weren't available.

Eventually, I grew up and moved to England. This irritated Mr Piper almost beyond measure. It was worse than being a Democrat. Whenever I was in town, Mr Piper would come over and chide me. 'I don't know what you're doing over there with all those Limeys,' he would say provocatively. 'They're not clean people.'

'Mr Piper, you don't know what you're talking about,' I would reply in my affected English accent. 'You are a cretin,' You could talk like that to Mr Piper because (1) he *was* a cretin and (2) he never listened to anything that was said to him.

'Bobbi and I went over to London two years ago and our hotel room didn't even have a *bathroom* in it,' Mr Piper would go on. 'If you wanted to take a leak in the middle of the night you had to walk about a mile down the hallway. That isn't a clean way to live.'

'Mr Piper, the English are paragons of cleanliness. It is a well-known fact that they use more soap per capita than anyone else in Europe.'

Mr Piper would snort derisively at this. 'That doesn't mean diddly-squat, boy, just because they're cleaner than a bunch of Krauts and Eyeties. My God, a *dog's* cleaner than a bunch of Krauts and Eyeties. And I'll tell you something else: if his Daddy hadn't bought Illinois for him, John F. Kennedy would never have been elected President.'

I had lived around Mr Piper long enough not to be thrown by this abrupt change of tack. The theft of the 1960 presidential election was a long-standing plaint of his, one that he brought into the conversation every ten or twelve minutes regardless of the prevailing drift of the discussion. In 1963, during Kennedy's funeral, someone in the Waveland Tap punched Mr Piper in the nose for making that remark. Mr Piper was so furious that he went straight out and crashed his car into a telephone pole. Mr Piper is dead now, which is of course one thing that Des Moines prepares you for.

When I was growing up I used to think that the best thing about coming from Des Moines was that it meant you didn't come from anywhere else in Iowa. By Iowa standards, Des Moines is a Mecca of cosmopolitanism, a dynamic hub of wealth and education, where people wear three-piece suits and dark socks, often simultaneously. During the annual state high school basketball tournament, when the hayseeds from out in the state would flood into the city for a week, we used to accost them downtown and snidely offer to show them how to ride an escalator or negotiate a revolving door. This wasn't always so far from reality. My friend Stan, when he was about sixteen, had to go and stay with his cousin in some remote, dusty hamlet called Dog Water or Dunceville or some such improbable spot – the kind of place where if a dog gets run over by a truck everybody goes out to have a look at it. By the second week, delirious with boredom, Stan insisted that he and his cousin drive the fifty miles into the county town, Hooterville, and find something to do. They went bowling at an alley with warped lanes and chipped balls and afterwards had a chocolate soda and looked at a *Playboy* in a drugstore, and on the way home the cousin sighed with immense satisfaction and said, 'Gee thanks, Stan. That was the best time I ever had in my whole life!' It's true.

I had to drive to Minneapolis once, and I went on a back road just to see the country. But there was nothing to see. It's just flat and hot, and full of corn and soya beans and hogs. Every once in a while you come across a farm or some dead little town where the liveliest thing is the flies. I remember one long, shimmering stretch where I could see a couple of miles down the highway and there was a brown dot beside the road. As I got closer I saw it was a man sitting on a box by his front yard, in some six-house town with a name like Spigot or Urinal, watching my approach with inordinate interest. He watched me zip past and in the rear-view mirror I could see him still watching me going on down the road until at last I disappeared into a heat haze. The whole thing must have taken about five minutes. I wouldn't be surprised if even now he thinks of me from time to time.

He was wearing a baseball cap. You can always spot an Iowa man because he is wearing a baseball cap advertising John Deere or a feed company, and because the back of his neck has been lasered into deep crevasses by years of driving a John Deere tractor back and forth in a blazing sun. (This does not do his mind a whole lot of good either.) His other distinguishing feature is that he looks ridiculous when he takes off his shirt because his neck and arms are chocolate brown and his torso is as white as a sow's belly. In Iowa it is called a farmer's tan and it is, I believe, a badge of distinction.

Iowa women are almost always sensationally overweight – you see them at Merle Hay Mall in Des Moines on Saturdays, clammy and meaty in their shorts and halter tops, looking a little like elephants dressed in children's clothes, yelling at their kids, calling out names like Dwayne and Shauna. Jack Kerouac, of all people, thought that Iowa women were the prettiest in the country, but I don't think he ever went to Merle Hay Mall on a Saturday. I will say this, however – and it's a strange, strange thing – the teenaged daughters of these fat women are always utterly delectable, as soft and gloriously rounded and naturally fresh-smelling as a basket of fruit. I don't know what it is that happens to them, but it must be awful to marry one of those nubile cuties knowing that there is a time bomb ticking away in her that will at some unknown date make her bloat out into something huge and grotesque, presumably all of a sudden and without much notice, like a self-inflating raft from which the stopper has been yanked.

Even without this inducement, I don't think I would have stayed in Iowa. I never felt altogether at home there, even when I was small. In about 1957, my grandparents gave me a Viewmaster for my birthday and a packet of discs with the title 'Iowa – Our Glorious State'. I can remember thinking even then that the selection of glories was a trifle on the thin side. With no natural features of note, no national parks, no battlefields or famous birthplaces, the Viewmaster people had to stretch their creative 3-D talents to the full. Putting the Viewmaster to your eyes and clicking the white handle gave you, as I recall, a shot of Herbert Hoover's birthplace, impressively three-dimensional, followed by Iowa's other great treasure, the Little Brown Church in the Vale (which inspired the song whose tune nobody ever quite knows), the highway bridge over the Mississippi River at Davenport (all the cars seemed to be hurrying towards Illinois), a field of waving corn, the bridge over the Missouri River at Council Bluffs and the Little Brown Church in the Vale again, taken from another angle. I can remember thinking even then that there must be more to life than that.

Then one grey Sunday afternoon when I was about ten I was watching TV and there was a documentary on about movie-making in Europe. One clip showed Anthony Perkins walking along some sloping city street at dusk. I don't remember now if it was Rome or Paris, but the street was cobbled and shiny with rain and Perkins was hunched deep in a trench coat and I thought, 'Hey, *c'est moi!'* I began to read – no, I began to *consume* – *National Geographics,* with their pictures of glowing Lapps and mist-shrouded castles and ancient cities of infinite charm. From that moment, I wanted to be a European boy. I wanted to live in an apartment across from a park in the heart of a city, and from my bedroom window look out on a crowded vista of hills and roof-tops. I wanted to ride trams and understand strange languages. I wanted friends named Werner and Marco who wore short pants and played soccer in the street and owned toys made of wood. I cannot for the life of me think why. I wanted my mother to send me out to buy long loaves of bread from a shop with a wooden pretzel hanging above the entrance, I wanted to step outside my front door and *be* somewhere.

As soon as I was old enough I left. I left Des Moines and Iowa and the United States and the war in Vietnam and Watergate, and settled across the world. And now when I came home it was to a foreign country, full of serial murderers and sports teams in the wrong towns (the Indianapolis Colts? the Toronto Blue Jays?) and a personable old fart who was President. My mother knew that personable old fart when he was a sportscaster called Dutch Reagan at WHO Radio in Des Moines. 'He was just a nice, friendly, kind of dopey guy,' my mother says.

Which, come to that, is a pretty fair description of most Iowans. Don't get me wrong. I am not for a moment suggesting that Iowans are mentally deficient. They are a decidedly intelligent and sensible people who, despite their natural conservatism, have always been prepared to elect a conscientious, clear-thinking liberal in preference to some cretinous conservative. (This used to drive Mr Piper practically insane.) And Iowans, I am proud to tell you, have the highest literacy rate in the nation: 99.5 per cent of grown-ups there can read. When I say they are kind of dopey I mean they are trusting and amiable and open. They are a tad slow, certainly – when you tell an Iowan a joke, you can see a kind of race going on between his brain and his expression – but it's not because they're incapable of high-speed mental activity, it's only that there's not much call for it. Their wits are dulled by simple, wholesome faith in God and the soil and their fellow man.

Above all, Iowans are friendly. You go into a strange diner in the South and everything goes quiet, and you realise all the other customers are looking at you as if they are sizing up the risk involved in murdering you for your wallet and leaving your body in a shallow grave somewhere out in the swamps. In Iowa you are the centre of attention, the most interesting thing to hit town since a tornado carried off old Frank Sprinkel and his tractor last May. Everybody you meet acts like he would gladly give you his last beer and let you sleep with his sister. Everyone is happy and friendly and strangely serene.

The last time I was home, I went to Kresge's downtown and bought a bunch of postcards to send back to England. I bought the most ridiculous ones I could find – a sunset over a feed lot, a picture of farmers bravely grasping a moving staircase beside the caption 'We rode the escalator at Merle Hay Mall!', that sort of thing. They were so uniformly absurd that when I took them up to the check-out, I felt embarrassed by them, as if I were buying dirty magazines, and hoped somehow to convey the impression that they weren't really for me. But the check-out lady regarded each of them with interest and deliberation – just as they always do with dirty magazines, come to that.

When she looked up at me she was almost misty-eyed. She wore butterfly glasses and a beehive hairdo. 'Those are real nice,' she said. 'You know, honey, I've bin in a lot of states and seen a lot of places, but I can tell you that this is just about the purtiest one I ever saw.' She really said purtiest. She really meant it. The poor woman was in a state of terminal hypnosis. I glanced at the cards and to my surprise I suddenly saw what she meant. I couldn't help but agree with her. They *were* purty. Together, we made a little pool of silent admiration. For one giddy, careless moment, I was almost serene myself. It was a strange sensation, and it soon passed.

My father liked Iowa. He lived his whole life in the state, and is even now working his way through eternity there, in Glendale Cemetery in Des Moines. But every year he became seized with a quietly maniacal urge to get out of the state and go on vacation. Every summer, without a whole lot of notice, he would load the car to groaning, hurry us into it, take off for some distant point, return to get his wallet after having driven almost to the next state, and take off again for some distant point. Every year it was the same. Every year it was awful.

The big killer was the tedium. Iowa is in the middle of the biggest plain this side of Jupiter. Climb onto a roof-top almost anywhere in the state and you are confronted with a featureless sweep of corn for as far as the eye can see. It is 1,000 miles from the sea in any direction, 400 miles from the nearest mountain, 300 miles from skyscrapers and muggers and things of interest, 200 miles from people who do not habitually stick a finger in their ear and swivel it around as a preliminary to answering any question addressed to them by a stranger. To reach anywhere of even passing interest from Des Moines by car requires a journey that in other countries would be considered epic. It means days and days of unrelenting tedium, in a baking steel capsule on a ribbon of highway.

In my memory, our vacations were always taken in a big blue Rambler station-wagon. It was a cruddy car – my dad always bought cruddy cars, until he got to the male menopause and started buying zippy red convertibles – but it had the great virtue of space. My brother, sister and I in the back were miles away from my parents up front, in effect in another room. We quickly discovered during illicit forays into the picnic hamper that if you stuck a bunch of Ohio Blue Tip matches into an apple or hard-boiled egg, so that it resembled a porcupine, and casually dropped it out the tailgate window, it was like a bomb. It would explode with a small bang and a surprisingly big flash of blue flame, causing cars following behind to veer in an amusing fashion.

My dad, miles away up front, never knew what was going on and could not understand why all day long cars would zoom up alongside him with the driver gesticulating furiously, before tearing off into the distance. 'What was that all about?' he would say to my mother in a wounded tone.

'I don't know, dear,' my mother would answer mildly. My mother only ever said two things. She said, 'I don't know, dear.' And she said, 'Can I get you a sandwich, honey?' Occasionally on our trips she would volunteer other pieces of intelligence like, 'Should that dashboard light be glowing like that, dear?' or, 'I think you hit that dog/man/blind person back there, honey,' but mostly she wisely kept quiet. This was because on vacations my father was a man obsessed. His principal obsession was with trying to economise. He always took us to the crummiest hotels and motor lodges, and to the kind of roadside eating-houses where they only washed the dishes weekly. You always knew, with a sense of doom, that at some point before finishing you were going to discover someone else's congealed egg-yolk lurking somewhere on your plate or plugged between the tines of your fork. This, of course, meant cooties and a long, painful death.

But even that was a relative treat. Usually we were forced to picnic by the side of the road. My father had an instinct for picking bad picnic sites – on the apron of a busy truck stop or in a little park that turned out to be in the heart of some seriously deprived ghetto, so that groups of children would come and stand silently by our table and watch us eating Hostess Cupcakes and crinkle-cut potato chips – and it always became incredibly windy the moment we stopped, so that my mother spent the whole of lunch-time chasing paper plates over an area of about an acre.

In 1957 my father invested $19.98 in a portable gas stove that took an hour to assemble before each use and was so wildly temperamental that we children were always ordered to stand well back when it was being lit. This always proved unnecessary, however, because the stove would flicker to life only for a few seconds before puttering out, and my father would spend many hours turning it this way and that to keep it out of the wind, simultaneously addressing it in a low, agitated tone normally associated with the chronically insane. All the while my brother, sister and I would implore him to take us some place with air-conditioning, linen table-cloths and ice-cubes clinking in glasses of clear water. 'Dad,' we would beg, 'you're a successful man. You make a good living. Take us to a Howard Johnson's.' But he wouldn't have it. He was a child of the Depression and where capital outlays were involved he always wore the haunted look of a fugitive who had just heard bloodhounds in the distance.

Eventually, with the sun low in the sky, he would hand us hamburgers that were cold and raw and smelled of butane. We would take one bite and refuse to eat any more. So my father would lose his temper and throw everything into the car and drive us at high speed to some roadside diner where a sweaty man with a floppy hat would sling hash while greasefires danced on his grill. And afterwards, in a silent car filled with bitterness and unquenched basic needs, we would mistakenly turn off the main highway and get lost and end up in some no-hope hamlet with a name like Draino, Indiana, or Tapwater, Missouri, and get a room in the only hotel in town, the sort of rundown place where if you wanted to watch TV it meant you had to sit in the lobby and share a cracked leatherette sofa with an old man with big sweat circles under his arms. The old man would almost certainly have only one leg and probably one other truly arresting deficiency, like no nose or a caved-in forehead, which meant that although you were sincerely intent on watching *Laramie* or *Our Miss Brooks,* you found your gaze being drawn, ineluctably and sneakily, to the amazing eaten-away body sitting beside you. You couldn't help yourself. Occasionally the man would turn out to have no tongue, in which case he would try to engage you in lively conversation. It was all most unsatisfying.

After a week or so of this kind of searing torment, we would fetch up at some blue and glinting sweep of lake or sea in a bowl of pine-clad mountains, a place full of swings and amusements and the gay shrieks of children splashing in water, and it would all almost be worth it. Dad would become funny and warm and even once or twice might take us out to the sort of restaurant where you didn't have to watch your food being cooked and where the glass of water they served you wasn't autographed with lipstick. This was living. This was heady opulence.

It was against this disturbed and erratic background that I became gripped with a curious urge to go back to the land of my youth and make what the blurb writers like to call a journey of discovery. On another continent, 4,000 miles away, I became quietly seized with that nostalgia that overcomes you when you have reached the middle of your life and your father has recently died and it dawns on you that when he went he took some of you with him. I wanted to go back to the magic places of my youth – to Mackinac Island, the Rocky Mountains, Gettysburg – and see if they were as good as I remembered them. I wanted to hear the long, low sound of a Rock Island locomotive calling across a still night and the clack of it receding into the distance. I wanted to see lightning bugs, and hear cicadas shrill, and be inescapably immersed in that hot, crazy-making August weather that makes your underwear scoot up every crack and fissure and cling to you like latex, and drives mild-mannered men to pull out handguns in bars and light up the night with gunfire. I wanted to look for Ne-Hi Pop and Burma Shave signs and go to a ball game and sit at a marble-topped soda-fountain and drive through the kind of small towns that Deanna Durbin and Mickey Rooney used to inhabit in the movies. I wanted to travel around. I wanted to see America. I wanted to come home.

So I flew to Des Moines and acquired a sheaf of roadmaps, which I studied and puzzled over on the living-room floor, drawing an immense circular itinerary that would take me all over this strange and giant semi-foreign land. My mother, meantime, made me sandwiches and said, 'Oh, I don't know, dear,' when I asked her questions about the vacations of my childhood. And one September dawn in my thirty-sixth year I crept out of my childhood home, slid behind the wheel of an ageing Chevrolet Chevette lent by my sainted and trusting mother and guided it out through the flat, sleeping streets of the city. I cruised down an empty freeway, the only person with a mission in a city of 250,000 sleeping souls. The sun was already high in the sky and promised a blisteringly hot day. Ahead of me lay about a million square miles of quietly rustling corn. At the edge of town I joined Iowa Highway 163 and with a light heart headed towards Missouri. And it isn't often you hear anyone say that.

Bill Bryson
The Lost Continent, 1989

Tokyo Pastoral

This is clearly one of those districts where it always seems to be Sunday afternoon. Somebody in a house by the corner shop is effortlessly practising Chopin on the piano. A dusty cat rolls in the ruts of the unpaved streetlet, yawning in the sunshine. Somebody's aged granny trots off to the supermarket for a litre or two of honourable saki. Her iron-grey hair is scraped into so tight a knot in the nape no single hair could ever stray untidily out, and her decent, drab kimono is enveloped in the whitest of enormous aprons, trimmed with a sober frill of cotton lace, the kind of apron one associates with Victorian nursemaids.

She is bent to a full hoop because of all the babies she has carried on her back and she bows formally before she shows a socially acceptable quantity of her gold-rimmed teeth in a dignified smile. Frail, omnipotent granny who wields a rod of iron behind the paper walls.

This is a district peculiarly rich in grannies, cats and small children. We are a 60 yen train ride from the Marunouchi district, the great business section; and a 60 yen train ride in the other direction from Shinjuku, where there is the world's largest congregation of strip-shows, clipjoints and Turkish baths. We are a pretty bourgeois enclave of perpetual Sunday wedged between two mega-highways.

The sounds are: the brisk swish of broom on tatami matting, the raucous cawing of hooded crows in a nearby willow grove; clickety-clackety rattle of chattering housewives, a sound like briskly plied knitting needles, for Japanese is a language full of Ts and Ks; and, in the mornings, the crowing of a cock. The nights have a rustic tranquility. We owe our tranquility entirely to faulty town planning; these streets are far too narrow to admit cars. The smells are: cooking; sewage; fresh washing.

It is difficult to find a boring part of Tokyo but, by God, I have done it. It is a very respectable neighbourhood and has the prim charm and the inescapable accompanying ennui of respectability.

I can touch the walls of the houses on either side by reaching out my arms and the wall of the house at the back by stretching out my hand, but the fragile structures somehow contrive to be detached, even if there is only a clearance of inches between them, as though they were stating emphatically that privacy, even if it does not actually exist, is, at least, a potential. Most homes draw drab, grey skirts of breeze-block walls around themselves with the touch-me-not decorum of old maids, but even the tiniest of gardens boasts an exceedingly green tree or two and the windowsills bristle with potted plants.

Our neighbourhood is too respectable to be picturesque but, nevertheless, has considerable cosy charm, a higgledy-piggledy huddle of brown-grey shingled roofs and shining spring foliage. In the mornings, gaudy quilts, brilliantly patterned mattresses and cages of singing birds are hung out to air on the balconies. If the Japanese aesthetic ideal is a subfusc, harmonious austerity, the cultural norm is a homey, cheerful clutter. One must cultivate cosiness; cosiness makes overcrowding tolerable. Symmetrical lines of very clean washing blow in the wind. You could eat your dinner off the children. It is an area of white-collar workers; it is a good area.

The absolute domestic calm is disturbed by little more than the occasional bicycle or a boy on a motorbike delivering a trayful of lacquer noodle bowls from the cafe on the corner for somebody's lunch or supper. In the morning, the men go off to work in business uniform (dark suits, white nylon shirts); in the afternoon, schoolchildren loll about eating ice-cream. High school girls wear navy-blue pleated skirts and sailor tops, very Edith Nesbitt, and high school boys wear high-collared black jackets and peaked caps, inexpressibly Maxim Gorki.

At night, a very respectable drunk or two staggers, giggling, down the hill. A pragmatic race, the Japanese appear to have decided long ago that the only reason for drinking alcohol is to become intoxicated and therefore drink only when they wish to be drunk. They all are completely unabashed about it.

Although this is such a quiet district, the streets around the station contain everything a reasonable man might require. There is a blue movie theatre; a cinema that specialises in Italian and Japanese Westerns of hideous violence; a cinema that specialises in domestic consumption Japanese weepies; and yet another one currently showing *My Fair Lady*. There is a tintinabulation of chinking *pachinko* (pinball) parlours, several bakeries which sell improbably luxurious European patisserie, a gymnasium and an aphrodisiac shop or two.

If it lacks the excitement of most of the towns that, added up, amount to a massive and ill-plumbed concept called Greater Tokyo, that is because it is primarily a residential area, although one may easily find the cluster of hotels which offer hospitality by the hour. They are sited sedately up a side street by the station, off a turning by a festering rubbish tip outside a Chinese restaurant, and no neighbourhood, however respectable, is complete without them – for, in Japan, even the brothels are altogether respectable.

They are always scrupulously clean and cosy and the more expensive ones are very beautiful, with their windbells, stone lanterns and little rock gardens with streams, pools and water lilies. So elegantly homelike are they indeed, that the occasional erotic accessory – a red light bulb in the bedside light, a machine that emits five minutes of enthusiastic moans, grunts and pants at the insertion of a 100 yen coin – seems like a bad joke in a foreign language. Repression operates in every sphere but the sexual, even if privacy may only be purchased at extortionate rates.

There are few pleasant walks around here; the tree-shaded avenue beside the river offers delight only to coprophiles. But it is a joy to go out shopping. Since this is Japan, warped tomatoes and knobbly apples cost half the price of perfect fruit. It is the strawberry season; the man in the open fruit shop packs martial rows of berries the size of thumbs, each berry red as a guardsman, into a polythene box and wraps each box before he sells it in paper printed with the legend, 'Strawberry for health and beauty.'

Non-indigenous foods often taste as if they had been assembled from a blueprint by a man who had never seen the real thing. For example, cheese, butter and milk have such a degree of hygienic lack of tang they are wholly alienated from the natural cow. They taste absolutely, though not unpleasantly, synthetic and somehow indefinably obscene. Powdered cream (trade-named 'Creap') is less obtrusive in one's coffee. Most people, in fact, tend to use evaporated milk.

Tokyo ought not be a happy city – no pavements; noise; few public places to sit down; occasional malodorous belches from sewage vents even in the best areas; and yesterday I saw a rat in the supermarket. It dashed out from under the seaweed counter and went to earth in the butchery. '*Asoka,*' said the assistant, which means, 'Well, well, I never did,' in so far as the phrase could be said to mean anything. But, final triumph of ingenuity, Megapolis One somehow contrives to be an exceedingly pleasant place in which to live. It is as though Fellini had decided to remake *Aphaville.*

Up the road, there is a poodle-clipping parlour; a Pepsi-Cola bottling plant heavily patrolled by the fuzz; a noodle shop which boasts a colour TV; a mattress shop which also sells wicker neckpillows of antique design; innumerable bookshops, each with a shelf or two of European books, souvenirs of those who have passed this way before – a tattered paperback of *The Rosy Crucifixion,* a treatise on budgerigar keeping, Marx and Engels on England; a dispenser from which one may purchase condoms attractively packed in purple and gold paper, trademarked 'Young Jelly'; and a swimming pool.

I am the first coloured family in this street. I moved in on the Emperor's birthday, so the children were all home from school. They were playing 'catch' around the back of the house and a little boy came to hide in the embrasure of the window. He glanced round and caught sight of me. He did not register shock but he vanished immediately. Then there was a silence and, shortly afterwards, a soft thunder of tiny footsteps. They groped round the windows, invisible, peering, and a rustle rose up, like the dry murmur of dead leaves in the wind, the rustle of innumerable small voices murmuring the word: '*Gaijin, gaijin, gaijin*' (foreigner), in pure, repressed surprise. We spy strangers. *Asoka.*

Angela Carter
New Society, 1970

On a Train

L arge ochre squashes sat plumply in fields of withering vines; people priming pumps and swinging buckets out of wells on long poles; tall narrow haystacks, and pepper fields in so many stages of ripeness I first took them for flower gardens. It is a feeling of utter quietness, deep rural isolation the train briefly penetrates. It goes on without a change for hours, this afternoon in Yugoslavia, and then all people disappear and the effect is eerie: roads without cars or bicycles, cottages with empty windows at the fringes of empty fields, trees heavy with apples and no one picking them. Perhaps it's the wrong time – 3.30; perhaps it's too hot. But where are the people who stacked that hay and set those peppers so carefully to dry? The train passes on – that's the beauty of a train, this heedless movement – but it passes on to more of the same. Six neat beehives, a derelict steam engine with wild flowers garlanding its smokestack, a stalled ox at a level crossing. In the heat haze of the afternoon my compartment grows dusty, and down at the front of the train Turks lie all over their seats, sleeping with their mouths open and children wakeful on their stomachs. At each river and bridge there were square brick emplacements, like Croatian copies of Martello towers, pocked by bombs. Then I saw a man, headless, bent over in a field, camouflaged by cornstalks that were taller than he; I wondered if I had missed all the others because they were made so tiny by their crops.

There was a drama outside Niš. At a road near the track a crowd of people fought to look at a horse, still in its traces and hitched to an overloaded wagon, lying dead on its side in a mud puddle in which the wagon was obviously stuck. I imagined its heart had burst when it tried to free the wagon. And it had just happened: children were calling to their friends, a man was dropping his bike and running back for a look, and farther along a man pissing against a fence was straining to see the horse. The scene was composed like a Flemish painting in which the pissing man was a vivid detail. The train, the window frame holding the scene for moments, made it a picture. The man at the fence flicks the last droplets from his penis and, tucking it in his baggy pants, begins to sprint; the picture is complete.

* * * * *

'I hate sightseeing,' said Molesworth. We were at the corridor window and I had just been reprimanded by a Yugoslav policeman for snapping a picture of a steam locomotive that, in the late afternoon sun, and the whirling dust the thousands of homeward-bound commuters had raised crossing the railway lines, stood amidst a magnificent exhalation of blue vapours mingling with clouds of gold gnats. Now we were in a rocky gorge outside Niš, on the way to Dimitrovgrad, the cliffs rising as we moved and holding occasional symmetries, like remainders of intelligent brickwork in the battlements of a ruined castle. The sight of this seemed to tire Molesworth, and I think he felt called upon to explain his fatigue. 'All that tramping around with guidebooks,' he said after a moment. 'In those horrible crocodiles of tourists, in and out of churches, museums, and mosques. No, no, no. I just like to be still, find a comfortable chair. Do you see what I mean? I like to *absorb* a country.'

He was drinking. We were both drinking, but drink made him reflective and it made me hungry. All I had had to eat during the day was a cheese bun in Belgrade, an envelope of pretzels, and a sour apple. The sight of Bulgaria, with its decrepit houses and skinny goats, did not make me hopeful of a good meal at Sofia Station, and at the fearfully named town of Dragoman a number of people, including several from Car 99, were taken off the train because they hadn't had cholera shots. Italy, the Bulgarians said, was stricken.

I found the Bulgarian conductor and asked him to describe for me a typical Bulgarian meal. Then I wrote down the Bulgarian words for the delicacies he had mentioned: cheese, potatoes, bread, sausages, salad with beans, and so forth. He assured me that there would be food in Sofia.

'This is an awfully slow train,' said Molesworth as the Direct-Orient creaked through the darkness. Here and there was a yellow lantern, a fire far off, a light in a hut at a remote halt where, barely visible, the stationmaster could be seen five paces from his hut, presenting his flag to the dawdling express.

I showed Molesworth my list of Bulgarian foods, and said I planned to buy what was obtainable at Sofia; it would be our last night on the Direct-Orient – we deserved a good meal.

'That should be very useful,' said Molesworth. 'Now, what are you going to use for money?'

'I haven't the slightest idea,' I said.

'They use the lev here, you know. But the snag is, I couldn't find a quotation for it. My bank manager said it was one of those hopeless currencies – I suppose it's not really money at all, just pieces of paper.' From the way he talked I could tell he wasn't hungry. He went on, 'I always use plastic. Plastic's incredibly useful.'

'Plastic?'

'Well, these things.' He set his drink down and took out a wad of credit cards, shuffled them, and read their names.

'Do you think the Barclaycard has hit Bulgaria yet?'

'Let's hope so,' he said. 'But if not, I still have some lire left.'

It was after eleven at night when we pulled into Sofia, and, as Molesworth and I leaped off the train, the conductor told us to hurry: 'Fifteen minutes, maybe ten.'

'You said we'd have a half-hour!'

'But we are running late now. Don't talk – hurry!'

We quick-marched down the platform, searching for food.

There was a cafeteria with a mob at the counter and then nothing more except, at the far end of the platform, a man with a steaming metal pushcart. He was bald. He held a small paper bag in one hand and with the other he flipped open the several tabernacles of his pushcart and stabbed at white buns and red, dripping sausages, the size of bananas, with pink meat showing in slightly burst seams. There were three customers ahead of us. He served them, taking his time, urging buns and sausages into the bags with his busy fork. When my turn came I showed him two fingers, changed my mind, three fingers. He bagged three of each.

'The same again,' said Molesworth and handed him a 1000-lire note.

'No, no,' said the man; he pushed my dollar away and at the same time took my bag from me and put it on the pushcart.

'He won't take our money,' said Molesworth.

'*Banka, banka,*' said the man.

He wants us to get change.'

'This is a dollar,' I said. 'Take the whole thing.'

'He won't wear it,' said Molesworth. 'Where's your *banka,* eh?'

The bald man pointed to the station. We ran in the direction his finger was pointing and found a teller's cage where a long line of disconsolate people stood clutching pieces of paper and kicking their luggage as the line inched forward.

'I think we'll have to give this up as a bad job,' said Molesworth.

'I'm dying for one of those sausages.'

'Unless you want to get duffilled*,' said Molesworth, 'you should get back on the train. I think I shall.'

We did and minutes later the whistle blew and the Bulgarian darkness swallowed Sofia. Enrico, seeing us empty-handed, got Italian crackers from his sister, the nun, and gave them to us; the Armenian lady presented a slab of cheese and even sat with us and had a drink, until her son wandered in wearing a pair of pyjamas. He saw his mother laughing; he burst into tears. 'Now I go,' she said, and went. Monique had gone to bed; so had Enrico. Car 99 was asleep, but we were picking up speed. 'And we're not badly off,' said Molesworth, slicing the cheese. 'Two more bottles of wine – that's one apiece and still some Orvieto to finish. Cheese and biscuits. We can call it a late supper.' We went on drinking, and Molesworth talked of India, how he had gone out for the first time on a P & O liner with thousands of enlisted men, tough mineworkers from the Durham coal fields. Molesworth and his fellow officers had plenty to drink, but the lower ranks were battened down. After a month they ran out of beer. There were fights, the men were mutinous, 'and by the time we reached

Bombay most of them were in chains. But I got an extra pip on my shoulder for behaving myself.'

'This is the idea,' said Molesworth. The train was racing, and he was uncorking the last bottle. 'It's usually a good rule to drink the wine of the country you're passing through.' He glanced out the window into the blackness. 'I suppose that's still Bulgaria. What a great pity.'

* Duffil is the name of another passenger they have met on the train.

Paul Theroux
The Great Railway Bazaar, 1975

First Train Journey

I had been travelling for more than ten years – in Europe, Asia and Africa – and it had not occurred to me to write a travel book. I had always somewhat disliked travel books: they seemed self-indulgent, unfunny and rather selective. I had an idea that the travel writer left a great deal out of his books and put the wrong things in. I hated sight-seeing, yet sight-seeing constituted much of the travel writer's material: the pyramids, the Taj Mahal, the Vatican, the paintings here, the mosaics there. In an age of mass tourism, everyone set off to see the same things, and that was what travel writing seemed to be about. I am speaking of the early 1970s. The travel book was a bore. A bore wrote it and bores read it. It annoyed me that a traveller would suppress the moments of desperation or fear or lust, the details of meals, the names of books read to kill time, the condition of toilets. I had done enough travelling to know that half of it was delay or nuisance – buses breaking down and hotel clerks being rude and market traders being rapacious. The truth of travel was interesting and off-key, and few people ever wrote about it.

Now and then one would read the truth: Evelyn Waugh being mistaken for his brother Alec in *Labels;* or Naipaul's good intentions and bad temper in parts of *An Area of Darkness;* or in a fragment like the following from Anthony Trollope's *The West Indies and the Spanish Main:*

> I was in a shoemaker's shop at St Thomas (Jamaica), buying a pair of boots, when a negro entered quickly and in a loud voice said he wanted a pair of pumps. He was a labouring man fresh from his labour. He had on an old hat – what in Ireland men would call a caubeen; he was in his shirt-sleeves, and was barefooted. As the only shopman was looking for my boots, he was not attended to at the moment.
>
> 'Want a pair of pumps – directerly,' he roared out in a very dictatorial voice.
>
> 'Sit down for a moment,' said the shopman, 'and I will attend to you.'
>
> He did sit down, but did so in the oddest fashion. He dropped himself suddenly into a chair, and at the same moment rapidly raised his legs from the ground; and as he did so fastened his hands across them just below his knees, so as to keep his feet suspended from his arms. This he

contrived to do in such a manner that the moment his body reached the chair his feet left the ground. I looked on in amazement, thinking he was mad. 'Give I a bit of carpet,' he screamed out; still holding up his feet, but with much difficulty.

'Yes, yes,' said the shopman, still searching for the boots.

'Give I a bit of carpet directerly,' he again exclaimed. The seat of the chair was very narrow, and the back was straight, and the position was not easy, as my reader will ascertain if he attempt it. He was half-choked with anger and discomfort. The shopman gave him the bit of carpet. Most men and women will remember that such bits of carpet are common in shoemakers' shops. They are supplied, I believe, in order that they who are delicate should not soil their stockings on the floor. The gentleman in search of the pumps had seen that people of dignity were supplied with such luxuries, and resolved to have his value for his money; but as he had on neither shoes nor stockings, the little bit of carpet was hardly necessary for his material comfort.

Something human had happened, and Trollope recorded it: that, it seemed to me, was the essence of good travel writing.

A traveller's itinerary was important too. Many travel books seemed to be accounts of a traveller becoming a resident. This was not travel at all, but rather a kind of extended visit that I knew well from having lived in Malawi and Uganda and Singapore. I had settled down in those places, I was working, I had a driver's licence, I went shopping every Saturday. It had never occurred to me to write a travel book about any of it. Travel had to do with movement and truth: with trying everything, offering yourself to experience and then reporting it.

Choosing the best route, the correct mode of travel, was the surest way, I felt, of gaining the experience that would lead to writing. It had to be total immersion, a deliberate trip through the hinterland rather than flying from one big city to another, which didn't seem to me to be travel at all. The travel books I liked were off-beat in some way – Trollope's and Naipaul's, Henry Miller's *The Air-Conditioned Nightmare* (America, coast to coast, by car), Mark Twain's *Following The Equator* (a lecture-tour around the world).

My speculations on travel writing took place in the autumn of 1972, when I was teaching for a semester at the University of Virginia. I was working on one novel, and awaiting the publication of another. In those days I began a new book as soon as I finished the one I was working on. My wife was in London with our two children, and she was working – indeed, earning a good living – but I still felt I was the bread-winner and that I was not earning enough. My fee for the new book was £250, and I assumed I would not get much more for the book I was writing. Money is a clumsy subject, but money was crucial in my decision to write my first travel book – simply, I needed it. When I mentioned the possibility of such a book to my American editor, she was delighted. She said, 'We'll give you an advance.' I had never before received an advance. Normally. I wrote a book and submitted it and was paid; I had never been given money for an unwritten book.

It is often the case that you begin to think clearly about your intentions when someone asks you very specific questions. I intended my travel book to be a series of long train journeys, but I had no idea where I wanted to go. I saw a book with lots of people and lots of dialogue and no sight-seeing. My editor's questioning made me think hard about it, and I thought: *Trains through Asia.* I was determined to start in London, and to take the Orient Express. My route would take me through Turkey, into Iran, into Baluchistan, and after a short bus ride I could catch a train in Zahedan, go into Pakistan and more or less chug through the rest of Asia – to Hanoi, through China, Mongolia and the Soviet Union. Much of this, on closer examination, proved impractical or impossible. The Chinese Embassy in 1972 simply hung up when I said I wanted a visa to take trains through China. I had to wait fourteen years before I was able to take that trip.

There was a war in Baluchistan – I rerouted myself through Afghanistan. I decided to include Japan and the whole of the Trans-Siberian. I didn't mind where I went as long as it was in Asia and had a railway system and visas were available. I saw myself puffing along from country to country, simply changing trains.

Meanwhile I was finishing my novel. It was about rural England and was rather ghostly and solemn. I wanted my next to be a sunny book. I had just about decided on my travel itinerary when I delivered my novel to my British publisher. He suggested we have lunch. Almost before we had started eating he told me he disliked it. 'It will hurt your reputation,' was how he put it. 'But I want to publish your travel book.' I had told him I had signed a contract for this with my American publisher. I said that if he published my novel he could have the travel book. 'If you twist my arm I'll publish your novel,' he said.

I found a new publisher in Britain. I had greater reason than ever for publishing the travel book: I doubted my ability to earn a living writing fiction.

I think of the circumstances surrounding *The Great Railway Bazaar* rather than the trip itself. I hated leaving my family behind in London. I had never taken such a trip, I felt encumbered by an advance on royalties – modest though it was; most of my writer friends mocked the idea.

I never got around to worrying about the trip itself. I was beset by an obscure ache that was both mental and physical – the lingering anxiety that I was going to die. I had always had the idea that my particular exit would be made via an appointment in Samarra, and that I would go a great distance and endure enormous discomfort in order to meet my death. If I chose to sit at home and eat and drink it would never occur. I imagined it would be a silly accident, like what happened to the monk and mystic Thomas Merton: he left his monastery in Kentucky after twenty-five years and accidentally electrocuted himself on the frayed wires of a fan in Bangkok a week later.

I left London on 19 September 1973. It was a grey day. I had a bad cold. My wife waved me goodbye. Almost immediately I felt I had made an absurd mistake. I hadn't the slightest idea of what I was doing. I became very gloomy and to cheer myself up and give myself the illusion that this was work I began to take voluminous notes. From the time I left until the moment I arrived back in England four months later I filled one notebook after another. I wrote everything down – conversations, descriptions of people and places, details of trains, trivia, even criticism of the novels I happened to be reading. I still have some of those books, and on the blank back pages of Joyce's *Exiles,* Chekhov's stories and Endo's *Silence,* I have scribbled small insectile notes, which I amplified when I transferred them to my large notebooks. I always wrote in the past tense.

The trip recorded is the trip I took. I changed the names of people I wished to protect, but many names I left. I had found a structure for the book in a series of train journeys, and I simply plunged in. I had never read a book quite like the one I was writing. This worried me as well as made me hopeful. The writing of the book took the same amount of time as the trip itself, four months.

That was almost fifteen years ago. *The Great Railway Bazaar* is still in print and sells well. Some people think it is the only book I have ever written, which annoys me. I have written other books that are more fluent and informative. For example, I mention in *The Great Railway Bazaar* that my train passed through Niš in Yugoslavia. But I never bothered to find out anything about Niš. I have just read that it was the birthplace of the Emperor Constantine. The *Blue Guide* continues: 'Though not a pleasant place in itself, Niš has several interesting monuments.' I now realize why I did not linger in Niš.

I did not know when I wrote my *Railway Bazaar* (I got the title from a street-name in India) that every journey is unique. My book is about my trip, not yours or anyone else's. If someone had come with me and written a book about the trip, it would have been a different book from mine. I also did not know that every trip has a historical dimension. After I returned home political changes occurred in the countries I had travelled through. The Shah was deposed and Iran became very dangerous for the traveller; Afghanistan went to war with itself; India and Pakistan restored their rail link. Laos shut its borders to foreigners and exiled its royalty. Vietnam repaired its railway, so that now it is possible to travel by train from Ho Chi Minh City (Saigon) to Hanoi. Many trains were taken out of service, most notably the Orient Express. The new train that plies from London to Venice under that name is for rich idle people who have selfish, sumptuous fantasies about travel that bear no relation to the real thing. However awful my old Orient Express was, at least it carried a range of passengers – rich and poor, old and young. It was cheap and friendly, and, like all great trains, it was a world on wheels.

When I wrote *The Great Railway Bazaar* I was groping in the dark – although I took care to disguise the fact. I may seem very self-assured in it, but it was simply my way of whistling to keep my spirits up. I knew that I had taken on a venerable genre, the travel book, and was writing it in my own way, to suit my peculiar trip and temperament. It was not like a novel: which requires inspiration and intense imagining and a long period alone in a room.

I began writing a novel soon after finishing my travel book. I got the idea for it in Vietnam and even mentioned it in *Railway Bazaar:* 'From the back of the train I could see market women and children reoccupying the track, and once – a swift sight of a leaping man – I thought I saw an American ... If one were to write about Vietnam in any coherent way one would have to begin with these outsiders.'

A travel book, I had discovered, was a deliberate act – like the act of travel itself. It took health and strength and confidence. When I finished a novel I never knew whether I would be able to write another one. But I knew, when I finished my first travel book, that I would be able to do it again.

Paul Theroux
New World, Granta 29, 1989

Travel Activities

A Journey to the Western Isles

Doctor Samuel Johnson and his companion James Boswell went on a journey to the Western Isles of Scotland in the 1770s. They both wrote separate accounts of their impressions.

1. Interrupted readings
● Work in pairs. Read aloud both versions of the same incident printed on Pages 23–26.
● Now take on the roles of Johnson and Boswell. As Johnson reads his account, Boswell should interrupt him, adding his reflections on the incident. Repeat this process for the second version.
e.g.

Johnson: Near the way, by the water-side...
Boswell: It was Loch Ness was it not?
Johnson: It may well have been but I was most interested in the hut. As I was saying, we espied a cottage.......

2. What's different?
● Make two parallel lists, in which you write down what you think Johnson and Boswell are each most interested in. Try numbering the points on the lists, to give a rank order for the writers' concerns. For instance, if you think Boswell is most interested in the bedroom, put a number one beside it and so on.
You could use these headings to construct your lists, along with any others you might want to add.

The construction of the hut
The details of the way the hut looks
The woman
The woman's misunderstanding
The bedroom
The children
How they manage to survive
The food they eat
The animals
The sleeping arrangements
Their travelling companion
Their amusing conversation

The woman's walk to church
Her snuff-taking
Her whisky

● Which of the two accounts did you find the more lively and engaging to read? Look at your parallel lists to see whether your preference had anything to do with what the writers chose to focus on. Is there a difference in style or tone between the pieces?

3. The old woman talks
● When the children return from their errands, what does the old woman tell them about Johnson and Boswell's visit? Imagine that you are the old woman and write her dialogue with her family.

4. Two versions of a journey
● Choose a memorable journey that you and one other person have been on, ideally someone else in your class e.g. a school outing or journey. Pick one day, event or incident from your journey. Write about it in whatever way you like, concentrating on the aspects you find most interesting. Try to make it a 'good read' . Ask the person who shared the journey with you to write about the same events from their own point of view.
● When both pieces of writing have been drafted, put the two versions together and analyse them in terms of the different perspectives and choices each of the two writers has made. Use these prompts to help you:

Were there any surprises for you in what the other person noticed or chose to mention?
Did s/he interpret any events differently from you?
Were there any differences of tone between the two pieces?
Did one of the pieces do more describing the scene/evoking emotions/ giving a personal perspective/telling it as a story?

● Write up your observations as a commentary that can be included with the two accounts as a piece of coursework.

Des Moines

'Des Moines' is the first chapter of a book by Bill Bryson called *The Lost Continent – Travels in Small Town America*.

1. Reading the opening
● Look closely at the first few sentences and annotate them, thinking about what kind of writing it is, what tone it is written in and what image is created of the place.

> 'I come from Des Moines. Somebody had to.
> When you come from Des Moines you either accept the fact without question
> and settle down with a local girl named Bobbi and get a job at the Firestone
> factory and live there for ever and ever, or you spend your adolescence moaning
> at length about what a dump it is and how you can't wait to get out, and then
> you settle down with a local girl named Bobbi and get a job at the Firestone
> factory and live there for ever and ever.'

● Try writing a few sentences about the place where you live, imitating the style of
the opening by experimenting with humour, irony and satire. Irony is when you say
one thing whilst meaning the opposite. Satire is when you reveal the faults in
something by sarcasm and mockery. You could pick just one fact about the place
where you live and develop it in a humorous way.

2. Group work on the text
● Having heard the text being read aloud to you, work in small groups, with each
group exploring a different aspect. Take notes on your discussion to help you plan a
presentation. Use the ideas below to help you, then when you are ready, present your
aspect of the text to the rest of the class.

Group 1 : People
Agree someone to act as the scribe for your ideas. Go through the text, listing
all the people who are described. For each one:

Talk about what s/he is like
Consider how s/he is presented by Bryson
Consider why Bryson has put them into the piece about Des Moines
Pick one or two short quotes that are particularly strong expressions of what
s/he is like

Plan a short presentation on the people in the text, what they have in common,
why they are there and your reactions to Bryson's presentation of them.

Group 2 : Purposes
Agree someone to act as the scribe for your ideas. Sketch out these headings on
a piece of paper:

Describe   **Inform**   **Entertain/Amuse**   **Tell a story**   **Make you think**

For each heading, find two or three examples from the text where the writer
seems to have this purpose in mind. Pick out short quotes (with page numbers).
Talk about which of these purposes seem to you most strongly at work in this
text.

Plan a short presentation on the different purposes of the text and which you
felt to be the most important and interesting.

Group 3 : Stories and Anecdotes

Agree someone to act as a scribe for your ideas. Bryson uses several little stories, or anecdotes, to tell us about Des Moines. Go through the text, listing each of the stories.

What do you think he achieves by telling each of the stories?
What do they have in common, if anything?
How effective are they?
Which one(s) did you enjoy most and why?

Plan a short presentation on the stories told, your reactions to them and the role they play in the text.

Group 4 : Tone

Agree someone to act as a scribe for your group. This opening chapter has a range of different tones at different times. Go through the text finding two or three examples of each of the different tones suggested below and write them on a chart, with page numbers. Discuss what makes you aware of the tone in each case. What do you think is the main tone of the piece?

Funny/Ironic   **Serious**   **Reflective**   **Chatty**   **Poetic**   **Nostalgic**

Plan a short presentation on the different tones you found in the piece and which you felt to be strongest.

Group 5 : Humour

Agree someone to act as a scribe for your group. Find as many examples as you can of Bryson trying to be funny in this piece. In each case, try to say what it is that makes it funny. These are some of the ways in which it might be humorous:

> The names used
> Exaggeration
> Funny situations
> Funny characters
> Teasing the reader
> Humorous comparisons
> Irony

Plan a presentation on the humour in the piece, in which you pick out some short quotes and sections and explain why you find them funny.

3. Writing about 'Des Moines'

● Write about your responses to 'Des Moines' using your discussion and notes to help you explore what the writer is trying to do and how he achieves his purposes.

4. Writing about your area

● Write an account of life in your area, using one of the angles listed below:

A description from the viewpoint of a tourist or visitor. If you have links with another country or region, write in the voice of someone visiting from there for the first time.

A personal account, in the style of Bryson, which sets out to present a humorous view of the place and supplies all kinds of examples and anecdotes to support that view.

Two different versions of your area e.g. an advert to go into a Tourist Information Centre, trying to attract visitors and a letter to the local newspaper setting out the problems in the area and suggesting improvements and solutions.

Tokyo Pastoral

1. Picture postcards

● Read the text out loud or listen to it being read to you.
● Working in small groups, skim through the text looking for five images of Tokyo that might make good picture postcards.
● Skim through the text looking for five images of Tokyo that might be used in a campaign leaflet to clean up the area, showing the deterioration of the community.

2. Exploring the text

● Each group will be given one area of the text to talk about, take notes on and present to the rest of the class. Pick out three or four key quotes, just short phrases, to help you explain to the class what Angela Carter is describing and how she creates a view of Tokyo and its inhabitants.

Sounds and Smells
Japanese Family Life
The Physical Environment
Houses and Homes
Shops and What They Reveal about Life in Tokyo
Angela Carter, the Outsider
Japanese Attitudes to Sex and Sexuality
Tokyo Women
Tokyo Men

3. A TV documentary

This is a very visual piece of writing. To explore this further, imagine the opening of a documentary programme about life in a district of Tokyo.

- Choose one of these titles for your documentary:

Tokyo: A Very Respectable Place
Sleaze and Slime in Tokyo
A Day in the Life of a District of Tokyo
Angela Carter in Tokyo
The Japanese Way of Life

- Produce a shooting script for the opening shots of the programme, using Angela Carter's account as the basis for the script. Decide what is going to be seen and what is going to be heard.

What is going to be seen should include:
Visual images, taken from Angela Carter's text
Ideas about visual style
Suggestions for camerawork

What is going to be heard should include:
Sound effects
Commentary (The commentary might be voice over or a narrator talking to camera and could include bits of Angela Carter's text.)
Music

On a Train

1. Talking about the text

- Having heard the text being read aloud, work in pairs or small groups. Talk about your first responses to this text. These might include:

Whether you enjoyed it
What it made you feel about foreign travel
What it made you feel about trains and train journeys

- The text could be said to divide into two parts. Decide where you think the divide is and give a sub-heading to each part. Look at the first and second parts in turn. Decide which of these words and phrases apply to each part:

Humorous
Dramatic
Exciting
Detailed
Poetic
Conversational
Reflective
Telling a story
Describing people

Describing places
Making you think
Creating a visual picture

● Which bit of the account did you enjoy most? Pick a short section, (5-10 lines), to look at closely. Talk about what you enjoyed about it. Practise reading it aloud.
● Share the bits of the text you have chosen as a whole class. Each group should read their section aloud and explain what they liked about it.

2. Observing the events

Paul Theroux writes about his own experiences. He writes in the first person, as 'I'. How would the piece be different if it were being observed by a more distanced commentator, who narrated the events without having participated in them?

● Experiment with re-writing a small section of the text using third person narration. You could choose any bit from ' 'I hate sight-seeing,' said Molesworth' to the end of the text.
e.g. Molesworth and Theroux stood at the corridor window, Molesworth chattering away about his dislike of sightseeing whilst Theroux remained silent. He was still feeling rather irritated by the incident with the Yugoslav policeman.

First Train Journey

1. Writing about journeys

In his first paragraph, Paul Theroux says,

> ‘The travel book was a bore. A bore wrote it and bores read it. It annoyed me that a traveller would suppress the moments of desperation or fear or lust, the details of meals, the names of books read to kill time, the condition of toilets. I had done enough travelling to know that half of it was delay or nuisance – buses breaking down and hotel clerks being rude and market traders being rapacious. The truth of travel was interesting and off-key, and few people ever wrote about it.’

● Choose one of the topics listed below. Tell someone else about it, allowing them to question you to jog your memory and add further detail. It does not have to be about a holiday abroad. It could be about a school trip or a visit to family or an outing, anything that took you away from your normal environment.

Travel memories:
Feeling ill
A delay
Feeling threatened or in danger
A misunderstanding
Missing a train/plane/boat

A meal
Seeing or meeting someone interesting or unusual
Money problems

2. The writer's views on the travel genre

● Read 'First Train Journey'.
● Look at this list of statements about travel writing. See if you can find places in the text where Theroux is either supporting or refuting these views.

> Good travel writing should tell the reader about visiting the sights in tourist destinations

> Travel writing should be about travelling, not about living in a different country

> Books that take an odd, or unusual angle are more interesting than ones which follow predictable travel-writing patterns

> There is no such thing as the truth about a journey: it is only one person's view of it

> The tiny details of experiencing a journey are what is interesting for a reader

> Travel writers shouldn't write about sordid or frightening things

> Travel writing is only interesting if it is about human behaviour

3. On a Train

● Look at the extract from *The Great Railway Bazaar*, which Theroux writes about in 'First Train Journey'. Annotate it with your views on what is happening in the extract and the extent to which Theroux is achieving what he sets out as his aims as a travel writer in 'First Train Journey'. e.g. Where is there human interest? Is it 'off-beat' in any way? Does it avoid the trap of being boring?

Comparing Travel Texts

1. Imagining and imitating
● Choose one of the three suggestions below, as a way of exploring differences between the travel writers in this section.

Angela Carter in the Western Isles
What if Angela Carter had written about the old woman and the hut described by Samuel Johnson and James Boswell? What would she have chosen to write about? What angle would she have taken? How might she have described the scene and the encounter? What might she have wanted to say to the woman?
● Experiment with writing her version of it.

Dr. Johnson and Boswell go to Des Moines
What would they have had to say about Des Moines? How might their views of the place differ? How might they have described Mr. Piper, Stan, or the woman selling postcards?
● Choose one character or incident from Bill Bryson's piece and try writing about it in the style of Johnson and Boswell.

Strangers on a train
Imagine the scene. The writers in this section on Travel are all going to a Writers' Conference in Blackpool. They meet up on the train. They don't know each other and begin to chat. Bit by bit they discover each other's identities and begin to talk about the train journey, their attitudes to travelling and their views on travel writing.
● In small groups roleplay the scene in the train, including as many writers as there are members of your group.

2. Looking through Theroux's eyes
● Use Paul Theroux's ideas about travel writing as a basis for reading and commenting on another piece of travel writing. Bear in mind that Theroux is expressing a viewpoint and that other writers may have very different purposes and ideas about what makes good travel writing.

3. Your own writing
Use the work you have done on travel writing to write about your own environment or a place you have travelled to. You could do it in the style of one of the writers you have read, take elements from different writers, or try to speak with a voice that is distinctively your own. These are first sentences from two of the texts, that could be adapted as a starting-point:
I come from ....Somebody had to.
This is clearly one of those districts where it always seems to be................

The Man With No Name

When it was raining hard the other day, a familiar silhouette appeared at my front door. I knew it was him, because, having rung the bell, he retreated to the gate: a defensive habit gained on the streets. 'It's the man', said my young daughter, 'with no name.'

He had on his usual tie and tweed jacket and was leaning against the hedge, though he said he hadn't had a drink. 'Just passing through,' he said as usual, and money passed between us with the customary clumsy handshake. 'I'd better give that a trim,' he said, as he always did, pointing at the hedge, and again I thanked him and said no; he was too unsteady for that. Collar up, he turned back into the rain.

I have known him for about three years. He comes to my door at least every week, and I see him out on the common in all weathers, asleep or reading or looking at the traffic. I see him nodding as if in silent discussion with himself on a weighty matter; or waving and smiling at a procession of women with small children in buggies. Understandably, women hurry away from him; others look through him.

He has no home, though he once told me he lived 'just around the corner'. That turned out to be a hostel. From what I can gather, he sleeps rough most of the time, often on a bench in front of a small powerboats clubhouse, or in a clump of large trees where sick and alcoholic men go and where there was a murder some years back. In winter, he has newspapers tucked inside his jacket. Perhaps he is fifty, or more; it's difficult to tell.

He vanishes from time to time, as the homeless tend to do; and when I last asked him about this, he said he went to 'visit my sister'. I very much doubted this; I know he goes to one of several seaside towns for a few weeks at a time. There he scans the local newspaper small ads for 'unemployed guests wanted'. These are inserted by the owners of bed-and-breakfast hotels and hostels, where homeless people are sent by local authorities and by the Department of Health and Social Security.

I can imagine a little of what it must be like for him. As a reporter I once ended up in one of these 'hotels'. When I couldn't produce the Social Security form that would allow the owner to collect every penny of his 'guest's' state benefit, I was thrown out. This wholesale diversion of public money is acknowledged as one of the fastest ways of getting rich in Britain since the Thatcher Government stopped councils spending on housing more than ten years ago. Hotel owners are said to make about £120 million a year. In the Enterprise Society, homelessness, like drinking water, has been 'privatised'; or is it 'restructured'?

My friend is one of 80,000 people who are officially homeless in London. This is the equivalent of the population of Stevenage, in Hertfordshire; the true figure is greater, of course. The national figure for homeless households is 169,000, ten times higher than a decade ago. The homeless are now a nation within a nation, whose suffering makes a good television story at Christmas or when there is snow and ice.

I have never been made homeless. To have nowhere to go, perhaps for the rest of my life, to face every day the uncertainty of the night and fear of the elements, is almost unimaginable. I say 'almost', because in writing about the homeless I have gleaned something of their powerlessness once they are snared in what used to be known as the 'welfare state'. This was true before Thatcher.

The difference these days is that there are no 'typical' homeless any more. They are also from the middle classes and the new software classes. They are both old and young – an estimated 35,000 children are homeless in London alone. My friend is typical in that he bears the familiar scars of homelessness: such as a furtiveness that gives the impression of a person being followed; a sporadic, shallow joviality that fails to mask his anxiety; and a deferential way that does not necessarily reflect his true self. The latter, because it is out of character, is occasionally overtaken by melodramatic declarations of independence. When he told me he had to go to hospital one day for a stomach operation and I offered to take him, he said, 'No! I can walk! Of course I can!' And he did.

I didn't know who or what he was until recently. It seemed an intrusion to ask. My place in his life was simply as a source of a few quid from time to time. Then one day he was telling me about a television programme about Asia he had seen, and it was clear he had been there in the Army. And that led to a statement of pride about what he had done with his life on leaving the Army. He had worked in a garage, training apprentice mechanics, until this was thwarted by a string of personal tragedies: a divorce and finally his 'redundancy': that wonderful expression of the Enterprise Society. He was then too old to start again; and he was taking to drink.

He has turned up with cuts and bruises, and blood caked on his cheek. Once, when I said I would go and call a doctor, I returned to the door to find him gone. On the common and in the streets, he is prey to thugs and to the police. He has little of the protection the rest of us assume as a right, provided by a civilised society. The defences that have been built up for the likes of him since the great Depression of sixty years ago continue to be dismantled with platitudes that are spoken, unchallenged, on the news almost every night.

Recently it was National Housing Week. The junior housing minister, Tim Yeo, said the government's 'rough sleepers initiative', which was launched during the freezing conditions of last winter, had halved the numbers of homeless sleeping out in London.

Anyone driving through London's West End knows this to be untrue. The homeless in the capital have become a tourist curiosity. Europeans are incredulous at having to step over so many human bundles on the pavement, in the Underground, on the steps of galleries and museums. Eavesdrop on a French tour guide describing the sights in the shopfronts of the Strand. 'They were hosed away,' she says, 'but they have come back.'

With the maximum publicity, the government allocated £300 million for 'rough sleepers'. As the London Housing Unit has pointed out, this has been wiped out by the £138 million in cuts in long-term housing investment by councils and by the abolition of £100 million-worth of special allowances for London boroughs. The minister, Tim Yeo, said: 'You will see a similar priority given to housing as to education and health between now and the general election.' In the circumstances this had to be irony; but it was not.

John Pilger
New Statesman, June 14, 1991

Beggars of Britain

Punk Beggars, drunk beggars, beggars with babies. Beggars in shell suits and beggars in rags. Beggars stinking of cheap lager with snot on their chin and a mangy mutt on the end of a piece of string. Lots of them.

And gypsy beggars who try to stuff a ratty flower into your button hole with some sentimental line – 'For the children,' coos some obese hag. Old beggars too shagged out to beg, young beggars who look like they could run a four-minute mile if they ever made it up off their fannies. Beggars in King's Cross, beggars in Covent Garden, beggars on the street where you live. All kinds of beggars everywhere in this city, and they will be with us forever now. They have no shame. Because begging is no longer taboo.

I think that my father would rather have seen us go hungry than have to go out there and ponce for our supper. I think that the old man, may he rest peacefully, would have preferred to rob, cheat or watch us wither with malnutrition before standing on a street corner with a Uriah Heep look in his eye asking for a hand-out. He would have been happier seeing us sleeping in a shoebox full of shit than he would have been *begging*.

The fact is that my father's generation was incapable of begging. The children they raised were also incapable of begging. There were standards that were not negotiable. There were certain lines you never crossed; there were taboos. Respect the elderly. Don't rat on your friends. Never hit a woman. Never stand on a street corner with snot on your chin and a dog on the end of a piece of string asking passers-by if they have any change. Of all the taboos, *don't beg* was the greatest of all. You could sleep with your sister before you went begging.

Somewhere between then and now, between our childhood and our thirties, all the old taboos disappeared. But taboos are good, taboos are the no-go areas that mark the parameters of society's moral code. When taboos fall, civilisation is built on dangerously shifting sands.

Liberals would blame the fall of the begging taboo on the let-the-bloody-orphans-take-care-of-themselves ethics of Thatcherism. Conservatives would blame the hey-you-guys-let's-catch-crabs permissiveness of the '60s. What is certain is that violence against women, children and the wrinklies is at an all-time high; and that begging is suddenly shame-free, an acceptable way to make a living. It is now quite all right to earn a crust with the crumbs you can ponce from strangers. Begging is a vocation. Soon beggars will have agents and accountants who will write off the food for their dogs-on-a-rope against tax. How low can you go? The British have become a nation of nappy-wearers.

In that underrated comedy classic *American Psycho,* Patrick Bateman is plagued by beggars at every turn. In the exchanges between Bateman and the beggars, Bret Easton Ellis reveals that he is really an old softie at heart. The beggars are invariably homeless and hungry and deserving of sympathy, easily reduced to tears of shame and regret. Meanwhile, the American Psycho himself is an archetype of right-wing heartlessness, saying things to the cry-baby beggars like, 'Listen – do you think it's fair to take money from people who do have jobs? Who do work?' just before he slices out their eyeballs with a platinum Am Ex card.

The most unrealistic thing about the beggars in *American Psycho* is their shame. It is quite believable that they are outside every restaurant. It is perfectly credible that they inspire nausea and disgust in Bateman. What smacks of pure invention, however, are the tears of self-loathing that course down their cheeks whenever Bateman gives them a stern look. I never saw a beggar yet who would recognise guilt if it bit him on his unwashed ass. In real life – over here and over there – beggars have no shame. Their whole schtick is a transference of guilt. Shame is meant to be in the eye of the beholder. Twenty years ago – five years ago! – the beggar might have felt guilty. Now it's the beggee who's meant to feel bad. Well, I'm sorry, but any liberal guilt I might feel about brushing past yet another beggar – and there are so many of the bastards – has long been overwhelmed by compassion fatigue.

Now that begging is an acceptable career option it is worth considering a few tips from poncing masterclass. Place yourself somewhere the public can't miss you, say outside a West End theatre or at the foot of some tube station steps. Consider the use of props – a child is good, a baby even better, though you would be surprised at the well of compassion you plumb when you have some flea-bitten mongrel at your side. Signs are fine. Knock out ones that say, 'Please give generously – No home, no job, no shame' or 'Take pity – Mohawk with run in tights' or 'Dog on a rope to support'. Make eye contact and be persistent, friendly – don't be too specific. Ask the beggees for 'loose change', rather than money for a cup of coffee or money to catch the bus to the Job Centre. Everybody knows you are going to piss it away.

You can always sing a little song or do a little dance, but a true beggar frowns on these gimmicks. Busking is begging with music (give me money because I am entertaining you) just as mugging is begging with menace (give me money or I will fill your face in). But begging purists want you to give them money because – what? Because you are better off than they are? Because life has dealt them a bad hand?

Well, I don't buy it. I don't believe that the people begging are the unluckiest people in town. They are merely the people with the least pride, dignity, self-respect – all the intangibles that hold the human spirit together. It's strange, but I don't recall ever seeing a black beggar in London, or a Hong Kong Chinese beggar or an Indian beggar. I must have seen hundreds, thousands of beggars in this town, and they have all been white trash. But when you look at the sick-making state of the white working class – all the men turning into fat farts at 20, all the girls turning into their mothers a year later – what possible hope could there be for the next rung down on the caste system? If the people with jobs have the aesthetic beauty and intellectual ability of a cow pat, what chance is there for the people without a job? Though of course by now begging is a job the newest profession.

I used to give, I used to give generously. These people disgusted me, but still I gave. I was appalled, but I felt sorry for them – and they knew it! Oh, they could spot old muggins a mile off! It was feeding frenzy time at the zoo when I came down the road! I was a soft touch – I thought it was the correct emotional response. In a way, my concern has simply been exhausted. So sorry, no change! Ponce your next bruise-blue can of Vomit Brew from some other sucker. There's just too many of them. But it goes beyond mere compassion fatigue. I think I have grown to truly hate them.

I hate the way they make a beautiful city ugly, the way they shuffle about in a lager haze first thing in the morning – booze is a bigger factor than bad luck in the begging world – and I hate it that my son came home one day saying he had given his tube fare to a man who really really needed it. I wish he could grow up thinking all men are brothers. But it is hard to think of a man as your brother when he has a brain addled by alcohol, snot on his chin and a dog on a rope. Then every man feels like an only child.

Begging defaces the city, degrades the spirit. It dehumanises you as well as them; it brutalises us all. You learn to walk past these people, you have to, and it makes it easier to turn away from the truly needy. These professional leeches, big strapping lads some of them, harden your heart, put callouses on your soul. They make every cry for help seem like junk mail.

In Africa you see beggars with deformed legs crawling, literally crawling, by the side of the road. In Africa you see old men with their eyes turned a horrible milky blue by river blindness being led around by their grandchildren. You see sights that make you feel like weeping – you see beggars with every excuse for begging. But London isn't the Third World. It just smells that way.

In America they have beggars who are suffering from AIDS – that's probably a couple of years away for us – which begs the question, what's so special about AIDS? Of course it's terrible, all terminal, all tragic. Because there is no social network to take care of these people, you say. Because the medical services can't cope. Well, you can believe that if you want. Or you can believe that begging is like eating human flesh, being cruel to animals or pushing your granny while she's shaving – something that no-one in the developed world should ever do, under any circumstances. The virus that we are truly blighted by is the one that attacks the human spirit. It is reflected in the general degeneracy of life in our capital, in the pathetically unctuous faces of all these healthy grown men whose best friend is a dog on a piece of string.

But it may not be very long before we look back on the good old days when the only beggars we had to contend with were gypsies, punks and drunks. The new hard times are not a northern, working-class, trouble-at-mill thing this time around. This time the recession has hit the middle class – it's wonderful, it's never been so easy to hail a black cab – and now that the last taboo is gone, how long before you are asked for loose change by a Channel 4 commissioning editor or a South Bank Show researcher, or an editor at Random House? How long before you look into the face of a beggar on Old Compton Street and realise – the horror, the horror – that you have had *lunch* with this person?

The taboos are coming down, and so are all the borders. The other day I saw a family of East Europeans jabbering away in some Slavic dialect. You wouldn't believe these people. The woman was wearing a little Porsche badge on clothes so synthetic they were a fire hazard. If you think that Thatcher has made us a nation of nappy wearers, then wait till you get a load of the paragons of dependency that Marx and Lenin have produced. The opening up of Europe creates all sorts of possibilities for the begging industry.

We owe it to ourselves to walk past them, metaphorically gobbing in the grubby palms of their outstretched hands, chanting our protest against a world that is forever changing for the worst. No change, we say, no change. Just say no change.

Tony Parsons
Arena, September/October 1991

An African Feast for Flies and Other Parasites

Once again Africans are dying, 'like flies' according to Isabel Pardigu of Médecins Sans Frontières, who is clearly gifted with a repellent turn of cliché. If you were there in Goma, you would know that flies never die, especially when there are so many corpses to feed on and breed in, and so many sticky eyes and runny noses to cluster on.

Flies all over the world are packing their bags and heading for Goma The congestion at Goma airport is being made worse by the pre-emptory demands of another kind of parasite, known collectively as the media. They will tell you that they are justified in crowding aid workers out of transport because they will be the ones to touch the hearts of the international community.

They will do it by stripping the Rwandan refugees of their last shred of dignity, poking cameras into their faces as they groan their lives away, posed to catch the hugest eyes on the very point of glazing. At breakfast and at dinner, we can sharpen our own appetites with a plentiful dose of the pornography of war, genocide, destitution and disease. The four horsemen are up and away, with the press corps stumbling along behind.

The media are involved in a revolting orgy, with the sole justification that it might produce some assistance. Why that means that every news organisation should be represented, why we can't at least be shown the same pictures of grim death, if that's what it takes, I don't know. There is actually a ghastly competition for the worst pictures on the spurious grounds that they are the most affecting. Dying children are slung on the scales so that a photographer can get a cover shot and maybe a Pulitzer, by clicking the shutter at the very instant the small heart stops.

The reporters trawl back and forth in search of a word that will get them the front page. They have their word and they are desperate to get someone to say it. The word is 'Cholera'. They can see it in four-inch type, maybe even in red. Tiredly, the aid workers admit that the people are at risk from diarrhoea disease. 'You mean cholera!' squeal the reporters. Everyone who has diarrhoea disease exhibits, according to the reporters, the symptoms of cholera. Rice-water faeces is not in the least photogenic; reporters don't crawl under the camp beds to see the hole cut for the infectious liquid to run out. They don't examine stools to see if they are bloody or mucous or rice-water, but they think they know the symptoms of cholera.

No aid worker will say cholera, when what is being dealt with is the whole gamut of diarrhoea disease, precisely because the word cholera is what the reporter is mad for, a buzz word. Shigellosis will kill as many or more in a situation like Goma, but you can't see shigellosis on the front page. I have seen people who were strong and healthy die in a few hours from the massive dehydration and shock that shigellosis can cause. There are a dozen kinds of typhus that can be as lethal as cholera but their names do not have the power to terrify as the dread word 'cholera'. It is beyond the imagination of most consumers of the pornography of war, genocide, destitution and disease that, disappearing under the tide of refugees, there is a real town with a real community. Look up and out of your window now; how would you feel if a horde of ragged, skinny people with absolutely nothing to lose was heading for your front door? Imagine then that they had infectious faeces dripping down their legs, or that you thought they had.

Do the reporters want the 50,000 healthy people of Goma to torch the sick refugees? Is more genocide what they would like to see? Panic is more dangerous in a situation like Goma than you and I could well imagine. We have already seen starving Hutus kicking starving Tutsis; we may see Zaireans fighting them both to save their own lives. Killing in self-defence is lawful, remember.

Cholera is said to be endemic in the Goma region. That cholera is endemic in the region is an absolute disgrace and reproach to the rich world. Cholera doesn't have to be endemic anywhere. The Rwandan catastrophe was a long time coming and could be seen afar off. That the information services of the rich world have joined the flies that swarm over the dying Rwandan people is the elaboration of a vile dereliction of duty. In frigging our sympathy glands for the people of Rwanda at this late stage, we do no more than indulge our sense of superiority at their expense.

The pretence that we do it so that the Rwandans may at last be assisted is absurd. You do not start to organise a fire brigade when the house is burning. You do not trot around the streets with collection boxes for the money to start buying water to throw on the house. Most people would be shocked and disgusted to know that there is an industry that exists to supply emergency aid. The greater the rush, the higher the price and the bigger the profit. 'You want tents, we got tents. You want them next week, fifty quid each, you want them tomorrow, £150.' The biggest entrepreneurs growing fat on the misery of Africa are British.

There is one more crowning obscenity in this mess. The organisations that are expected to handle it are charities. Charities! How can anyone dare to imagine for a second that what is going on in Rwanda is an opportunity to exercise charity! Let alone an opportunity to demonstrate the excellence of one god over another, one sect over another, one culture over another. If there is a God he should not allow himself to be mocked in this way.

If the name 'human' is not to be shameful in the universe, we have got now to accept our global responsibility. We have to organise and fund a disaster brigade, with the right to requisition supplies and logistical support, and to cross frontiers – in just the same way that the fire brigade can empty a private swimming pool or cut through a door. Every day we show Rwandan humiliation, destitution and despair in vivid colour on our screens and in our newspapers, we defile ourselves and all that is human. The truth is that we have failed to deal with every catastrophe that has befallen the poor world, principally because that world is so poor by contrast to ourselves. After all this knowledge, there can be no forgiveness.

Germaine Greer
The Guardian, July 25 1994

A Response to Germaine Greer

Germaine Greer's wrong-headed analysis (July 25) has crudely exposed her own ignorance of the refugee crisis in Goma.

First, she argues for a single television news organisation to cover the crisis. Does she want a single newspaper correspondent too? Or just one photo journalist? Perhaps Pravda could do the job for everyone.

Second, she would be correct to call the television coverage 'pornography' if it had sought to focus solely on the misery that has afflicted the refugees. But their exodus and subsequent hardship is a direct result of careful planning by the former Rwandan government who have actively forced the Hutu population to flee their country. The news media has been rigorous in ensuring that the horrific images shown to their audiences are placed in that full vertical context.

Third, she is quite wrong to state that 'cholera' is a word seized upon by journalists to sensationalise the story and is a word not used by aid workers. Both UNHCR and MSF stated on July 20 that cholera was rife in the camps and they have been saying that ever since.

Fourth, the population of Goma is 150,000, not 50,000.

Fifth, Miss Greer may dismiss the effect of the television reportage of the crisis but President Clinton and Baroness Chalker have publicly stated that it was the television pictures from Goma that forced them to act. If Miss Greer had her way it is likely that the hundreds of thousands of refugees would face an even bleaker future than the one already open to them.

Before Miss Greer sounds off again on the subject I invite her to leave the comfort of her home and visit Goma, check out the facts, and then attempt to write a column that approximates something close to the truth.

David Belton
The Guardian, 3rd August 1994

Media Duty that Begins When the Dying Stops

Acry of rage and desperation such as I uttered in my last column about Rwanda has been denounced by David Belton as a wrong-headed analysis. Only a TV journalist could have imagined that the piece offered an analysis of any kind or that it argued for the presence of a single media organisation in disaster areas when it was actually arguing for a single secular international professional disaster relief organisation.

The argument that massive media coverage gets a degree of logistical support is by now so thin that many journalists can no longer bring themselves to utter it. You do not have to see pictures of burnt people before you call the fire brigade. We should not have to see pictures of people dying in their own excrement before we send in the military engineers. It is vile that there has to be a market in the most horrendous images of human anguish before anything will be done about it.

Even so, Belton is wrong to claim that the story is being told. Where does he think I got the figure of 50,000 inhabitants for Goma from? From the *Guardian*, that's where. He says the figure should be 150,000, so why has not a single reporter interviewed a single Zairean inhabitant of Goma? There are three 'camps', we hear. One is Kibumba, one is Goma, and I defy anyone to tell me what the other one is supposed to be. And as for the historical and political context, you would never think, to read any of our papers, that the Hutu have been doing their best to exterminate the Tutsi for the last 30 years, let alone the historic reasons why this is so and will continue to be so. The massacre was a peasant uprising; the condition of many of the refugees should be taken as evidence that there was something pretty serious to rise up against.

Most insidiously, however, the media all tell the same story: black victims, white saviours. Black equals skinny, filthy, mute and sick; white equals healthy, strong, good, brave and articulate.

Aid agencies screw up often and badly. When the League of Red Cross Societies commissioned a review of its own performance in the Ethiopian famine, the ultimate judgment was that the organisation should involve itself in no further famine relief activity until it had acquired a better understanding of what was needed, but any journalist's reports about agency blunders will have been spiked. Traditionally, aid agencies distrust local authorities and often involve themselves in futile struggles for control, unmindful of the fact that the locals have to live not only with the current crisis but with the fall-out when the foreigners are long gone.

Belton tells me to leave the comfort of my home, 'visit Goma and check out the facts'. Like him I don't speak the local languages; for any serious analysis, the official Francophone version is not enough. Flying visits don't produce much in the way of facts, though I would be able to determine from the medical supplies that were in use what kinds of diarrhoea disease were being treated and in what proportion. I certainly would not be under the impression that oral rehydration salts were a treatment for cholera, as a BBC radio reporter confidently stated.

I saw my first refugee shelters in 1971, when nine million people fled Pakistani genocide in East Bengal to the neighbouring Indian states. Then too reporters ran about desperately seeking cholera. There must have been some cases. That there were not more was mostly because of the self-discipline of the refugees themselves and partly because vaccine guns were to deliver hundreds of thousands of doses of vaccine. What happened in 1971-1972 is that one of the poorest nations in the world carried out the greatest relief operation the world has ever seen, but because catastrophe did not eventuate, the story was never told. Then I saw marasmic children dying because they could not digest the infant food that was sent by European and American charities. The right things could have been, and largely were, locally available. What was needed was money to pay for them; what was supplied was everything but money. The story was, as it always is in these cases, that the local authorities could not be trusted. The proof was that unwanted supplies were sold on the black market. The Indian government did what no international refugee programme has ever succeeded in doing; the refugees survived to go home and create the new nation of Bangladesh. If we had studied the Bengali experience we might have learnt how such situations can be handled. As it is we have learnt less than nothing because when the dying stops, there is no sensational imagery to keep our attention.

We are told that cholera, which was rife in Goma, has now been 'tamed' or 'has peaked'. Oh yeah? Are we to believe that though infectious excrement has been deposited randomly all over the encampment area, seriously weakened and exhausted people have begun to resist the contagion even as they grow ever weaker and more demoralised?

Who worked this miracle? Now we are told that dysentery has taken over as chief threat. Dysentery is Greek for painful gut; you might as well call it 'diarrhoeal disease', and you'd be sure to be right. Amoebic, malarial, bacterial, viral, all infections kill when people are huddled in their excrement with inadequate food, water and fuel. The agencies know that when the rains come the death toll will soar again, cholera or no.

Refugees' diseases kill aid workers too, but only when they are locals. When I was in Ethiopia, two university undergraduates working in Bati shelter died of cerebral malaria. The one I knew died on the bus on his way to the district hospital. If he had been European he would have been airlifted out.

I asked at Mengistu's Ministry of Information if the boys could be made heroes of the revolution. Oh no, they said. If parents knew that their children were in danger while they were working for the relief effort, they would send them out of the country. One of the things we should be prepared to do when this agony is over is to use our media to give credit where credit is due. Zaireans and Rwandans cannot come back to a clean, luxurious world and put what has happened behind them. We should put at least some of our effort into rebuilding their dignity and enhancing their self-esteem, rather than glorifying our own self-image at their expense.

Germaine Greer
The Guardian, Monday 8th August 1994

The Brutal Truth

This year, two programmes I am involved with, *Brookside* and *Emmerdale*, have been criticised by the industry watchdogs who regulate British television. I am learning to come to terms with this, for ever since creating *Grange Hill* in 1976, I have elicited a variety of criticism from the TV censors. Back then, the complaints were all about the working-class accents of the characters, and issues like student militancy and smoking behind the bike sheds.

In the eighties I found myself in trouble over *Brookside* and a teenage drama called *What Now?* Both the programmes featured something that is common to most people – swearing. Over the years, I have also found myself having to defend a range of issues on *Brookside*, from showing a packet of contraceptives on screen to the more recent debate over the length and the timing of the kiss between Beth and Margaret.

My experience is that what tends to upset the regulators changes with time and is stimulated by what else is going on around them. At the moment, the vogue seems to be violence, but interestingly enough, most surveys of what the general public finds offensive tend to list swearing, violence and sex in that order of priority. People appear much more ready to put up with naughty bits than naughty language – and violence falls somewhere in the middle.

The portrayal of violence on television is a fascinating subject. While researching for the police series *Waterfront Beat*, I discovered from the police that criminal statistics appear to show that violence within society remains at a constant level. Since the Home Office started keeping crime statistics in 1900, the percentage of violent crime in relation to all other crimes has remained constant at around six per cent.

The point, then, is this: why does fear of crime and violence seem to have risen so dramatically over the past few years? The answer lies not in an increase in violent crime, but in the increase in the amount of media coverage given to both factual and fictional crime, as well as the massive expansion of media outlets themselves. Whether these be the proliferating number of national newspapers, magazines and video shops, or the increasing numbers of satellite and cable TV channels, the truth is that today there is an incredible number of ways people come into contact with violent material.

Most obvious has been the rise of programmes depicting real-life crimes. After the BBC launched *Crimewatch* as a perfectly legitimate public service to try to get more information for the police, ITV followed, after seeing the huge audience appeal, with shows that were clearly designed to be bigger, better and more 'realistic' than the BBC offering. In other words, they were after ratings.

Yet we should not even look to the BBC as the initiator of these programmes, but to the usual source of sensational television – America. Shows like *America's Most Wanted* and *911* (America's equivalent of our 999) had been running for years and proved very successful. From there, they travelled via satellite television to Britain – and coming from the gun-culture society of America, they were obviously going to be of the 'blow them away' variety. For British commercial television chiefs, the idea looked great but a British bobby jotting down details of a video theft wouldn't really cut the mustard. So they had to respond with big, sensational crimes.

As these went out on national television, concern about violence was increased from a local worry. Not only did you have the odd madman around the corner – the nation was full of them. However, it is well known to the police that 95 per cent of all crime committed by any age group is committed by the same five per cent of offenders. In other words, society is 95 per cent honest, and, as we know, there are always a few idiots knocking about. Similarly, every major urban area in Britain has about 13 murders a year – of which about 11 are carried out by someone who knows the victim. The other two are usually related to some other criminal activity. Comparing our annual national total of about 670 murders with the 4,000 and more killings in Washington DC alone, this makes the chances of your being killed by a deranged serial killer as very slim.

So why an increase in crime shows? For a start, they are cheaper to produce than drama, and history shows that most box-office hits have been adventure movies – from John Wayne's westerns through the James Bond action movies to Schwarzenegger's *Terminator*. The good guys beat up the bad guys and the white hats beat the black hats. People like heroes to beat villains, to give them their just deserts. This reinforces the creed of social order: that good should triumph over evil. Even more interesting is that violence in movies or television programmes is accepted because the stories are detached from everyday life and are often pure fantasy. Very few focus on the real lives of the majority of the population. It is when they do – as in *Brookside* – that the outcry is loudest.

Although it needs only a glance through any morning's national newspapers to see the level of violence perpetrated throughout the world, the isolating factor is that it doesn't directly affect the reader. The outcry against the realism of violence in films and on television is fuelled by fear of violence, yet it is very rare for newspapers, or factual television programmes, to explain the relatively low level of violence experienced by the majority of the people. No one ever tries to calm the fear of violence. Why? Because fear sells newspapers.

It is too convenient for people to blame television or cinema for society's problems. Of course, there is concern over the rising use of weapons in crimes such as robbery, but before people turn to television as the reason, they should consider social causes first. One is obviously drugs, and we often hear that most crime is drug-related. But again, historical precedent shows that drugs are a cyclical concern. The gin and opium problems of the 19th century and the drug culture of the Sixties were treated with the same levels of concern – and television was nowhere near as widespread as it is now.

The same applies to weapons. Factual and fictional accounts of life in the Fifties are littered with armed robberies, as the interest for both journalists and writers was the enormous amount of ex-service weapons in the country after the Second World War. If you talk to any drug officer today, he will tell you about the ready supply of cheap weapons following the collapse of the old Soviet Union.

Before our moral guardians reach for their regulations, they should perhaps review those regulations more regularly and realise that in the past 10 years the world has embarked on a media revolution. Like the cinema before them, the BBC and ITV are no longer the dominant forces they once were. More importantly, viewers are no longer as passive or naive as they were assumed to be when the regulations were written in the Fifties.

While I am not advocating the unrestricted transmission of anything, it seems to me slightly ridiculous to have a specific regulation that states that because knives are the most common weapons used in domestic violence, care must be shown in depicting their use in case it gives people ideas. If someone is in a kitchen and wants to injure somebody, they will pick up whatever is readily to hand – not stop and consider what they have recently seen on television.

Apart from the nanny factor and playing the dubious and impossible role of moral arbiter, the whole role of regulation seems to me to be based on two false premises. The first is that there are hordes of deranged individuals lining up to inflict their own particular deviant behaviour on viewers. Although I have met a few odd people in the business, there are armies of lawyers and accountants running most broadcast companies whose sole purpose is not to let anything get on air that might offend their viewers and therefore cause them to switch off.

The second is that most people aren't stupid. They know more about the real world than the average bureaucrat because they live it, experience it, shape it. If they don't like it, they won't watch it. How do I know? Because on 2 November 1982, *Brookside* started off with about four million people watching the first episode. Six months later, the figure was below one million. The reason? They didn't like the swearing, and used the one device open to them to register their displeasure. They switched off.

This may seem an easy answer, but I believe that 99 per cent of the population can tell the difference between reality and fantasy. I am familiar with the argument that although some young people may not be able to read, they all can see visual images, and I think this can be dealt with on three counts.

The first is the generally accepted but not yet fully defined principle of the watershed: there are different times for different material. The second is that we need greater programme information about content, not just from broadcasters but from the rest of the media, who tend to publicise programmes by titillation rather than information. The third is greater acceptance of viewers' responsibility to control what goes on in their own lives and homes. The broadcasters can do only so much by agreeing to schedule at particular times and giving better information. After that, people must take responsibility for who views what.

I am also familiar with the copycat argument. This is that someone somewhere will watch a television programme, and then go off and commit an evil deed. This is why I have always vetoed stories about glue-sniffing in my programmes, because one sniff of the wrong solvent can cause brain damage, even death.

Finally, which form of television is preferable? That which comes from a different country and culture with different social values, so that the use of sex and violence is seen simply as entertainment, or programmes like *Brookside* and *Emmerdale* where things are shown in a context we can understand?

Is it preferable to show people or cartoon characters fighting each other to the death, and then walking away without a hair out of place? Or to show the bloodied face of someone in a fight – or even the psychological trauma of killing someone? Which will leave the lasting impression?

It has been a good 12 years for *Brookside*, and it is pleasing that with stories about the Jordache family's domestic and sexual violence and the Farnham's Down's syndrome child, the series is still taking a provocative role appreciated by over five million regular viewers. If we occasionally upset the watchdogs that is a price we must pay. Otherwise we are doomed to a diet of television pap – and that is something you will not get from *Brookside*.

Phil Redmond
Brookside, The Magazine, 1994

Argument Activities

The Man with No Name

Magazines and newspapers try to attract readers by asking well known journalists to write articles giving their opinions and views about a variety of social issues. Journalists who write this kind of column become well known to the reader, who looks forward to reading what they have to say about topical issues and events. The first two articles in this section are by two such writers, John Pilger and Tony Parsons, both writing on the subject of begging. Pilger's piece was first printed in the *New Statesman,* a left of centre weekly magazine, and Tony Parson's article comes from *Arena,* a fortnightly style magazine aimed at men.

1. You and money
● In groups of three exchange any personal experiences you may have had of talking to beggars or the homeless and the nearest you have got to asking for money yourself.

2. What the bible says
In the New Testament, the treatment of the poor is seen as being a very important test of Christian faith.
● Look at these quotes from the bible, in which Jesus preaches to his followers. Talk about what the quotes tell us about Christian beliefs about the poor and about charity.

> ‘Blessed are the meek: for they shall inherit the earth.’
> *St. Matthew 5:3*

> ‘It is easier for a camel to go through the eye of a needle, than for a rich man to enter into the kingdom of God.’
> *St. Matthew 19:24*

> ‘For I was an hungred, and ye gave me meat:
> I was thirsty and ye gave me drink:
> I was a stranger, and ye took me in:
> Naked, and ye clothed me: I was sick and ye visited me:
> I was in prison, and ye came to me.’
> *St Matthew 25:35*

> 'Inasmuch as ye have done it unto one of the least of these my brethren, ye have done it unto me.'
> *St Matthew 25:40*

3. What is the argument?

● Having read the article, or heard it read aloud, work in small groups and see if you can decide what points John Pilger is trying to make. You could choose from the list below the statements that seem to sum up Pilger's arguments most clearly.

Pilger is arguing that:

> The homeless are to blame for their plight and shouldn't be given money when they beg

> The Department of Health and Social Security's rules help to make people homeless

> It's a disgrace that public money from the Department of Health and Social Security is going into the pockets of hotel owners, rather than being spent on homes for the homeless

> It's really only a very small part of the population that is homeless

> Homelessness and begging will decrease if the Government makes tougher laws to stop people from loitering on the streets and begging

> The 'welfare state', which was supposed to help people has trapped the homeless in their situation

> Homeless people can't be identified as a typical group. Anyone can become homeless, from any class or age group

> Homeless people are people who are especially inadequate and that's why they have become homeless

> The homeless are not given the same rights as the rest of society

> Homeless people shouldn't have the same rights as everyone else

4. Making a point with a story

John Pilger uses a particular incident to make a general point about society, in this case the plight of the homeless and the government's response to the problem. By telling a story Pilger intends to get the sympathy of the reader which in turn enables him to make his point.
● Find two examples of Pilger telling the story of the man and two examples of Pilger giving his broader viewpoint on homelessness and government policy.
● List the ways that Pilger tries to create the sense of a real human being in his description of the homeless man.
● Where do the comment and story appear in the article? (e.g. is it all story at the beginning and comment at the end?) Talk about why you think Pilger has structured the article in this way.

5. No name's story

When a writer uses a slice of life to make a point it is equally possible that the people being written about might have another point of view.
● Re-read 'The Man with No Name' and write a piece of your own, as if written by the homeless man. How might he see 'The Middle Class Journalist with No Name.' It might help to imagine it as a dialogue with another homeless person in a hostel.

Beggars of Britain

1. The title

When this article first appeared, it was called 'Street Trash', with the words 'Beggars of Britain' as a smaller title.
● Talk about your response to the full title. What expectations does it raise for you?

2. The tone of voice

In threes read the first two paragraphs aloud. Each person should try reading it with a different tone of voice. Which one seems most appropriate to the way the author uses words?

Angry
Sneering and full of contempt
Patronising
Cruel
Sympathetic and concerned
Depressed

3. Who is he talking to?
● *Arena* is a magazine aimed at men. Can you learn anything about the readership of the article from Parson's:

use of language
use of vocabulary
level of formality
emotional appeal

What does his language tell you about the way he sees the reader?

4. How strong is his case?
● Make a list of the reasons why Tony Parsons dislikes begging. Do they add up to a reasonable case against begging?
● Do you feel that the author is breaking any taboos in this article, saying things that most people would feel shouldn't be said?

5. What do you learn about the author?
● Try to write a character analysis of the author based on the way he writes and the kinds of points that he makes.

e.g. Tony Parsons is young enough to feel comfortable challenging older people's views on the world.....etc.

6. The weapon of sarcasm
At one point Parsons seems to be writing a guide on how to beg. Clearly, given his point of view, these instructions are not meant to be taken seriously. He is pretending to give advice but is in fact only using this as a device to reinforce his argument. This technique is called sarcasm or irony.
● Write 'A Beginner's Guide to Being...' in which you target your anger and contempt at a particular group, attacking them through sarcasm. You could choose from the list below:

Politicians
Head teachers
Bullies
DJs.

7. Parsons and Pilger meet
Write an imaginary dialogue between John Pilger and Tony Parsons about the subject of begging and homelessness. Use all the work you have done on the two texts to help you identify what is different about their viewpoints and their likely styles of arguing with each other.

An African Feast for Flies and Other Parasites

1. Photos from Rwanda

Patience ... child at a Unicef camp for Hutu children separated from their parents, and, right, women forced from the Kibeho and Ndago camps wait for their food rations

The Guardian, 23 April 1995

Camp terror: violence in Rwanda's refugee sites is common as this flashback to last summer shows. Now, hundreds more are feared dead in the latest outbreak   *The Sunday Times*, 23 April 1995

PHOTOGRAPHS: JEAN-MARC BOUJU AND DAVID GUTTENFELDER

● In pairs, talk about these photos of Rwandan refugee camps, sold by journalists to the press.

What information do these pictures give you about the situation in Rwanda?

What is your emotional reaction to each one – sympathy, horror, anger, respect, compassion?

What has each photo set out to do and how has it achieved this? Talk about type of shot (close-up, long-shot, one person or a group, camera angle etc.), framing, choice of subject and caption.

2. Photographers as witnesses

● In pairs list the disasters that spring immediately to mind which you have seen on television and which made a strong impression on you.

● Talk about how you have dealt with your feelings about the tragedies of others that TV and newspaper reports bring you. Have you seen things from real disasters and tragedies that you think should not have been shown?

3. The main points of the argument

● When you have read the article 'An African Feast for Flies and other Parasites' look back over a photocopy and annotate it to show the following:

The main points of each paragraph, down the left hand margin
Greer's tone of voice down the right hand margin, e.g. outrage, disbelief, sarcasm, disgust, desperation.

● In pairs, summarise her argument in 50 words. Get into fours to compare summaries and discuss the similarities and differences.

4. Devices used

● Talk about the intentions and effects of Greer's use of the following images and phrases:

> 'Flies all over the world are packing their bags and heading for Goma'

> 'poking cameras into their faces as they groan their lives away'

> 'Dying children are slung on the scale so that a photographer can get a cover shot'

> 'the pornography of war, destitution and disease'

5. A response to Germaine Greer

● Imagine that you are a television or press journalist who has been reporting from Rwanda. Identify and respond to five parts of Germaine Greer's argument. One way of doing this is to write your responses up as speech bubbles and paste them onto the relevant parts of her article.

Now read David Belton's response to Germaine Greer.
● Talk about the intentions and effects of some of the devices he uses in his piece:

Short paragraphs
Numbering each point
Sarcasm
Factual evidence

Media Duty that Begins When the Dying Stops

● Listen to Germaine Greer's reply to David Belton being read and talk about whose attitudes and style of argument you agree with most.

6. Your own writing

Germaine Greer describes her first article as a 'cry of rage and desperation'. Like some other commentators, Germaine Greer writes with great energy and anger. As a result the reader gets a strong sense of the personality and voice of the writer.
● Try writing a piece of argument about something you feel very strongly about. You could try imitating the two different styles illustrated by Greer and Belton. The suggestions below are deliberately worded in a provocative manner to get you going:

All dangerous dogs should be taken from their owners and put to death

Any driver who causes a fatal accident while under the influence of alcohol should be given a life sentence

All cars should be painted yellow to make them more visible

Air pollution caused by traffic has become so damaging to children's health that private cars should be banned in cities

Abortion is the right of every woman to choose

All children should be allowed to leave school at 14

The Brutal Truth

1. Before reading
● In threes, consider the statements below. Give a few minutes to each statement and try to list points for and against each one.

There is growing concern about violence in society and in the media

Sex and bad language on TV offends a lot of people

Factual programmes about crimes (*999* and *Crimewatch*) increase people's fear of crime and violence

Newspapers and TV producers know that fear creates large audiences

Actual statistics about violence are not well explained or understood

Violence on TV should be shown happening to ordinary people with real consequences

When people watch violence they copy it

There is no need for any censors or regulation on what we read or watch

2. Headlining
● Once you have heard the article read aloud, look at it again and then write a headline for each paragraph which summarises the main points.

When you have done this, try to decide whether Redmond has made a convincing and consistent argument. Think about the following:

Are his points made clearly?
Does one point link to the previous one logically?

Do any of his points contradict each other?
What kind of evidence does he use?

3. Questioning the author

● Make a list of any points in the article that you don't understand or which you disagree with. Alongside each point, write down your doubts and comments and make an additional list of questions you would like to ask the author or another expert.

4. Becoming a feature writer

● Imagine that you have just recorded a long interview with Phil Redmond for your newspaper/magazine. Your editor tells you s/he only has space for a very short piece of 750 words written *about* Redmond's views, not a full interview. Have a go at writing an article of 700 – 750 words which does the following:

Explains in your own words who Phil Redmond is, and his past experiences of problems with public criticism and censorship
Explains his views on fear of crime and violence, using quotes from his own words wherever you can
Explains what he thinks about TV regulation (again using quotes)
Explains how he justifies the use of violence in *Brookside* and *Emmerdale Farm*
Gives your own summary and opinion of his arguments

While drafting your feature:
Check that your writing is clear and to the point by asking 'Who? What? Why? Where? When?' at any stage in the article and being able to get the answers.

Look over your paragraphs and check that you could provide a headline for each one to be sure that it is making an identifiable point.

Think of the structure of the whole piece. This could be an upside-down pyramid which begins with a broad look at all the issues and ideas, gradually narrowing them down and finishing with one final point. Or you could think of the structure as a diamond shape which begins with one sharp observation, comment or stance, widens out to look at other ideas and then narrows down again to form its concluding point.

No Name Woman

'You must not tell anyone,' my mother said, 'what I am about to tell you. In China your father had a sister who killed herself. She jumped into the family well. We say that your father has all brothers because it is as if she had never been born.

'In 1924 just a few days after our village celebrated seventeen hurry-up weddings – to make sure that every young man who went "out on the road" would responsibly come home – your father and his brothers and your grandfather and his brothers and your aunt's new husband sailed for America, the Gold Mountain. It was your grandfather's last trip. Those lucky enough to get contracts waved good-bye from the decks. They fed and guarded the stowaways and helped them off in Cuba, New York, Bali, Hawaii. 'We'll meet in California next year,' they said. All of them sent money home.

'I remember looking at your aunt one day when she and I were dressing; I had not noticed before that she had such a protruding melon of a stomach. But I did not think, 'She's pregnant,' until she began to look like other pregnant women, her shirt pulling and the white tops of her black pants showing. She could not have been pregnant, you see, because her husband had been gone for years. No one said anything. We did not discuss it. In early summer she was ready to have the child, long after the time when it could have been possible.

'The village had also been counting. On the night the baby was to be born the villagers raided our house. Some were crying. Like a great saw, teeth strung with lights, files of people walked zigzag across our land, tearing the rice. Their lanterns doubled in the disturbed black water, which drained away through the broken bunds. As the villagers closed in, we could see that some of them, probably men and women we knew well, wore white masks. The people with long hair hung it over their faces. Women with short hair made it stand up on end. Some had tied white bands around their foreheads, arms, and legs.

'At first they threw mud and rocks at the house. Then they threw eggs and began slaughtering our stock. We could hear the animals scream their deaths – the roosters, the pigs, a last great roar from the ox. Familiar wild heads flared in our night windows; the villagers encircled us. Some of the faces stopped to peer at us, their eyes rushing like searchlights. The hands flattened against the panes, framed heads, and left red prints.

'The villagers broke in the front and the back doors at the same time, even though we had not locked the doors against them. Their knives dripped with the blood of our animals. They smeared blood on the doors and walls. One woman swung a chicken, whose throat she had slit, splattering blood in red arcs about her. We stood together in the middle of our house, in the family hall with the pictures and tables of the ancestors around us, and looked straight ahead.

'At that time the house had only two wings. When the men came back, we would build two more to enclose our courtyard and a third one to begin a second courtyard. The villagers pushed through both wings, even your grandparents' rooms, to find your aunt's, which was also mine until the men returned. From this room a new wing for one of the younger families would grow. They ripped up her clothes and shoes and broke her combs, grinding them underfoot. They tore her work from the loom. They scattered the cooking fire and rolled the new weaving in it. We could hear them in the kitchen breaking our bowls and banging the pots. They overturned the great waist-high earthenware jugs; duck eggs, pickled fruits, vegetables burst out and mixed in acrid torrents. The old woman from the next field swept a broom through the air and loosed the spirits-of-the-broom over our heads. 'Pig.' 'Ghost.' 'Pig,' they sobbed and scolded while they ruined our house.

'When they left, they took sugar and oranges to bless themselves. They cut pieces from the dead animals. Some of them took bowls that were not broken and clothes that were not torn. Afterwards we swept up the rice and sewed it back up into sacks. But the smells from the spilled preserves lasted. Your aunt gave birth in the pigsty that night. The next morning when I went for the water, I found her and the baby plugging up the family well.

'Don't let your father know that I told you. He denies her. Now that you have started to menstruate, what happened to her could happen to you. Don't humiliate us. You wouldn't like to be forgotten as if you had never been born. The villagers are watchful.'

Whenever she had to warn us about life, my mother told stories that ran like this one, a story to grow up on. She tested our strength to establish realities. Those in the emigrant generations who could not reassert brute survival died young and far from home. Those of us in the first American generations have had to figure out how the invisible world the emigrants built around our childhoods fits in solid America.

The emigrants confused the gods by diverting their curses, misleading them with crooked streets and false names. They must try to confuse their offspring as well, who, I suppose, threaten them in similar ways – always trying to get things straight, always trying to name the unspeakable. The Chinese I know hide their names; sojourners take new names when their lives change and guard their real names with silence.

Chinese-Americans, when you try to understand what things in you are Chinese, how do you separate what is peculiar to childhood, to poverty, insanities, one family, your mother who marked your growing with stories, from what is Chinese? What is Chinese tradition and what is the movies?

If I want to learn what clothes my aunt wore, whether flashy or ordinary, I would have to begin. 'Remember Father's drowned-in-the-well sister?' I cannot ask that. My mother has told me once and for all the useful parts. She will add nothing unless powered by Necessity, a riverbank that guides her life. She plants vegetable gardens rather than lawns; she carries the odd-shaped tomatoes home from the fields and eats food left for the gods.

Whenever we did frivolous things, we used up energy; we flew high kites. We children came up off the ground over the melting cones our parents brought home from work and the American movie on New Year's Day – *Oh, You Beautiful Doll* with Betty Grable one year, and *She Wore a Yellow Ribbon* with John Wayne another year. After the one carnival ride each, we paid in guilt; our tired father counted his change on the dark walk home.

Adultery is extravagance. Could people who hatch their own chicks and eat the embryos and the heads for delicacies and boil the feet in vinegar for party food, leaving only the gravel, eating even the gizzard lining – could such people engender a prodigal aunt? To be a woman, to have a daughter in starvation time was a waste enough. My aunt could not have been the lone romantic who gave up everything for sex. Women in the old China did not choose. Some man had commanded her to lie with him and be his secret evil. I wonder whether he masked himself when he joined the raid on her family.

Perhaps she had encountered him in the fields or on the mountain where the daughters-in-law collected fuel. Or perhaps he first noticed her in the marketplace. He was not a stranger because the village housed no strangers. She had to have dealings with him other than sex. Perhaps he worked an adjoining field, or he sold her the cloth for the dress she sewed and wore. His demand must have surprised, then terrified her. She obeyed him; she always did as she was told.

When the family found a young man in the next village to be her husband, she had stood tractably beside the best rooster, his proxy, and promised before they met that she would be his for ever. She was lucky that he was her age and she would be the first wife, an advantage secure now. The night she first saw him, he had sex with her. Then he left for America. She had almost forgotten what he looked like. When she tried to envision him, she only saw the black and white face in the group photograph the men had had taken before leaving.

The other man was not, after all, much different from her husband. They both gave orders: she followed. 'If you tell your family, I'll beat you. I'll kill you. Be here again next week.' No one talked sex, ever. And she might have separated the rapes from the rest of living if only she did not have to buy her oil from him or gather wood in the same forest. I want her fear to have lasted just as long as rape lasted so that the fear could have been contained. No drawn-out fear. But women at sex hazarded birth and hence lifetimes. The fear did not stop but permeated everywhere. She told the man, 'I think I'm pregnant.' He organized the raid against her.

On nights when my mother and father talked about their life back home, sometimes they mentioned an 'outcast table' whose business they still seemed to be settling, their voices tight. In a commensal tradition, where food is precious, the powerful older people made wrongdoers eat alone. Instead of letting them start separate new lives like the Japanese, who could become samurais and geishas, the Chinese family, faces averted but eyes glowering sideways, hung on to the offenders and fed them leftovers. My aunt must have lived in the same house as my parents and eaten at an outcast table. My mother spoke about the raid as if she had seen it, when she and my aunt, a daughter-in-law to a different household, should not have been living together at all. Daughters-in-law lived with their husbands' parents, not their own; a synonym for marriage in Chinese is 'taking a daughter-in-law'. Her husband's parents could have sold her, mortgaged her, stoned her. But they had sent her back to her own mother and father, a mysterious act hinting at disgraces not told me. Perhaps they had thrown her out to deflect the avengers.

She was the only daughter; her four brothers went with her father, husband, and uncles 'out on the road' and for some years became western men. When the goods were divided among the family, three of the brothers took land, and the youngest, my father, chose an education. After my grandparents gave their daughter away to her husband's family, they had dispensed all the adventure and all the property. They expected her alone to keep the traditional ways, which her brothers, now among the barbarians, could fumble without detection. The heavy, deep-rooted women were to maintain the past against the flood, safe for returning. But the rare urge west had fixed upon our family, and so my aunt crossed boundaries not delineated in space.

The work of preservation demands that the feelings playing about in one's guts not be turned into action. Just watch their passing like cherry blossoms. But perhaps my aunt, my forerunner, caught in a slow life, let dreams grow and fade and after some months or years went towards what persisted. Fear at the enormities of the forbidden kept her desires delicate, wire and bone. She looked at a man because she liked the way the hair was tucked behind his ears, or she liked the question-mark line of a long torso curving at the shoulder and straight at the hip. For warm eyes or a soft voice or a slow walk – that's all – a few hairs, a line, a brightness, a sound, a pace, she gave up family. She offered us up for a charm that vanished with tiredness, a pigtail that didn't toss when the wind died. Why, the wrong lighting could erase the dearest thing about him.

It could very well have been, however, that my aunt did not take subtle enjoyment of her friend, but, a wild woman, kept rollicking company. Imagining her free with sex doesn't fit, though. I don't know any women like that, or men either. Unless I see her life branching into mine, she gives me no ancestral help.

To sustain her being in love, she often worked at herself in the mirror, guessing at the colours and shapes that would interest him, changing them frequently in order to hit on the right combination. She wanted him to look back.

On a farm near the sea, a woman who tended her appearance reaped a reputation for eccentricity. All the married women blunt-cut their hair in flaps about their ears or pulled it back in tight buns. No nonsense. Neither style blew easily into heart-catching tangles. And at their weddings they displayed themselves in their long hair for the last time. 'It brushed the backs of my knees,' my mother tells me. 'It was braided, and even so, it brushed the backs of my knees.'

At the mirror my aunt combed individuality into her bob. A bun could have been contrived to escape into black streamers blowing in the wind or in quiet wisps about her face. but only the older women in our picture album wear buns. She brushed her hair back from her forehead, tucking the flaps behind her ears. She looped a piece of thread, knotted into a circle between her index fingers and thumbs, and ran the double strand across her forehead. When she closed her fingers as if she were making a pair of shadow geese bite, the string twisted together catching the little hairs. Then she pulled the thread away from her skin, ripping the hairs out neatly, her eyes watering from the needles of pain. Opening her fingers, she cleaned the thread, then rolled it along her hairline and the tops of her eyebrows. My mother did the same to me and my sisters and herself. I used to believe that the expression 'caught by the short hairs' meant a captive held with a depilatory string. It especially hurt at the temples, but my mother said we were lucky we didn't have to have our feet bound when we were seven. Sisters used to sit on their beds and cry together, she said, as their mothers or their slaves removed the bandages for a few minutes each night and let the blood gush back into their veins. I hope that the man my aunt loved appreciated a smooth brow, that he wasn't just a tits-and-ass man.

Once my aunt found a freckle on her chin, at a spot that the almanac said predestined her for unhappiness. She dug it out with a hot needle and washed the wound with peroxide.

More attention to her looks than these pullings of hairs and pickings at spots would have caused gossip among the villagers. They owned work clothes and good clothes, and they wore good clothes for feasting the new seasons. But since a woman combing her hair hexes beginnings, my aunt rarely found an occasion to look her best. Women looked like great sea snails – the corded wood, babies, and laundry they carried were the whorls on their backs. The Chinese did not admire a bent back; goddesses and warriors stood straight. Still there must have been a marvellous freeing of beauty when a worker laid down her burden and stretched and arched.

Such commonplace loveliness, however, was not enough for my aunt. She dreamed of a lover for the fifteen days of New Year's, the time for families to exchange visits, money, and food. She plied her secret comb. And sure enough she cursed the year, the family, the village, and herself.

Even as her hair lured her imminent lover, many other men looked at her. Uncles, cousins, nephews, brothers would have looked, too, had they been home between journeys. Perhaps they had already been restraining their curiosity, and they left, fearful that their glances, like a field of nesting birds, might be startled and caught. Poverty hurt, and that was their first reason for leaving. But another, final reason for leaving the crowded house was the never-said.

She may have been unusually beloved, the precious only daughter, spoiled and mirror gazing because of the affection the family lavished on her. When her husband left, they welcomed the chance to take her back from the in-laws: she could live like the little daughter for just a while longer. There are stories that my grandfather was different from other people, 'crazy ever since the little Jap bayoneted him in the head'. He used to put his naked penis on the dinner table, laughing. And one day he brought home a baby girl, wrapped up inside his brown western-style greatcoat. He had traded one of his sons, probably my father, the youngest, for her. My grandmother made him trade back. When he finally got a daughter of his own, he doted on her. They must have all loved her, except perhaps my father, the only brother who never went back to China having once been traded for a girl.

Brothers and sisters, newly men and women, had to efface their sexual colour and present plain miens. Disturbing hair and eyes, a smile like no other threatened the ideal of five generations living under one roof. To focus blurs, people shouted face to face and yelled from room to room. The immigrants I know have loud voices, unmodulated to American tones even after years away from the village where they called their friendships out across the fields. I have not been able to stop my mother's screams in public libraries or over telephones. Walking erect (knees straight, toes pointed forward, not pigeon-toed, which is Chinese-feminine) and speaking in an inaudible voice, I have tried to turn myself American-feminine. Chinese communication was loud, public. Only sick people had to whisper. But at the dinner table, where the family members came nearest one another, no one could talk, not the outcasts nor any eaters. Every word that falls from the mouth is a coin lost. Silently they gave and accepted food with both hands. A preoccupied child who took his bowl with one hand got a sideways glare. A complete moment of total attention is due everyone alike. Children and lovers have no singularity here, but my aunt used a secret voice, a separate attentiveness.

She kept the man's name to herself throughout her labour and dying; she did not accuse him that he be punished with her. To save her inseminator's name she gave silent birth.

He may have been somebody in her own household, but intercourse with a man outside the family would have been no less abhorrent. All the village were kinsmen, and the titles shouted in loud country voices never let kinship be forgotten. Any man within visiting distance would have been neutralized as a lover – 'brother', 'younger brother', 'older brother' – one hundred and fifteen relationship titles. Parents researched birth charts probably not so much to assure good fortune as to circumvent incest in a population that has but one hundred surnames. Everybody has eight million relatives. How useless then sexual mannerisms, how dangerous.

As if it came from an atavism deeper than fear, I used to add 'brother' silently to boys' names. It hexed the boys, who would or would not ask me to dance, and made them less scary and as familiar and deserving of benevolence as girls.

But, of course, I hexed myself also – no dates. I should have stood up, both arms waving, and shouted out across libraries, 'Hey, you! Love me back.' I had no idea, though, how to make attraction selective, how to control its direction and magnitude. If I made myself American – pretty so that the five or six Chinese boys in the class fell in love with me, everyone else – the Caucasian, Negro, and Japanese boys – would too. Sisterliness, dignified and honourable, made much more sense.

Attraction eludes control so stubbornly that whole societies designed to organize relationships among people cannot keep order, not even when they bind people to one another from childhood and raise them together. Among the very poor and the wealthy, brothers married their adopted sisters, like doves. Our family allowed some romance, paying adult brides' prices and providing dowries so that their sons and daughters could marry strangers. Marriage promises to turn strangers into friendly relatives – a nation of siblings.

In the village structure, spirits shimmered among the live creatures, balanced and held in equilibrium by time and land. But one human being flaring up into violence could open up a black hole, a maelstrom that pulled in the sky. The frightened villagers, who depended on one another to maintain the real, went to my aunt to show her a personal, physical representation of the break she had made in the 'roundness'. Misallying couples snapped off the future, which was to be embodied in true offspring. The villagers punished her for acting as if she could have a private life, secret and apart from them.

If my aunt had betrayed the family at a time of large grain yields and peace, when many boys were born, and wings were being built on many houses, perhaps she might have escaped such severe punishment. But the men – hungry, greedy, tired of planting in dry soil – had been forced to leave the village in order to send food-money home. There were ghost plagues, bandit plagues, wars with the Japanese, floods. My Chinese brother and sister had died of an unknown sickness. Adultery, perhaps only a mistake during good times, became a crime when the village needed food.

The round moon cakes and round doorways, the round tables of graduated sizes that fit one roundness inside another, round windows and rice bowls – these talismans had lost their power to warn this family of the law: a family must be whole, faithfully keeping the descent line by having sons to feed the old and the dead, who in turn look after the family. The villagers came to show my aunt and her lover-in-hiding a broken house. The villagers were speeding up the circling of events because she was too shortsighted to see that her infidelity had already harmed the village, that waves of consequences would return unpredictably, sometimes in disguise, as now, to hurt her. This roundness had to be made coin-sized so that she would see its circumference; punish her at the birth of her baby. Awaken her to the inexorable. People who refused fatalism because they could invent small resources insisted on culpability. Deny accidents and wrest fault from the stars.

After the villagers left, their lanterns now scattering in various directions towards home, the family broke their silence and cursed her. 'Aiaa, we're going to die. Death is coming. Death is coming. Look what you've done. You've killed us. Ghost! Dead ghost! Ghost! You've never been born.' She ran out into the fields, far enough from the house so that she could no longer hear their voices, and pressed herself against the earth, her own land no more. When she felt the birth coming, she thought that she had been hurt. Her body seized together. 'They've hurt me too much,' she thought. 'This is gall, and it will kill me.' Her forehead and knees against the earth, her body convulsed and then released her on to her back. The black well of sky and stars went out and out and out for ever; her body and her complexity seemed to disappear. She was one of the stars, a bright dot in blackness, without home, without a companion, in eternal cold and silence. An agoraphobia rose in her, speeding higher and higher, bigger and bigger; she would not be able to contain it; there would be no end to fear.

Flayed, unprotected against space, she felt pain return, focusing her body. This pain chilled her – a cold, steady kind of surface pain. Inside, spasmodically, the other pain, the pain of the child, heated her. For hours she lay on the ground, alternately body and space. Sometimes a vision of normal comfort obliterated reality: she saw the family in the evening gambling at the dinner table, the young people massaging their elders' backs. She saw them congratulating one another, high joy on the mornings the rice shoots came up. When these pictures burst, the stars drew yet further apart. Black space opened.

She got to her feet to fight better and remembered that old-fashioned women gave birth in their pigsties to fool the jealous, pain-dealing gods, who do not snatch piglets. Before the next spasms could stop her, she ran to the pigsty, each step a rushing out into emptiness. She climbed over the fence and knelt in the dirt. It was good to have a fence enclosing her, a tribal person alone.

Labouring, this woman who had carried her child as a foreign growth that sickened her every day, expelled it at last. She reached down to touch the hot, wet, moving mass, surely smaller than anything human, and could feel that it was human after all – fingers, toes, nails, nose. She pulled it up on to her belly, and it lay curled there, butt in the air, feet precisely tucked one under the other. She opened her loose shirt and buttoned the child inside. After resting, it squirmed and thrashed and she pushed it up to her breast. It turned its head this way and that until it found her nipple. There, it made little snuffling noises. She clenched her teeth at its preciousness, lovely as a young calf, a piglet, a little dog.

She may have gone to the pigsty as a last act of responsibility: she would protect this child as she had protected its father. It would look after her soul, leaving supplies on her grave. But how would this tiny child without family find her grave when there would be no marker for her anywhere, neither in the earth nor the family hall? No one would give her a family hall name. She had taken the child with her into the wastes. At its birth the two of them had felt the same raw pain of separation, a wound that only the family pressing tight could close. A child with no descent line would not soften her life but only trail after her, ghostlike, begging her to give it purpose. At dawn the villagers on their way to the fields would stand around the fence and look.

Full of milk, the little ghost slept. When it awoke, she hardened her breasts against the milk that crying loosens. Towards morning she picked up the baby and walked to the well.

Carrying the baby to the well shows loving. Otherwise abandon it. Turn its face into the mud. Mothers who love their children take them along. It was probably a girl; there is some hope of forgiveness for boys.

'Don't tell anyone you had an aunt. Your father does not want to hear her name. She has never been born.' I have believed that sex was unspeakable and words so strong and fathers so frail that 'aunt' would do my father mysterious harm. I have thought that my family, having settled among immigrants who had also been their neighbours in the ancestral land, needed to clean their name, and a wrong word would incite the kinspeople even here. But there is more to this silence: they want me to participate in her punishment. And I have.

In the twenty years since I heard this story I have not asked for details nor said my aunt's name; I do not know it. People who can comfort the dead can also chase after them to hurt them further – a reverse ancestor worship. The real punishment was not the raid swiftly inflicted by the villagers, but the family's deliberately forgetting her. Her betrayal so maddened them, they saw to it that she would suffer for ever, even after death. Always hungry, always needing, she would have to beg food from other ghosts, snatch and steal it from those whose living descendants give them gifts. She would have to fight the ghosts massed at crossroads for the buns a few thoughtful citizens leave to decoy her away from village and home so that the ancestral spirits could feast unharassed. At peace, they could act like gods, not ghosts, their descent lines providing them with paper suits and dresses, spirit money, paper houses, paper automobiles, chicken, meat, and rice into eternity – essences delivered up in smoke and flames, steam and incense rising from each rice bowl. In an attempt to make the Chinese care for people outside the family, Chairman Mao encourages us now to give our paper replicas to the spirits of outstanding soldiers and workers, no matter whose ancestors they may be. My aunt remains forever hungry. Goods are not distributed evenly among the dead.

My aunt haunts me – her ghost drawn to me because now, after fifty years of neglect, I alone devote pages of paper to her, though not origamied into houses and clothes. I do not think she always means me well. I am telling on her, and she was a spite suicide, drowning herself in the drinking water. The Chinese are always very frightened of the drowned one, whose weeping ghost, wet hair hanging and skin bloated, waits silently by the water to pull down a substitute.

Maxine Hong Kingston
Woman Warrior, 1978

I Know Why the Caged Bird Sings

> *'What you looking at me for?*
> *I didn't come to stay ...'*

I hadn't so much forgot as I couldn't bring myself to remember. Other things were more important.

> *'What you looking at me for?*
> *I didn't come to stay ...'*

Whether I could remember the rest of the poem or not was immaterial. The truth of the statement was like a wadded-up handkerchief, sopping wet in my fists, and the sooner they accepted it the quicker I could let my hands open and the air would cool my palms.

> *'What you looking at me for ... ?'*

The children's section of the Colored Methodist Episcopal Church was wiggling and giggling over my well-known forgetfulness.

The dress I wore was lavender taffeta, and each time I breathed it rustled, and now that I was sucking in air to breathe out shame it sounded like crepe paper on the back of hearses.

As I'd watched Momma put ruffles on the hem and cute little tucks around the waist, I knew that once I put it on I'd look like a movie star. (It was silk and that made up for the awful color.) I was going to look like one of the sweet little white girls who were everybody's dream of what was right with the world. Hanging softly over the black Singer sewing machine, it looked like magic, and when people saw me wearing it they were going to run up to me and say, 'Marguerite [sometimes it was 'dear Marguerite'], forgive us, please, we didn't know who you were,' and I would answer generously, 'No, you couldn't have known. Of course I forgive you.'

Just thinking about it made me go around with angel's dust sprinkled over my face for days. But Easter's early morning sun had shown the dress to be a plain ugly cut down from a white woman's once-was-purple throwaway. It was old-lady-long too, but it didn't hide my skinny legs, which had been greased with Blue Seal Vaseline and powdered with the Arkansas red clay. The age-faded color made my skin look dirty like mud, and everyone in church was looking at my skinny legs.

Wouldn't they be surprised when one day I woke out of my black ugly dream, and my real hair, which was long and blond, would take the place of the kinky mass that Momma wouldn't let me straighten? My light-blue eyes were going to hypnotize them, after all the things they said about 'my daddy must of been a Chinaman' (I thought they meant made out of china, like a cup) because my eyes were so small and squinty. Then they would understand why I had never picked up a Southern accent, or spoke the common slang, and why I had to be forced to eat pigs' tails and snouts. Because I was really white and because a cruel fairy stepmother, who was understandably jealous of my beauty, had turned me into a too-big Negro girl, with nappy black hair, broad feet and a space between her teeth that would hold a number-two pencil.

'What you looking ...' The minister's wife leaned toward me, her long yellow face full of sorry. She whispered, "I just come to tell you, it's Easter Day.' I repeated, jamming the words together, 'Ijustcometotellyouit'sEasterDay,' as low as possible. The giggles hung in the air like melting clouds that were waiting to rain on me. I held up two fingers, close to my chest, which meant that I had to go to the toilet, and tiptoed toward the rear of the church. Dimly, somewhere over my head, I heard ladies saying, "Lord bless the child," and "Praise God." My head was up and my eyes were open, but I didn't see anything. Halfway down the aisle, the church exploded with 'Were you there when they crucified my Lord?' and I tripped over a foot stuck out from the children's pew. I stumbled and started to say something, or maybe to scream, but a green persimmon, or it could have been a lemon, caught me between the legs and squeezed. I tasted the sour on my tongue and felt it in the back of my mouth. Then before I reached the door, the sting was burning down my legs and into my Sunday socks. I tried to hold, to squeeze it back, to keep it from speeding, but when I reached the church porch I knew I'd have to let it go, or it would probably run right back up to my head and my poor head would burst like a dropped watermelon, and all the brains and spit and tongue and eyes would roll all over the place. So I ran down into the yard and let it go. I ran, peeing and crying, not toward the toilet out back but to our house. I'd get a whipping for it, to be sure, and the nasty children would have something new to tease me about. I laughed anyway, partially for the sweet release; still, the greater joy came not only from being liberated from the silly church but from the knowledge that I wouldn't die from a busted head.

If growing up is painful for the Southern Black girl, being aware of her displacement is the rust on the razor that threatens the throat.

It is an unnecessary insult.

Maya Angelou
I Know Why the Caged Bird Sings, 1969

Black Boy

One winter morning in the long-ago, four-year-old days of my life I found myself standing before a fireplace, warming my hands over a mound of glowing coals, listening to the wind whistle past the house outside. All morning my mother had been scolding me, telling me to keep still, warning me that I must make no noise. And I was angry, fretful, and impatient. In the next room Granny lay ill and under the day and night care of a doctor and I knew that I would be punished if I did not obey. I crossed restlessly to the window and pushed back the long fluffy white curtains – which I had been forbidden to touch – and looked yearningly out into the empty street. I was dreaming of running and playing and shouting, but the vivid image of Granny's old, white, wrinkled, grim face, framed by a halo of tumbling black hair, lying upon a huge feather pillow, made me afraid.

The house was quiet. Behind me my brother – a year younger than I – was playing placidly upon the floor with a toy. A bird wheeled past the window and I greeted it with a glad shout.

'You better hush,' my brother said.

'You shut up,' I said.

My mother stepped briskly into the room and closed the door behind her. She came to me and shook her finger in my face.

'You stop that yelling, you hear?' she whispered. 'You know Granny's sick and you better keep quiet!'

I hung my head and sulked. She left and I ached with boredom.

'I told you so,' my brother gloated.

'You shut up,' I told him again.

I wandered listlessly about the room, trying to think of something to do, dreading the return of my mother, resentful of being neglected. The room held nothing of interest except the fire and finally I stood before the shimmering embers, fascinated by the quivering coals. An idea of a new kind of game grew and took root in my mind. Why not throw something into the fire and watch it burn? I looked about. There was only my picture book and my mother would beat me if I burned that. Then what? I hunted around until I saw the broom leaning in a closet. That's it........Who would bother about a few straws if I burned them? I pulled out the broom and tore out a batch of straws and tossed them into the fire and watched them smoke, turn black, blaze, and finally become white wisps of ghosts that vanished. Burning straws was a teasing kind of fun and I took more of them from the broom and cast them into the fire. My brother came to my side, his eyes drawn by the blazing straws.

'Don't do that,' he said.

'How come?' I asked.

'You'll burn the whole broom,' he said.

'You hush,' I said.

'I'll tell,' he said.

'And I'll hit you,' I said.

My idea was growing, blooming. Now I was wondering just how the long fluffy white curtains would look if I lit a bunch of straws and held it under them. Would I try it? Sure. I pulled several straws from the broom and held them to the fire until they blazed; I rushed to the window and brought the flame in touch with the hems of the curtains. My brother shook his head.

'Naw,' he said.

He spoke too late. Red circles were eating into the white cloth; then a flare of flames shot out. Startled, I backed away. The fire soared to the ceiling and I trembled with fright. Soon a sheet of yellow lit the room. I was terrified; I wanted to scream but was afraid. I looked around for my brother; he was gone. One half of the room was now ablaze. Smoke was choking me and the fire was licking at my face, making me gasp.

I made for the kitchen; smoke was surging there too. Soon my mother would smell that smoke and see the fire and come and beat me. I had done something wrong, something which I could not hide or deny. Yes, I would run away and never come back. I ran out of the kitchen and into the back yard. Where could I go? Yes, under the house! Nobody would find me there. I crawled under the house* and crept into a dark hollow of a brick chimney and balled myself into a tight knot. My mother must not find me and whip me for what I had done. Anyway, it was all an accident; I had not really intended to set the house afire. I had just wanted to see how the curtains would look when they burned. And neither did it occur to me that I was hiding under a burning house.

Presently footsteps pounded on the floor above me. Then I heard screams. Later the gongs of fire wagons and the clopping hoofs of horses came from the direction of the street. Yes, there was really a fire, a fire like the one I had seen one day burn a house down to the ground, leaving only a chimney standing black. I was stiff with terror. The thunder of sound above me shook the chimney to which I clung. The screams came louder. I saw the image of my grandmother lying helplessly upon her bed and there were yellow flames in her black hair. Was my mother afire? Would my brother burn? Perhaps everybody in the house would burn! Why had I not thought of those things before I fired the curtains? I yearned to become invisible, to stop living. The commotion above me increased and I began to cry. It seemed that I had been hiding for ages, and when the stomping and the screaming died down I felt lonely, cast forever out of life. Voices sounded near-by and I shivered.

'Richard!' my mother was calling frantically.

I saw her legs and the hem of her dress moving swiftly about the back yard. Her wails were full of an agony whose intensity told me that my punishment would be measured by its depth. Then I saw her taut face peering under the edge of the house. She had found me! I held my breath and waited to hear her command me to come to her. Her face went away; no, she had not seen me huddled in the dark nook of the chimney. I tucked my head into my arms and my teeth chattered.

'Richard!'

The distress I sensed in her voice was as sharp and painful as the lash of a whip on my flesh.

'Richard! The house is on fire. Oh, find my child!'

Yes, the house was afire, but I was determined not to leave my place of safety. Finally I saw another face peering under the edge of the house; it was my father's. His eyes must have become accustomed to the shadows, for he was now pointing at me.

'There he is!'

'Naw!' I screamed.

'Come here, boy!'

'Naw ! '

'The house is on fire!'

'Leave me 'lone!'

He crawled to me and caught hold of one of my legs. I hugged the edge of the brick chimney with all of my strength. My father yanked my leg and I clawed at the chimney harder.

'Come outta there, you little fool!'

'Turn me loose!'

I could not withstand the tugging at my leg and my fingers relaxed. It was over. I would be beaten. I did not care any more. I knew what was coming. He dragged me into the back yard and the instant his hand left me I jumped to my feet and broke into a wild run, trying to elude the people who surrounded me, heading for the street. I was caught before I had gone ten paces.

From that moment on things became tangled for me. Out of the weeping and the shouting and the wild talk, I learned that no one had died in the fire. My brother, it seemed, had finally overcome enough of his panic to warn my mother, but not before more than half the house had been destroyed. Using the mattress as a stretcher, Grandpa and an uncle had lifted Granny from her bed and had rushed her to the safety of a neighbour's house. My long absence and silence had made everyone think, for a while, that I had perished in the blaze.

'You almost scared us to death,' my mother muttered as she stripped the leaves from a tree limb to prepare it for my back.

I was lashed so hard and long that I lost consciousness. I was beaten out of my senses and later I found myself in bed, screaming, determined to run away, tussling with my mother and father who were trying to keep me still. I was lost in a fog of fear. A doctor was called – I was afterwards told – and he ordered that I be kept abed, that I be kept quiet, that my life depended upon it. My body seemed on fire and I could not sleep. Packs of ice were put on my forehead to keep down the fever. Whenever I tried to sleep I would see huge wobbly white bags, like the full udders of cows, suspended from the ceiling above me. Later, as I grew worse, I could see the bags in the daytime with my eyes open and I was gripped by the fear that they were going to fall and drench me with some horrible liquid. Day and night I begged my mother and father to take the bags away, pointing to them, shaking with terror because no one saw them but me. Exhaustion would make me drift toward sleep and then I would scream until I was wide awake again; I was afraid to sleep. Time finally bore me away from the dangerous bags and I got well. But for a long time I was chastened whenever I remembered that my mother had come close to killing me.

Each event spoke with a cryptic tongue And the moments of living slowly revealed their coded meanings. There was the wonder I felt when I first saw a brace of mountainlike, spotted, black-and-white horses clopping down a dusty road through clouds of powdered clay.

There was the delight I caught in seeing long straight rows of red and green vegetables stretching away in the sun to the bright horizon.

There was the faint, cool kiss of sensuality when dew came on to my cheeks and shins as I ran down the wet green garden paths in the early morning.

There was the vague sense of the infinite as I looked down upon the yellow, dreaming waters of the Mississippi River from the verdant bluffs of Natchez.

There were the echoes of nostalgia I heard in the crying strings of wild geese winging south against a bleak, autumn sky.

There was the tantalising melancholy in the tingling scent of burning hickory wood.

There was the teasing and impossible desire to imitate the petty pride of sparrows wallowing and flouncing in the red dust of country roads.

There was the yearning for identification loosed in me by the sight of a solitary ant carrying a burden upon a mysterious journey.

There was the disdain that filled me as I tortured a delicate, blue-pink crawfish: that huddled fearfully in the mudsill of a rusty tin can.

There was the aching glory in masses of clouds burning gold and purple from an invisible sun.

There was the liquid alarm I saw in the blood-red glare of the sun's afterglow mirrored in the squared panes of whitewashed frame houses.

There was the languor I felt when I heard green leaves rustling with a rainlike sound.

There was the incomprehensible secret embodied in a whitish toadstool hiding in the dark shade of a rotting log.

There was the experience of feeling death without dying that came from watching a chicken leap about blindly after its neck had been snapped by a quick twist of my father's wrist.

There was the great joke that I felt God had played on cats and dogs by making them lap their milk and water with their tongues.

There was the thirst I had when I watched clear, sweet juice trickle from sugar cane being crushed.

There was the hot panic that welled up in my throat and swept through my blood when I first saw the lazy, limp coils of a blueskinned snake sleeping in the sun.

There was the speechless astonishment of seeing a hog stabbed through the heart, dipped into boiling water, scraped, split open, gutted, and strung up gaping and bloody.

There was the love I had for the mute regality of tall, mossclad oaks.

There was the hint of cosmic cruelty that I felt when I saw the curved timbers of a wooden shack that had been warped in the summer sun.

There was the saliva that formed in my mouth whenever I smelt clay dust pitted with fresh rain.

There was the cloudy notion of hunger when I breathed the odour of new-cut, bleeding grass.

And there was the quiet terror that suffused my senses when vast hazes of gold washed earthward from star-heavy skies on silent nights ...

* The house is built on a wooden frame, with a gap between the ground and the floor.

Richard Wright
Black Boy, 1970

An Evil Cradling

It is always difficult to find a beginning. All good stories have one, no matter how inconclusive or unexpected their end may be. The end of this story has not yet come, so it is particularly difficult to know where to begin. Were I older and had I lived fully the greater part of what life has been given me, then perhaps as in any good autobiography it would be easy to find a starting point, a rationale or a structure for my life: a place from where memory might begin to unfold the full and meaningful pattern of my time and how I have lived it.

But here is a different kind of search for a beginning. I do not wish to tell of a whole life, but only of an incident: an episode in time, a short sequence, yet one that seems dreadfully long and meaningful to me.

I think of the opening lines of the Bible: 'In the beginning was the Word, and the Word was with God.' Somehow those lines kept ringing back to me in the long captive silences, with a head full of words, a confusion of images, a mind not sane enough to find a rational perspective from which I could understand what was happening to me. Again I recall that ancient prologue to try to convey to you something of that imprisoned time and hopefully to explain something of what it meant and how it continues to have meaning; sometimes good, sometimes bad, and sometimes I don't know. Those easy definitions of good and bad, right and wrong seem inadequate to my purpose: the same inadequacy that overcomes so many things that we as human beings are forced to deal with and to understand.

So now I try to find a starting point from which I can share with you part of the self that I knew, and to find the self that I may have become as a result of my strange sojourn in the Lebanon. Because 'myself' could never again be an easily defined and well-summed thing. I have been asked so many times 'Why did you go? What took you to that place?' In answering, I can at last find my beginning.

All of us are beings of our age and time. All of us are a consequence of the depth or limitation of our understanding of the world about us, sometimes faulted in our development by the kind of commitment we make to that world, the people who share it with us and the historical events that touch our lives. I am a product of my city and of this awful period in its history. Before I left

Belfast, I had been torn with a desperate kind of love and distaste for my place and my people and even after coming back these scars of anger and of desire still mark me.

A love that cannot find an outlet turns inward, and not being able to reach out and touch the thing it loves, be it a place or the people in that place, turns to anger and becomes confused. I have lived through a terrible time, but seen something of the loveliness that is in a people and a country, and have known people who struggle, who insist on trying to rise above the forces that threaten them. But we all become tired, like a man struggling with a great load: Sisyphus pushing his awful stone only to feel it roll back and topple him down to the bottom of that hill from which again he must begin his upward heave.

When I think of my choice to leave Ireland, I constantly ask myself was it a wearisome walking away? Was it time to find another set of values, breathe another kind of air? One in which I would have to recharge myself with new ideas, new thoughts, new relationships, new feelings? I remember talking to a friend before I made my decision to go. I said to him 'There comes a time when you get so utterly empty that you've got to move somewhere else to satisfy an inner hunger.'

So I sought change, not knowing fully what form that change would take. I suppose it was a kind of inner compulsion that I had not then articulated or understood. As we sat, my friend and I, over a few pints in a local pub, we talked of ageing. We had been friends from school days – one of those few constant friendships that a man or woman has in their lives. I remember remarking how I suddenly felt myself becoming afraid of never going anywhere, afraid of the challenge that life itself presents.

My departure was a way of taking up that challenge. All my friends and professional colleagues in teaching and from community work in Belfast had married, bought homes, started families; settled into a cosy domesticity which I had avoided and had perhaps feared. Lines from W. B. Yeats's poem 'The Choice' had imprinted themselves on and directed my understanding of life's trajectory:

> *The intellect of man is forced to choose*
> *Perfection of the life, or of the work,*
> *And if it take the second must refuse*
> *A heavenly mansion, raging in the dark.*

That 'heavenly mansion,' domesticity, love, marriage, eluded me for so many reasons, and I was fearful that I was going to be swallowed up in the emptiness that was encroaching upon me. I was gripped by the irresolution of life that seems to drive us to take decisions.

Unlike many of my contemporaries, I was not tempted to take up the cudgels of full-time politics. Politics can only be a small part of what we are. It's a way of seeing, it's not all-seeing in itself, and people like me, who were fortunate enough to be born and educated before the start of the tragedy that has engulfed the North of Ireland, found the panacea of politics to be a bitter cul-de-sac. What was happening around us had moved beyond meaningful reality. So it was for me a time to move, to find out if I could remould myself. The energizing effect of politics had dissipated, the vibrant radicalism of our generation had become ghettoized and subterranean; the rival slogans of 'Ourselves Alone' and 'Who Shall Separate Us' marked political backwaters, stagnating and debilitating. At worst they were full of perverse arrogance, vindictive and malign. At best they were a sheltering place from the long war of attrition: bursting full of community and fellowship, they were a loud testimony to people's determination not to be subdued.

I think of that decision to move as one which many men must face. I speak of men because I am one and because I understand as a man. I think something happens to us; people looking for a colourful expression call it the male menopause. We come to an age when choice is forced upon us. Some of us choose to change our job, knowing that in our late thirties it will be the last and final change we might comfortably make. Therefore we make it with some urgency, perhaps with fear, certainly with anxiety. Alternatively we decide on a change of house. It will be the last house we will ever be able to buy for we will never be able to increase our income. Some seek out the companionship of a younger partner, a kind of emotional assurance that we can still achieve, that we are still valued.

During my period of incarceration I felt that perhaps this urge to change is not unlike a woman's in her late thirties or early forties when she decides to have her first or final child. Maybe something in the male psyche wants a child and since we cannot have it we redirect our inner compulsion towards something that vaguely declares itself as a renewing of love, a revitalizing of what is creative in us.

In the grey back streets of Belfast, aware of people's unresolved desire and need and sensing myself becoming rooted and dead, burdened with a feeling that I had ceased to choose life, I forced myself to change, and consequently to go.

I had a half-formed notion about the effects of change on the personality. We seem to undergo a reactive process before any transition. A person's initial reaction to change is one of immobilization. We feel overwhelmed, and the more unfamiliar the change, the greater our paralysis. With the growing negative expectations resulting from this paralysis we feel ourselves frozen up. Such was my experience. I felt the debilitating cold of ice-floes gathering about me. I knew that I must find some free water, an open channel through which I might escape before I was trapped. How was I to know that I was to confront the same entrapment in another place? Literally as well as metaphorically, it seemed that islands of ice followed and gathered about me: dry ice, so cold that it burned the skin, melted into it. My resolution to action, as it turned out, simply drove me further into blinding snowfields of the mind.

My personal history is quite ordinary. I grew up in a working-class family in Protestant East Belfast, the only male child, the middle of the family. Being the son, I was given advantages over my two sisters. When I sought out books and education, my family facilitated me. With scholarships and reasonably good exam results under my belt I was able to continue my education.

But first I left school at fifteen. I was an academically bright lad, who was cajoled by some of his teachers not to leave, but I wanted out, to see life and not to reach beyond the expectations of the mates who left school with me. I worked for a year in a laundry, as a van-boy delivering dry cleaning.

On turning sixteen and feeling destined for an apprenticeship, I applied, and eventually began working my trade as a heating engineer with a medium-sized company in East Belfast. I still remember my first pair of overalls. They were strange, after the black blazer and grey flannels of secondary school. I can't remember if they made me feel any older or more of a man. I just remember that the bloody things were so baggy. I walked to work every morning and walked home again in the evening, with my 'piece-box' snug under my arm.

As with most apprenticeships, those first months were boring. The work was not demanding but I found the environment of a factory tiresome. I remember my first week. I left the factory to meet up with a friend in a pub next door – the usual Friday evening occupation for all workers in Belfast. I realized after having my first drink that I had forgotten to collect my wages. My friend thought I was an idiot.

After many months working in the factory, I was sent off to the 'Tech', as it was called, to study for my City & Guilds in Heating Engineering. This different kind of classroom routine became oppressive. I remember feeling a sense of limitation. Five years of this, to end up a glorified plumber and continue with that for the foreseeable future, was not an enthralling prospect to me.

Although I had left school against the advice of my teachers I had, without telling anyone, tried to continue my studies in literature at night school. It was a tedious walk from one end of the city to the other every Tuesday night, and to sit amongst adults studying for 'O' levels was confusing. I was the youngest in the class, so the companionship that I knew at school was absent here. I stuck it for a short period. It was too long a walk on cold winter's nights, and then to try to concentrate on Shakespeare with wet shoes and soaking trousers, wondering how I was going to get home when the buses stopped. So I persisted in reading books at home, and compensated for the boredom of the days in the factory and the hours studying for my City & Guilds by going away every weekend.

From the age of fourteen I would catch a train or a bus every weekend to somewhere outside Belfast, and as I got older I would go off youth-hostelling. It was a need simply to go somewhere, anywhere, with a sleeping bag and stay wherever luck would take me for as long as I could. The seeds of the need to travel and to be free of immediate pressures – the home, the family, the streets that I grew up in – sprang up early. Something always nags, especially in the young. I wanted more.

By freak of circumstance, for which I am not sure I am entirely grateful, I won some prizes and literary awards in national competitions. A young woman from the BBC came to the Tech one day. She told me in the quiet of the corridor that I had won a national poetry award. I stared at her in astonishment and disbelief. She wanted to film a small piece, to which I said: 'No, I couldn't do that.' Not that I had any real excuse. I was just frightened. She eventually persuaded me that I should do it the following day, and it was her good looks, her charm and my sudden rise in the estimation of my friends that made me grudgingly agree.

Off I went to Shaws Bridge, on the outskirts of Belfast. They made a short film piece of me reading one of my poems and I was thence and forever condemned, I think, to a fascination with words. I wondered what I should do after this, and decided some weeks later that I could not bear to weld pipes for the rest of my days in broken-down factories. So coming home one evening from work, I fumblingly told my parents that I wanted to return to school. They were shocked, and I think a little afraid. But they never tried to dissuade me. They wanted to know if I was sure; if I knew what it meant; and whether I was aware that if I left my apprenticeship it would be very difficult to get a good job – to get a trade. But nothing would deflect me, and they pursued the matter no further.

I returned to education and the following year received another national award. My commitment to language was doubly stamped. And thus alone among my friends in East Belfast I went to university and I suppose to another world, another way of understanding, which set me at a remove from all those things that were familiar to me. This was my first real leave-taking.

Brian Keenan
An Evil Cradling, 1992

Autobiography Activities

The First Sentence

1. Reading the sentences
- Read the opening sentences of these six pieces of autobiographical writing.

A.
> 'It is always difficult to find a beginning.'

B.
> 'Like most people I lived for a long time with my mother and father.'

C.
> 'One winter morning in the long-ago, four-year-old days of my life I found myself standing before a fireplace, warming my hands over a mound of glowing coals, listening to the wind whistle past the house outside.'

D.
> 'Under the volcanoes, beside the snow-capped mountains, among the huge lakes, the fragrant, the silent, the tangled Chilean forest..........'

E.
> ''What are you looking at me for?''

F.
> ''You must not tell anyone,' my mother said, 'what I am about to tell you.''

- Talk about what these sentences tell you about the person writing (e.g. male? female? age at this point in the story? cultural identity? personality?)
- Write as many statements as you can about the sentences, in this form:

Sentence 1 is.................whereas Sentence 5 is.......................
e.g. Sentence 6 uses suspense to get you interested, whereas Sentence 4 is descriptive.

- Which of these openings makes you most interested to read on?

2. Writing your own first sentence

● Try some opening sentences of your own autobiography. Experiment with four or five different versions, then choose the one you like best.

Experiment with: using suspense
  being descriptive
  using humour
  being surprising or a bit wacky
  being reflective

No Name Woman

1. Secrets

Before reading, the class should be divided in half, work in pairs and do one of the following:

● Improvise a conversation between a mother and a daughter that begins: 'You must not tell anyone what I am about to tell you...'

● Tell each other stories, real or made up, on the subject of 'Family Secrets'.

After a few minutes get into groups of about eight and find out what each pair talked about. List any similarities.

2. The mother's story of the aunt

● Listen to the story as the writer remembers her mother telling it which ends on Page 83 with the line 'The villagers are watchful.' Make notes on the following:

All the facts about life in rural China in the 1920s that you can gather from this story
Any phrases or words which strike you for any reason
Any questions about this story that you want to ask

● Share your work with the rest of the class or another pair.

3. Whose viewpoint?

● Listen to the rest of the text being read and then choose one of the following short writing assignments:

The second or third time the daughter hears this story, she writes about her reactions to it in her private journal where she explores the unanswered questions it raises.

After telling her daughter the story, the mother sits alone thinking. Write down her thoughts, memories and feelings in the form of an internal monologue.

4. The title

'No Name Woman' is the title of the first chapter of Maxine Hong Kingston's autobiography.

- Write the title onto a sheet of paper and annotate it to show its links with the extract and the associations and ideas it suggests. Annotate these alternative titles in the same way:

No Name Girl
Nameless Lady
Father's Drowned-in-the-Well Sister

5. Roots and inheritance

In most of this extract, Maxine Hong Kingston is trying to make sense of the story about her aunt. In doing so she tells the reader quite a bit about herself and her roots, as the child of emigrant parents.

- Listen to the rest of the text being read aloud and then work in a small group to examine what you discover about the writer and why her aunt is important to her. Make a list of the five most interesting quotes onto a chart like this one:

Quote	What this tells us
Always trying to get things straight, always trying to name the unspeakable	Questioning the story of her aunt is part of the struggle a child of emigrant parents has to understand cultural differences and conflicts

6. Your own autobiographical writing

- Find out and write about forerunners in your family that you are curious about. You could make a recording of different relatives talking about them or you could just ask about them and listen to the stories and memories. One way of writing this up would be as an imaginary conversation with them where they are as interested to hear about you and your life as you are about them and their life.

- Read the quote below. Write about the range of influences and experiences which help shape your sense of who you are as you grow up. If you have connections to more than one culture you could also write about how the different cultural traditions have influenced your identity.

> 'Chinese-Americans, when you try to understand what things in you are Chinese, how do you separate what is peculiar to childhood, to poverty, insanities, one family, your mother who marked your growing with stories, from what is Chinese? What is Chinese tradition and what is the movies?'

- Read the quote below. The story of the aunt is one where sexism has been taken to horrific extremes. Write about your reactions to the story and the light it throws on cultural attitudes to males and females.

> 'It was probably a girl; there was some hope of forgiveness for boys.'

● Read the quote below. Write about two or three warning tales that you know or have heard. These might be spoken tales, read or read-aloud tales, tales on television, film or in some other form. Think about the purpose of such tales, their effect on the listener, their connection with reality and what they reveal about the culture from which they come.

> 'Whenever she had to warn us about life, my mother told stories that ran like this one, a story to grow up on.'

Starting-points for Wider Reading

In this section there are three openings of autobiographical texts. Work in small groups, each group focusing on one of the texts to present to the rest of the class.

Black Boy by Richard Wright
I Know Why the Caged Bird Sings by Maya Angelou
An Evil Cradling by Brian Keenan

1. Reading your text
● Read the text aloud in your small group, sharing the reading by dividing the text into manageable chunks (e.g. a few paragraphs at a time for each person).
● Talk about first impressions and first responses:

Is it interesting?
What kind of life is being described?
What kind of personality emerges from the writing?
Does it make you want to read on? Why?

2. Exploring your text further
● Think about what the writer was intending to do in the opening. Look down the list of writers' intentions and pick out the ones that seem to you to fit your text. Write them down as a list. Choose the three most important intentions and find three short quotes from your text to show the writer doing this.

Writers' intentions
To tell a story
To present his/her childhood
To introduce issues, beliefs or ideas that are an important part of his/her whole life
To describe his/her cultural identity and background
To describe his/her physical environment
To explain about his/her country, to audiences from another country
To grab the reader's attention
To be amusing or entertaining
To let thoughts and feelings out in an unstructured way

● Talk about how important the following issues seem in the text itself and in your reading and response to it:

The fact that the writer is male or female
The writer's cultural or racial identity

3. Presenting your text
● Choose what you think is the best extract from your text to read aloud to the rest of the group. Pick a chunk that is long enough to give a good sense of the writer's style. Decide how to read it aloud (choosing the best reader, sharing out the reading, putting it on an audiotape, with music?)
● Pull together all of the notes around your discussion. Decide on one key point that you want to make on each of the topics you have discussed. Find quotes from the text to back up what you want to say.
● Present your text to the rest of the class.

4. Comparing openings
You have worked closely on one text and heard about two others.
Choose two of the openings to compare, using a grid like the one shown below.

	OPENING 1		OPENING 2	
	Statement	Quote/evidence	Statement	Quote/evidence
Gender				
Race/Culture				
Presentation of Childhood				
Themes				
Style and Language (e.g.descriptive, poetic, using dialogue etc.)	Poetic language gives a strong	'the faint, cool kiss of sensuality when dew		
Voice				
How it begins				

● Use your chart to write a comparison between the two openings you have chosen. Do a first draft timed, to give you practice at writing about texts in exam conditions. Re-draft it more carefully and slowly if you want to use it for coursework.

5. Writing the opening of your autobiography

● Choose five or six facts or feelings about yourself and one incident from early childhood. Write them down as a list.
● Write five or six different opening paragraphs, which take different angles and try to achieve different things.

e.g. one humorous opening, one opening which begins to tell a story from your childhood, one opening describing your physical environment, one opening which focuses on your gender or cultural identity.

You could try writing in the style of one of the writers you have read.

● Pick the one that you like best and continue it, writing the whole opening section of your autobiography. When you have completed a first draft and worked on it to polish it up, write a commentary to go with it, in which you explain what you were trying to do and how it compares with the openings you have read by other writers.

6. The facts revealed

The openings you have looked at have all been from written autobiographies, or autobiographical works. There are other ways in which non-fictional material about people's lives can be presented e.g. as biographies (where someone else writes about a famous person's life), in newspaper articles, letters, diaries, interviews, radio phone-ins, chat shows and so on. Sometimes writers use their life experiences as the basis for fiction or drama.
● Take the opening of your autobiography and try turning it into a different genre, taking an idea from the list above.

7. Wider reading

The texts in this section are all extracts from longer autobiographical works.
● Choose one that you would like to read on your own and use as the basis for a piece of coursework on wider reading.

The Eruption of Vesuvius

My uncle was stationed at Misenum, in active command of the fleet. On 24 August, in the early afternoon, my mother drew his attention to a cloud of unusual size and appearance. He had been out in the sun, had taken a cold bath, and lunched while lying down, and was then working at his books. He called for his shoes and climbed up to a place which would give him the best view of the phenomenon. It was not clear at that distance from which mountain the cloud was rising (it was afterwards known to be Vesuvius); its general appearance can best be expressed as being like an umbrella pine, for it rose to a great height on a sort of trunk and then split off into branches, I imagine because it was thrust upwards by the first blast and then left unsupported as the pressure subsided, or else it was borne down by its own weight so that it spread out and gradually dispersed. In places it looked white, elsewhere blotched and dirty, according to the amount of soil and ashes it carried with it. My uncle's scholarly acumen saw at once that it was important enough for a closer inspection, and he ordered a boat to be made ready, telling me I could come with him if I wished. I replied that I preferred to go on with my studies, and as it happened he had himself given me some writing to do.

As he was leaving the house he was handed a message from Rectina, wife of Tascus whose house was at the foot of the mountain, so that escape was impossible except by boat. She was terrified by the danger threatening her and implored him to rescue her from her fate. He changed his plans, and what he had begun in a spirit of inquiry he completed as a hero. He gave orders for the warships to be launched and went on board himself with the intention of bringing help to many more people besides Rectina, for this lovely stretch of coast was thickly populated. He hurried to the place which everyone else was hastily leaving, steering his course straight for the danger zone. He was entirely fearless, describing each new movement and phase of the portent to be noted down exactly as he observed them. Ashes were already falling, hotter and thicker as the ships drew near, followed by bits of pumice and blackened stones, charred and cracked by the flames: then suddenly they were in shallow water, and the shore was blocked by the debris from the mountain. For a moment my uncle wondered whether to turn back, but when the helmsman advised this he refused, telling him that Fortune stood by the courageous and they must make for Pomponianus at Stabiae. He was cut off there by the breadth of the bay (for the shore gradually curves round a basin filled by the sea) so that he was not as yet in danger, though it was clear that this would come nearer as it spread. Pomponianus had therefore already put his belongings on board ship, intending to escape if the contrary wind fell. This wind was of course full in my uncle's favour, and he was able to bring his ship in. He embraced his terrified friend, cheered and encouraged him, and thinking he could calm his fears by showing his own composure, gave orders that he was to be carried to the bathroom. After his bath he lay down and dined; he was quite cheerful, or at any rate he pretended he was, which was no less courageous.

Meanwhile on Mount Vesuvius broad sheets of fire and leaping flames blazed at several points, their bright glare emphasized by the darkness of night. My uncle tried to allay the fears of his companions by repeatedly declaring that these were nothing but bonfires left by the peasants in their terror, or else empty houses on fire in the districts they had abandoned. Then he went to rest and certainly slept, for as he was a stout man his breathing was rather loud and heavy and could be heard by people coming and going outside his door. By this time the courtyard giving access to his room was full of ashes mixed with pumice stones, so that its level had risen, and if he had stayed in the room any longer he would never have got out. He was wakened, came out and joined Pomponianus and the rest of the household who had sat up all night. They debated whether to stay indoors or take their chance in the open, for the buildings were now shaking with violent shocks, and seemed to be swaying to and fro as if they were torn from their foundations. Outside, on the other hand, there was the danger of falling pumice stones, even though these were light and porous; however, after comparing the risks they chose the latter. In my uncle's case one reason outweighed the other, but for the others it was a choice of fears. As a protection against falling objects they put pillows on their heads tied down with cloths.

Elsewhere there was daylight by this time, but they were still in darkness, blacker and denser than any ordinary night, which they relieved by lighting torches and various kinds of lamp. My uncle decided to go down to the shore and investigate on the spot the possibility of any escape by sea, but he found the waves still wild and dangerous. A sheet was spread on the ground for him to lie down, and he repeatedly asked for cold water to drink. Then the flames and smell of sulphur which gave warning of the approaching fire drove the others to take flight and roused him to stand up. He stood leaning on two slaves and then suddenly collapsed, I imagine because the dense fumes choked his breathing by blocking his windpipe which was constitutionally weak and narrow and often inflamed. When daylight returned on the 26th – two days after the last day he had seen – his body was found intact and uninjured, still fully clothed and looking more like sleep than death.

Meanwhile my mother and I were at Misenum ... After my uncle's departure I spent the rest of the day with my books, as this was my reason for staying behind. Then I took a bath, dined, and then dozed fitfully for a while. For several days past there had been earth tremors which were not particularly alarming because they are frequent in Campania: but that night the shocks were so violent that everything felt as if it were not only shaken but overturned. My mother hurried into my room and found me already getting up to wake her if she were still asleep. We sat down in the forecourt of the house, between the buildings and the sea close by. I don't know whether I should call this courage or folly on my part (I was only seventeen at the time) but I called for a volume of Livy and went on reading as if I had nothing else to do. I even went on with the extracts I had been making. Up came a friend of my uncle's who had just come from Spain to join him. When he saw us sitting there and me actually reading, he scolded us both – me for my foolhardiness and my mother for allowing it. Nevertheless, I remained absorbed in my book.

By now it was dawn, but the light was still dim and faint. The buildings round us were already tottering, and the open space we were in was too small for us not to be in real and imminent danger if the house collapsed. This finally decided us to leave the town. We were followed by a panic-striken mob of people wanting to act on someone else's decision in preference to their own (a point in which fear looks like prudence), who hurried us on our way by pressing hard behind in a dense crowd. Once beyond the buildings we stopped, and there we had some extraordinary experiences which thoroughly alarmed us. The carriages we had ordered to be brought out began to run in different directions though the ground was quite level, and would not remain stationary even when wedged with stones. We also saw the sea sucked away and apparently forced back by the earthquake: at any rate it receded from the shore so that quantities of sea creatures were left stranded on dry sand. On the landward side a fearful black cloud was rent by forked and quivering bursts of flame, and parted to reveal great tongues of fire, like flashes of lightning magnified in size.

At this point my uncle's friend from Spain spoke up still more urgently, 'If your brother, if your uncle is still alive, he will want you both to be saved; if he is dead, he would want you to survive him – why put off your escape?' We replied that we would not think of considering our own safety as long as we were uncertain of his. Without waiting any longer, our friend rushed off and hurried out of danger as fast as he could.

Soon afterwards the cloud sank down to earth and covered the sea; it had already blotted out Capri and hidden the promontory of Misenum from sight. Then my mother implored, entreated and commanded me to escape as best I could – a young man might escape, whereas she was old and slow and could die in peace as long as she had not been the cause of my death too. I refused to save myself without her, and grasping her hand forced her to quicken her pace. She gave in reluctantly, blaming herself for delaying me. Ashes were already falling, not as yet very thickly. I looked round: a dense black cloud was coming up behind us, spreading over the earth like a flood. 'Let us leave the road while we can still see,' I said, 'or we shall be knocked down and trampled underfoot in the dark by the crowd behind.' We had scarcely sat down to rest when darkness fell, not the dark of a moonless or cloudy night, but as if the lamp had been put out in a closed room. You could hear the shrieks of women, the wailing of infants, and the shouting of men; some were calling their parents, others their children or their wives, trying to recognize them by their voices. People bewailed their own fate or that of their relatives, and there were some who prayed for death in their terror of dying. Many besought the aid of the gods, but still more imagined there were no gods left, and that the universe was plunged into eternal darkness for evermore. There were people, too, who added to the real perils by inventing fictitious dangers: some reported that part of Misenum had collapsed or another part was on fire, and though their tales were false they found others to believe them. A gleam of light returned, but we took this to be a warning of the approaching flames rather than daylight. However, the flames remained some distance off; then darkness came on once more and ashes began to fall again, this time in heavy showers. We rose from time to time and shook them off, otherwise we should have been buried and crushed beneath their weight. I could boast that not a groan or cry of fear escaped me in these perils, but I admit that I derived some poor consolation in my mortal lot from the belief that the whole world was dying with me and I with it.

At last the darkness thinned and dispersed like smoke or cloud; then there was genuine daylight, and the sun actually shone out, but yellowish as it is during an eclipse. We were terrified to see everything changed, buried deep in ashes like snowdrifts. We returned to Misenum where we attended to our physical needs as best we could, and then spent an anxious night alternating between hope and fear. Fear predominated, for the earthquakes went on, and several hysterical individuals made their own and other people's calamities seem ludicrous in comparison with their frightful predictions. But even then, in spite of the dangers we had been through and were still expecting, my mother and I had still no intention of leaving until we had news of my uncle.

Of course these details are not important enough for history, and you will read them without any idea of recording them; if they seem scarcely worth putting in a letter, you have only yourself to blame for asking for them.

Pliny the Younger
Letters, 24 August, 79 AD

The Street-sellers of 1851

Street-sellers of tape and cotton are usually elderly females; and during my former inquiry I was directed to one who had been getting her living in the street by such means for nine years. I was given to understand that the poor woman was in deep distress, and that she had long been supporting a sick husband by her little trade, but I was wholly unprepared for a scene of such startling misery, sublimed by untiring affection and pious resignation, as I there discovered.

I wish the reader to understand that I do not cite this case as a type of the sufferings of this particular class, but rather as an illustration of the afflictions which frequently befall those who are soley dependent on their labour, or their little trade, for their subsistence, and who, from the smallness of their earnings, are unable to lay by even the least trifle as a fund against any physical calamity.

The poor creatures lived in one of the close alleys at the east end of London. On inquiring at the house to which I was directed, I was told I should find them in 'the two-pair back.' I mounted the stairs, and on opening the door of the apartment I was terrified with the misery before me. There, on a wretched bed, lay an aged man in almost the last extremity of life. At first I thought the poor old creature was really dead, but a tremble of the eyelids as I closed the door, as noiselessly as I could, told me that he breathed. His face was as yellow as clay, and it had more the cold damp look of a corpse than that of a living man. His cheeks were hollowed in with evident want, his temples sunk, and his nostrils pinched close. On the edge of the bed sat his heroic wife, giving him drink with a spoon from a tea-cup. In one corner of the room stood the basket of tapes, cottons, combs, braces, nutmeg-graters, and shaving-glasses, with which she strove to keep her old dying husband from the workhouse. I asked her how long her good man had been ill, and she told me he had been confined to his bed five weeks last Wednesday, and that it was ten weeks since he had eaten the size of a nut in solid food. Nothing but a little beef-tea had passed his lips for months. 'We have lived like children together,' said the old woman, as her eyes flooded with tears, 'and never had no dispute. He hated drink, and there was no cause for us to quarrel. One of my legs, you see, is shorter than the other,' said she, rising from the bed-side, and showing me that her right foot was several inches from the ground as she stood. 'My hip is out. I used to go out washing, and walking in my pattens I fell down. My hip is out of the socket three-quarters of an inch, and the sinews is drawn up. I am obliged to walk with a stick.' Here the man groaned and coughed so that I feared the exertion must end his life. 'Ah, the heart of stone would pity that poor fellow,' said the good wife.

'After I put my hip out, I couldn't get my living as I'd been used to do. I couldn't stand a day if I had five hundred pounds for it. I must sit down. So I got a little stall, and sat at the end of the alley here with a few laces and tapes and things. I've done so for this nine year past, and seen many a landlord come in and go out of the house that I sat at. My husband used to sell small articles in the streets – black lead and furniture paste, and blacking. We got a sort of a living by this, the two of us together. It's very seldom though we had a bit of meat. We had 1s. 9d. rent to pay – Come, my poor fellow, will you have another little drop to wet your mouth?' said the woman, breaking off. 'Come, my dearest, let me give you this,' she added, as the man let his jaw fall, and she poured some warm sugar and water flavoured with cinnamon – all she had to give him – into his mouth.

'He's been an ailing man this many a year. He used to go of errands and buy my little things for me, on account of my being lame. We assisted one another, you see. He wasn't able to work for his living, and I wasn't able to go about, so he used to go about and buy for me what I sold. I am sure he never earned above 1s. 6d. in a week. He used to attend me, and many a time I've sat for ten and fourteen hours in the cold and wet and didn't take a sixpence. Some days I'd make a shilling, and some days less; but whatever I got I used to have to put a good part into the basket to keep my little stock.' [A knock here came to the door; it was for a half-penny-worth of darning cotton.]

'You know a shilling goes further with a poor couple that's sober than two shillings does with a drunkard. We lived poor, you see, never had nothing but tea, or we couldn't have done anyhow. If I'd take 18d. in the day I'd think I was grandly off, and then if there was 6d. profit got out of that it would be almost as much as it would. You see these cotton braces here' (said the old woman, going to her tray). 'Well, I gives 2s. 9d. a dozen for them here, and I sells 'em for 4½d. and oftentimes 4d. a pair. Now, this piece of tape would cost me seven farthings in the shop, and I sells it at six yards a penny. It has the *name* of being eighteen yards. The profit out of it is five farthings. It's beyond the power of man to wonder how there's a bit of bread got out of such a small way. And the times is so bad, too! I think I could say I get 8d. a day profit if I have any sort of custom, but I don't exceed that at the best of times. I've often sat at the end of the alley and taken only 6d., and that's not much more than 2d. clear – it ain't 3d. I'm sure.

'I think I could safely state that for the last nine years me and my husband has earned together 5s. a week, and out of that the two of us had to live and pay rent – 1*s.* 9*d.* a week. Clothes I could buy none, for the best garment is on me; but I thank the Lord still. I've paid my rent all but three weeks, and that isn't due till tomorrow. We have often reckoned it up here at the fire. Some weeks we have got 5*s.* 3*d.,* and some weeks less, so that I judge we have about 3*s.* to 3*s.* 6*d.* a week to live upon the two of us, for this nine years past. Half-a-hundred of coals would fit me the week in the depths of winter. My husband had the kettle always boiling for me against I came in. He used to sit here reading his book – he never was fit for work at the best – while I used to be out minding the basket. He was so sober and quiet too. His neighbours will tell that of him.

'Within the last ten weeks he's been very ill indeed, but still I could be out with the basket. Since then he's never earn't me a penny – poor old soul, he wasn't able! All that time I still attended to my basket. He wasn't so ill then but what he could do a little here in the room for hisself; but he wanted little, God knows, for he couldn't eat. After he fell ill, I had to go all my errands myself. I had no one to help me, for I had nothing to pay them, and I'd have to walk from here down to Sun-street with my stick, till my bad leg pained me so that I could hardly stand. You see the hip being put out has drawn all the sinews up into my groin, and it leaves me uncapable of walking or standing constantly; but I thank God that I've got the use of it anyhow. Our lot's hard enough, goodness knows, but we are content. We never complain, but bless the Lord for the little he pleases to give us. When I was on my errands, in course I couldn't be minding my basket; so I lost a good bit of money that way. Well, five weeks on Wednesday he has been totally confined to his bed, excepting when I lifted him up to make it some nights; but he can't bear *that* now. Still the first fortnight he was bad, I did manage to leave him, and earn a few pence; but, latterly for this last three weeks, I haven't been able to go out at all, to do anything.'

'She's been stopping by me, minding me here night and day all that time,' mumbled the old man, who now for the first time opened his grey glassy eyes and turned towards me, to bear, as it were, a last tribute to his wife's incessant affection. 'She has been most kind to me. Her tenderness and care has been such that man never knew from woman before, ever since I lay upon this sick bed. We've been married five-and-twenty years. We have always lived happily – very happily indeed – together; until sickness and weakness overcome me I always strove to help myself a bit, as well as I could; but since then she has done all in her power for me – worked for me – ay, she has worked for me, surely – and watched over me. My creed through life has been repentance towards God, faith in Jesus Christ, and love to all my brethren. I've made up my mind that I must soon change this tabernacle, and my last wish is that the good people of this world will increase her little stock for her. She cannot get her living out of the little stock she has, and since I lay here it's so lessened, that neither she nor no one else can live upon it. If the kind hearts would give her but a little stock more, it would keep her old age from want, as she has kept mine. Indeed, indeed, she does deserve it. But the Lord, I know, will reward her for all she has done to me.' Here the old man's eyelids dropped exhausted.

'I've had a shilling and a loaf twice from the parish,' continued the woman. 'The overseer came to see if my old man was fit to be removed to the workhouse. The doctor gave me a certificate that he was not, and then the relieving officer gave me a shilling and a loaf of bread, and out of that shilling I bought the poor old fellow a sup of port wine. I bought a quarter of wine; which was 4*d.*, and I gave 5*d.* for a bit of tea and sugar, and I gave 2*d.* for coals; a halfpenny rushlight I bought, and a short candle, that made a penny – and that's the way I laid out the shilling. If God takes him, I know he'll sleep in heaven. I know the life he's spent, and am not afraid; but no one else shall take him from me – nothing shall part us but death in this world. Poor old soul, he can't be long with me. He's a perfect skeleton. His bones are starting through his skin.'

I asked what could be done for her, and the old man thrust forth his skinny arm, and laying hold of the bed-post, he raised himself slightly in his bed, as he murmured 'If she could be got into a little parlour, and away from sitting in the streets, it would be the saving of her.' And, so saying, he fell back overcome with the exertion, and breathed heavily.

The woman sat down beside me, and went on. 'What shocked him most was that I was obligated in his old age to go and ask for relief at the parish. You see, he was always a spiritful man, and it hurted him sorely that he should come to this at last, and for the first time in his lifetime. The only parish money that ever we had was this, and it *does* hurt him every day to think that he must be buried by the parish after all. He was always proud, you see.'

I told the kind-hearted old dame that some benevolent people had placed certain funds at my disposal for the relief of such distress as hers; and I assured her that neither she nor her husband should want for anything that might ease their sufferings.

The day after the above was written, the poor old man died. He was buried out of the funds sent to the 'Morning Chronicle,' and his wife received some few pounds to increase her stock; but in a few months the poor old woman went mad, and is now, I believe, the inmate of one of the pauper lunatic asylums.

Henry Mayhew
Mayhew's Characters, 1851

Baghdad Under Fire

Hussein stood alone in the carpet souk on the eastern bank of the Tigris, fingering his ivory worrybeads and gazing at the huge sun setting behind the Ottoman tenements on the far side of the river. The dying sunlight washed his *dishdasha* robe a wintry red.

The market square of the souk usually bustled at this time of early evening as people stopped to gossip or do last-minute shopping on the way home from work. But it was January 15, the United Nations' deadline for Iraq's withdrawal from Kuwait. Baghdad was silent and edgy. The souk was deserted.

Hussein greeted me with far more warmth than our acquaintance merited. I had visited him on and off in his shop over the past five months, using the excuse of fingering a Kurdish bangle, or looking at a carpet, to pick up the rumours and rhythms of daily life in Baghdad. For him, it had been an excuse for a rare talk with a foreigner, something that for an Iraqi is akin to a visit to the confessional.

Now, in this chance encounter, we seemed the only people left in the capital. We walked to his shop under the vaulted roof of the souk. Inside, there was none of the usual salesmanship or the ritual cup of sugared tea. 'Would you like a whisky?' he asked, and picked up a half-full bottle of Whyte & Mackay. He poured us two tea glasses full.

Amid the clutter of piled-up carpets, silver necklaces, antique frames, heavy Kurdish belts – and, beside the ubiquitous picture of Saddam Hussein, a likeness of President John F. Kennedy beaten into a copper plate – we discussed whether he should stay in Baghdad or take his family to a place safe from American bombs, as other merchants had.

Tareq, who owned the House of Antiquities across the street, had taken his wife and sons to Kurdistan in northern Iraq. 'The Americans like the Kurds, they won't bomb them,' he had said.

Hussein agonised. Baghdad was home; perhaps thieves would come to the empty souk and steal his carpets; but there was no business anyway because everybody was hoarding their money.

We drank another tea glass of whisky, standing up, too edgy to sit down. His wife, five children aged two to 12, younger brother and a mother were at home waiting. His children had their school exams on the 20th: if they missed, it would mean losing a year of school. 'But perhaps it is better that they lose a year than that they lose their lives,' he said.

Darkness was falling and we walked out of the shop. He said: 'If you have any problems you can come to my house. Really.' For an Iraqi, it was an enormous act of faith. A visit by a foreigner in this tightly controlled society meant a follow-up visit by the security police. But these were extraordinary times. It was a way of saying we were not enemies. I drove back to the Rashid hotel through dark and deserted streets.

Baghdad is normally a bustling city. Although its glorious antiquity was long ago buried under drab concrete, its spirit was irrepressible, even at the height of the first Gulf war, when taxis returning from the front with coffins on their roofs raced among the fierce traffic on its highways. To see the city now was chilling.

Many middle-class families had closed their homes and left to stay with relatives in the country after the failure of the talks in Geneva between Tariq Aziz, the foreign minister, and James Baker, the American secretary of state. Others held out, fiddling for good news between the BBC, Voice of America and the Pan-Arab station, Monte Carlo.

They had heard the ominous tone in Saddam's speech on Friday to an Islamic conference in Baghdad. They had heard Joe Wilson, the American chargé d'affaires, dramatically announce as he left on Saturday: 'This is the last flight out.' They knew most Western diplomats had left with him.

But even illiterate taxi drivers held an irrational faith that Javier Pérez de Cuéllar, the United Nations secretary-general, might be able to avert war when he arrived to see Saddam at the weekend. 'Maybe Saddam will leave Kuwait,' the taxi driver said as he drove me to Pérez de Cuéllar's news conference at the airport. When the secretary-general said 'only God knows' if there would be a war, it was the last straw. Iraqis knew Saddam was ready to take on the world.

Everybody was jumpy. We lost our way leaving the airport and when we drove up to a checkpoint to ask a soldier for directions, there was an audible click as he flipped the safety catch off his AK-47 and walked up to the car with the barrel pointed through the window.

There were many poignant moments in those days overshadowed by the deadline. The most striking thing perhaps, to somebody who had been visiting Iraq on and off since the crisis began, was the sudden openness of the usually careful and closed Iraqis.

This is a society that usually keeps its head down and offers no political opinions. Most dissidents are dead or in exile. The tiny middle class would, in general, be glad to see Saddam's regime fall; but the merchants did well out of the war against Iran and reached an accommodation with those in power. The urban poor, who have enjoyed cheap, and even free, housing and subsidised food under Saddam, are compliant to his will. The long war against Iran united society and now I found that his stand against the world was filling many Iraqis with pride as well as fear.

After seeing Hussein in the souk hours before the deadline expired, I went into the Al-wiyah club with Falah, an Iraqi businessman. It is a former British club now frequented by Iraq's elite, a place of contrasts. A huge Saddam portrait greets arrivals in the club car park, but members still leave their own private bottles of whisky behind the bar, their names printed on them, in the old British club tradition. We were the only customers, but there was still food, some salads and chicken.

Falah spoke over dinner about statistics, trying to put on a brave face that Iraq would somehow continue. He had been helping as a consultant to the government in what he called 'food security' since the crisis began. He had managed to cut sugar consumption by 60 per cent by closing down ice-cream and confectionery shops; Iraq was now making its own liquid sugar from dates. Farmers had had to kill most of Iraq's chickens because of the shortage of grain, but cows had been switched to grass and still gave milk. Wheat was a problem; Iraq produced 4 million tons annually and consumed 6.5 million but increased subsidies for farmers would make up much of the shortage. Meanwhile, rationing filled the gap: his office had made charts of human consumption, added 20 per cent and produced rationing amounts and distributed coupons.

Such statistics are usually impossible to come by; but I had barely the energy to commit them to memory (you don't take notes in public in Iraq). Falah relaxed, dropped his beloved subject and lapsed into tales of his childhood.

The club was significant to him and to the current situation. He had come here first as a young and proud university student, the first Arab of his generation to visit it, brought by a British professor as a reward for being number one in his class. 'You realise for us this is much more than a war between Iraq and America. For us, even for the Arabs who are not with Saddam, it is a struggle for our dignity. The West has humiliated us and we see Saddam as a leader who has finally stood up to the West and said we want our dignity.'

On the way home, I went by the French embassy where André Jenier, the last Western diplomat in Baghdad, was preparing to leave in proper French style. He had laid out the embassy's last French cheeses, pâtés and salamis and served champagne until midnight, when he and his few remaining staff clambered into their cars and drove through the night to the Jordanian border.

At the Hotel Palestine, previously the Meridian but now run-down and shabby after a change from French to Iraqi ownership at the start of the economic embargo five months ago, I stopped at a 'challenge the deadline' celebration, an Iraqi version of an end-of-the-world party.

Kadum Al-Sahir, a popular singer, was on the floor amid a group of men who danced and waved Iraqi flags. But most of the rest of the hall was filled with sombre beer drinkers, sitting at their table without much enthusiasm. Most were government recruits; the only guests who seemed to have paid the 20 dinar ($35) entry price were 10 Palestinians who had come in a delegation from Jordan to show solidarity with Iraq. A wedding party had been recruited to build up the numbers.

I went to bed in my room at the Rashid hotel and waited for the worst.

The Americans had announced that the deadline would fall at mid-night New York time, 8.00am local time next day, Wednesday the 16th. When I woke, a heavy fog had settled across the flat city. For a moment, looking out of the hotel window, unable to see anything but white mist obscuring the skyline, I thought perhaps the attack had come and I had slept through it.

Downstairs, among the government 'minders' who watched the comings and goings of the few of the 40 or so journalists left at the Rashid hotel, there was premature euphoria. 'You see, I told you there would not be war,' said Karim, one of the men from the information ministry.

Baghdad thought otherwise. Driving around town, I saw only a few knots of men in quiet discussions. Rashid Street, the main thoroughfare, lined with colonnaded mock-Ottoman buildings from the 1930s, was usually packed with cars. Instead, it was a wide deserted avenue at 9.00am.

Windows were taped over against bombs for the first time. The Mandarin restaurant on Karada Street, once Baghdad's busiest fast food joint but closed for months because of a ban on serving meals, had its wide windows taped in large Xs. At the Shorjah souk, Baghdad's most popular market because of its cheap clothing, household items and canned goods, only four of the 200 stores had opened. One man, hanging up flannel robes from the ceiling of his shop, said: 'We still open for an hour. If it stays like this, we will close.' Schools had opened, but with few teachers and fewer students they quickly closed for the day.

There was no sign of backing off by Saddam. The headline of the government newspaper, *Al-Jumhuriya*, said: 'We shall never compromise on Iraqi and Arab rights.' Midday television news showed perhaps the unluckiest people in the world that day: 177 former prisoners of war descending from an Iraqi Airways flight to Baghdad after years of captivity in Iran.

Sources were fast disappearing. I telephoned the foreign ministry to try to see Nizar Hamdoun, the under-secretary. But the ministry's number had changed and its officials had moved to a new location. The last time I had seen Hamdoun, he was sitting in his office, morosely watching CNN television. 'I feel like I'm watching a bad fiction movie,' he had said.

During his tenure as Iraqi ambassador to Washington, Hamdoun had been the architect of the Iraqi-American *rapprochement* of the 1980s. He still felt Iraq could be America's best ally in the Middle East. It was the only local power able to enforce stability in the region under Bush's new world order; it had oil America needed; it was a potentially wealthy market; and it would guarantee American interests. But by January 16, 1991, policy was long out of the hands of thoughtful diplomats such as Hamdoun.

At the ministry of information that evening, the receptionist at the office of Naji Hadithi, the director-general, was watching cartoons. Inside, Hadithi and I watched a film showing Saddam visiting troops in Kuwait. The president looked confident as he had in every appearance that week, although rather awkward as he sat wrapped in a huge greatcoat with troops who looked terrified by his presence. He asked them oddly personal questions. 'Have you had your dinner?' he said to one. A long pause ... 'Is this place warm?' he said to another.

Hadithi switched to CNN and we watched a demonstration of allied fire control in Dhahran, where Saudi, American and British forces are based. A lieutenant-commander was interviewed, saying his men were prepared. Hadithi commented: 'The only thing missing from this is reality.'

He meant on the allied side. It was a cherished belief of many Iraqis I spoke to, even those who were desperate to avoid war, that if it came to a battle, Iraqi soldiers, hardened in the war against Iran, would defeat their better armed but inexperienced enemy.

As Wednesday evening drew on, Marlin Fitzwater, Bush's spokesman, caused the first real worry among the foreign press corps. He said any journalists in Baghdad were in danger and should leave immediately. All American print reporters had left on the 14th, but the American television networks remained. Now they started getting prearranged signals from Pentagon sources that an attack was imminent.

Larry Doyle of CBS received the message: 'Your family is fine but your children have colds.' Doyle, a veteran journalist who reported on the Vietnam war, put down the phone and said simply: 'Shit.'

A delegation of journalists hurried to Hadithi's office. Some wanted to move out of the Rashid hotel, located in central Baghdad near most of the ministries and the presidential palace, all obvious targets for attack. But Hadithi said: 'We are still here. Our ministry is a dangerous place and yet we did not evacuate.'

John Simpson of BBC Television said in his understated manner: 'The Americans have 2,000lb bombs which could make things extremely unpleasant.'

Latis Jassim, the information minister, arrived and reassured us. 'You are safe. This is a commitment on our part. We are willing and eager to offer you the necessary services so that you can report the facts as you see them. But at no time will communications fail completely.'

It was midnight. We went back to the hotel. The attack could come at any moment. Nobody knew how bad it might be. We waited.

I took a small bag down to the bomb shelter below the hotel, just in case. Already women and children were huddled along the walls wrapped in blankets. Somehow the warning had swept through the hotel.

The lights in the shelter flickered. I had to see what was happening. I turned and started up the steps but was met by a flood of panicked people coming down the stairs, women with crying children, Sudanese waiters still in uniform, an Iranian delegation staying at the hotel.

At entrance-hall level, I could hear booms from outside. Upstairs, from the 5th-floor BBC office, we saw out of the window a spectacular display of tracer fire shooting across the sky. Tracers spewed up as if from a roman candle. Others shot across the sky as if following an unseen and unheard enemy. White flashes illuminated the tops of buildings on which, during the last five months, we had watched the crews of anti-aircraft guns shelter first from the August sun and lately from January's rain and cold.

Strange video game noises filled the air. The staccato thud-thud-thud of heavy artillery sounded. Bob Simpson of BBC Radio had a microphone out of the open window and leaned on his elbows on the windowsill as he calmly described the spectacular display. Down the hall, a CBS cameraman knelt on the floor, his camera out of the window, and filmed through a down-tilted eye scope.

Huge yellow flashes appeared on the horizon. Something to the right thudded and the impact threw me back across the room. Smoke rose from the building. There could no longer be any suspicion that it was a false alarm or jittery anti-aircraft gunners. It was 2.35am Iraqi time and Baghdad was under attack.

Doyle, spotting the flashes on the horizon, narrated for those of us less knowledgeable about armaments. 'Those are the big boys, the cute 2,000lb bombs,' he said. 'Unfortunately I've been through this before. They are just pounding the hell out of that place.'

The bombing appeared to be about 20 miles off, probably at the Rashid military complex. The attack slackened off, then started again at 3.35am. The city, which had remained lit up, went completely black. The anti-aircraft fire stopped and started again in almost 15-minute intervals, sometimes directed above our hotel, filling the skies but seeming to have little effect.

About 4.25am, hotel security guards came into the room and tried to drag us downstairs to the shelter. They settled for taping over the emergency light that had gone on when the hotel lights failed. From below, during a lull, an earnest ABC reporter yelled up: 'What are your departure plans?' Somebody yelled down: 'Up in the air at the moment.'

I wandered back to my room at 6.00am as dawn broke and the attack appeared to have stopped. A man I had never seen before was asleep in my bed still wearing large boots. I went down the hall and took a nap on the floor of the BBC office.

Morning came cold and misty again when I woke at 7.30am. After the drama of the night, it was strange to see the city skyline unchanged. Smoke from a fire behind the hotel drifted through the hallways. But little damage was visible from the hotel room.

We clustered around to hear Baghdad radio for the first communiqué of the war. 'This is communiqué number one. The mother of battles has begun. President Bush will regret this attack. Victory is near.' The voice announced the immediate call-up of reserve soldiers born in 1954, 1955 and 1956. The radio returned to martial music.

My driver had disappeared. He was born in 1955 and had been worrying about the call-up for the last month. 'War is very bad,' he had said to me. 'I fought eight years in the war with Iran. No wife, no children. Now maybe I have to go to Kuwait.' His fears had been realised.

I grabbed a taxi on the street and drove around the city. The first evidence of attack was at the international post and telecommunications building. It had been hit by at least four missiles that had left gaping holes and dangling wires. Chunks of building and glass littered the streets, but no surrounding buildings suffered damage more than broken windows.

A bit further on the Ba'ath party headquarters had taken a direct hit in the roof. Again, no surrounding buildings were touched. On Abunawas Street, across the river from the presidential palace, a car tilted crazily into a 30-foot crater already filled with water. But, other than that, there seemed to be almost no damage to civilian targets.

Anti-aircraft guns sounded again at 9.00am and 10.00am. Soldiers in uniform lined the roads at bus stations trying to flag down cabs or cars to head south to register with their units. The few families that had left it too late to leave stood, suitcases and children in hand, trying to do the same.

At 10.30am I was standing in front of the ministry of information, now deserted despite the minister's brave words just hours earlier, as a thud sounded and a mushroom of smoke went up from the defence ministry about half a mile away. Two more thuds shook the building. Neither a plane had been visible nor an engine heard. Anti-aircraft fire went up but it was too late.

Driving by the ministry – an old Ottoman building still marked the Abbassid Palace on tourist maps and so secret that a government official once told me it was a musuem – I could see flames in the central section. A wing had been flattened as if by a giant fist.

The reaction from soldiers in the barracks across the street from the defence ministry was as surprising as the suddenness of the attack. They stood standing and watching the fire as if it was a show unconnected to them. Nobody seemed to be in much of a hurry to put it out. Like the foreign ministry, the defence department must have transferred its operations elsewhere in the days before the deadline.

As I drove around town, the calm and lack of panic were impressive. Orderly lines formed for bread and cars queued for petrol. It was a far cry from the day after the bombing of the Libyan city of Tripoli, when Libyans crashed their cars into each other trying to flee, the government disappeared and rumours that Colonel Gadaffi had been overthrown filled the capital.

Baghdad's militiamen had appeared overnight to keep order. In the Amriyah area, a civilian neighbourhood, six teenagers dressed in jeans and jackets walked along the streets with Kalashnikov assault rifles casually slung over their shoulders. A man in a cheap suit and a *keffiyeh* Arab headdress manned an anti-aircraft gun placed in the back of a Nissan pick-up truck at a crossroads. But there were no new checkpoints, nor was there hostility towards foreigners.

Saddam came on Baghdad radio at 12.40 in the afternoon, speaking in calm and confident tones: 'At 12.30am the great duel started. The valiant sons of Iraq, your brothers, sons and fathers confronted the invaders. Damn King Fahd, the traitor of Mecca, damn the invaders, damn these criminals. We shall win. The dawn will break and they will be damned.'

My taxi driver, taking me back to the hotel, said he was not at the front because he had a piece of shrapnel still in his head from the Iran war. It hurt when the weather got cold. Like most Iraqis that day, he appeared worried but unfazed. 'I did not think we should have taken Kuwait,' he said. 'I don't agree with this. But the Americans should not come to Iraq. Iraqi soldiers will fight for Iraq and for Saddam. We have fought for eight years against Iran and they cannot frighten us.'

This was the mood of Baghdad under fire. An Iraqi businessman explained to me why people were so calm. Listening for weeks to the propaganda from Washington, they had expected Armageddon. Now that the bombing had come at last and they had survived, he said, their attitude was: 'Well, if that's it, we can take it.'

People had even begun to listen for the first time to Iraqi radio, and to believe its propaganda, because they felt that the BBC and Voice of America had lied about allied successes against the air force and missile sites in the first attack.

In addition, the government maintained at least a semblance of control. The city was without water or electricity, and the streets began to smell of sewage and cordite. But soldiers directed traffic in place of traffic lights, papers continued to publish daily, and the television news appeared every night at the same time, with its usual announcer, and on the same television studio set.

Only a few shops opened; and prices were astonishing: I saw a bottle of whisky, a packet of cigarettes and three Mars bars bought for 147 dinars, the equivalent of $441 at the official rate and equal to three-quarters of the monthly salary of a middle-ranking government official.

But in the poor neighbourhoods such as Saddam City, where more people had remained because they had no way of escape, and which the regime regards as its centres of support, government lorries distributed bread under normal ration regulations.

Anti-aircraft fire erupted sporadically during the day. Tracer fire, the thud of guns and falling bombs filled the night, but there were few civilian casualties.

There were makeshift shelters to be found almost anywhere in the city. Driving back to the Rashid, I ducked into the Baghdad hotel when anti-aircraft guns went off at the nearby presidential palace. The discotheque had been turned into a bomb shelter and guests were handed candles at the door. People were worried but there was still an air of unreality. 'Palestine seems closer than it has for 40 years,' said a Palestinian businessman also sheltering inside.

Baghdad's survival – and the news that Saddam had launched Scud rockets at Israel – had many Palestinians and their Iraqi supporters still believing that he would achieve his goal of somehow freeing Palestinian land from Israel.

As the sun set on Friday, I watched two orbs of light streak low across the city skyline, just missing the rooftops, and smash into the Dora oil refinery. A huge ball of fire erupted and smoke drifted back over Baghdad.

Bombing continued sporadically that night and at dawn the refinery had only three instead of four chimneys. The 20-storey communications tower – which had lost its top three storeys to an unseen missile on Friday, as if to an invisible hand – had completely disappeared from the skyline by Saturday morning.

On Saturday afternoon, I was gazing idly from a 5th-floor window across the Zawra zoo park opposite the hotel when I suddenly realised that a cruise missile was heading above the trees straight for us. It seemed to be white. I could see its little fins. There was no smoke trail coming from it.

I thought it was going to hit the hotel, and I yelled out. But it turned right and skirted the building, as if following a street map, and hit the old parliament building about half a mile away, sending up a white pall of smoke.

Another cruise landed even closer, disappearing with a deafening crash into breeze-block staff quarters next to the hotel. The huts burst into flames and shrapnel showered the lawn and swimming pool. Glass from broken windows littered the hotel lobby as hotel workers dragged an electronic circuit board into the air-raid shelter, dancing around it, ululating and shouting that they had downed an American plane.

It was a relentless afternoon attack. At least two more missiles hit the Dora refinery again, sparking a fire that lit Baghdad with a beautiful rose glow late into the night.

Conditions at the Rashid hotel were becoming primitive. Electricity remained off and journalists worked at night by candlelight. Sanitation had broken down, toilets could not flush, and we had been washing in the swimming pool.

The officials minding us had had enough. They had stayed in the shelter for days and had not seen their families nor been able to contact them by telephone. They were worried about our safety and about the detail of what we were reporting. We were ordered to leave.

On Saturday night, as I packed and sat up late with other journalists discussing our departure, a Palestinian friend stopped by to say farewell. An articulate, educated man, he was trying to explain why so much of the Arab world had come out in support of Saddam despite his invasion of Kuwait and oppressive policies.

'You must understand that if Saddam goes, no Westerner will be safe walking down an Arab street. I will pick up a machine gun and fight the Americans. A year ago I would have told you I hated Saddam and his regime. But he has become a symbol for us. Saddam is the result of the humiliation of the war of 1967 and of all the humiliations we have suffered from the West. If we let you destroy Saddam now, you will destroy all of us Arabs again.' He added: 'It is a question of dignity. Saddam came along with his rockets and stood up to you and we said, 'Why not?'

I rose at 5.00am to the incongruous sounds of a cock crowing and another barrage of anti-aircraft fire, this time a light and sparkling scattering of shots of tracer into the air. The government newspaper headline read: 'Hussein rockets answer the call of Palestine. The road to Jerusalem is open.' Uniting under attack behind Saddam, people might even believe this hyperbole.

Downstairs the taxi drivers demanded the exorbitant sum of $3,000 a car to the Jordanian border, because a convoy of cars that had left on Saturday had been bombed near the town of Rutba in the western desert.

We drove out of Baghdad on the deserted highway, past military camps on the city's perimeter that appeared surprisingly intact, with anti-aircaft guns still manned on mounds along their boundaries. Government army lorries trundled south towing anti-aircraft guns, but there was little other traffic. The journey through flat, unbroken rocky desert was uneventful. Iraqi guards stamped exit visas into our passports at the desolate border station of Trebil. Among the shabby breeze-block buildings we left behind the stacks of abandoned cheap luggage from earlier refugees and drove across the no man's land into Jordan.

Marie Colvin
The Sunday Times, January 27, 1991

When the Wolves Stopped Howling

W hen the wolves stopped howling, the people began to move again. Now thousands of them were stumbling in the lead-coloured water of violent little rivers, passing babies across fallen logs.

The valleys were full of snow and lightning and the babies stared cold and hungry through a wrap of wet blankets at the miserable sky.

Sometimes the infants fell and mothers screamed after them with snow squeezing through the toes of their bare feet.

Then the columns of people joined up below the snowline at 6,000 feet. And afterwards it was a human avalanche filling the mountainside. The sound of wailing and crying began as a small noise way up there and became something that covered the slopes with its awful sound.

These were the Kurds of Iraq, desperate in their search for sanctuary from the murderous pursuit of Saddam Hussein.

The Turkish Army waited for them in the village of Isikveren. It is a nothing collection of wood huts and stone hovels which is all any place is up here in the Zakho Mountains dividing East Turkey from Iraq. Soon, though, Isikveren will be part of history.

The great columns of refugees shuffled around the last turn of the lowest valley. They came in a huge mass, a haunting sight of families, children half-blind with exhaustion, old men with their chests pumping, mothers and girls carrying babies, some of them in buckets.

President Bush worries about his 8-iron golf shots pulling up short of the putting greens in Florida. But there is no golf in Isikveren. Just people falling into pits of mud and fighting with vanishing strength to live another day in the hell of the Zakho Mountains.

The soldiers raised their rifles and fired suddenly over the heads of the people. The mountains roared back the echo of the shooting. The sound changed from wailing to the noise of battle.

It wasn't a single shot here and there. Thousands of rounds went over their heads, even a rip of machine-gun fire, and behind that the thud of something heavier. But the people just walked on to face the guns and the soldiers stepped back and fired wildly. They didn't change step. The front rank went right up to the soldiers and almost touched noses. The soldiers raised their guns higher and more long volleys shook the ground.

Bullets ricocheted from the boulder-strewn hillsides and whined everywhere. The people kept walking.

A woman in a blue coat was killed when a shot came off a rock. She fell down dead, and her friends, or people walking with her anyway, got around her body and carried it with them.

'An accident, a terrible accident,' an army lieutenant came over and said. He was distressed. They had not meant to hurt anybody, he said.

Why are you shooting? 'We can't have all of them scattering into the countryside,' he explained his orders. 'We have to keep them together. We are building a camp with good facilities.'

When the mountains petered out into level ground the area was Uludere province. The provincial governor went to Isikveren in a dark blue suit and a white shirt and a black tie. He looked like he had an appointment with a bank manager. He slapped his forehead when he heard the woman was shot and babbled something into a hand radio.

Nothing stopped the Kurds. All they did was walk on in this huge crowd, 20,000 maybe.

'We are told there are hundreds of thousands more up there,' the lieutenant said, pointing behind him.

Another fury of shooting cut him short.

'Try to tell them we are not going to send them back to Iraq,' he pleaded, 'try, please try.'

A refugee who spoke English was brought through the crowd. 'This officer says you are not being sent back to Iraq but you must stay together here,' he was told.

The man screamed with anger. 'Many children have died in the mountains there, why can't we be let into Turkey?'

The officer had gone before he could answer.

'Saddam, Saddam, die, die,' one group shouted. They all drew flat hands across their throats.

'In hospital in Zakho (a Kurdish city in North Iraq) Saddam's soldiers killed 30 people, children and women,' another man said. 'We will all be killed if we go back.'

How were they killed? 'Stab,' he said, 'stab all over and shooting.'

Children sat exhausted on bed-rolls and old coats under the storm of bullets which went in sheets over their heads. The sound of shooting meant nothing. 'We've been shot at by Saddam for days,' somebody said.

Mothers fed babies in a rainstorm holding bits of carpets over their little heads. Dark-faced boys, six or seven years old, hunted for their families in the mass where it stopped next to the village.

When you talked to them, smoothed their mud-stiff hair, they smiled.

A tiny boy, perhaps seven, wore the jacket of a man. His little hands were 12 inches up the sleeves. He struggled to get his hand out to shake yours. The jacket was nearly an overcoat for him.

Where did he get it? 'From somebody who died in the snow,' the man with good English said.

The child saluted with the end of the sleeve hanging over his hand.

When did he last eat? 'Two days ago at least,' the man said. He told the story.

'We are all Kurds. Saddam wants us killed. The army shelled us in Zakho. All the people tried to cross the mountains to escape.'

Some of them were in the bucket of a bulldozer.

'When we cross first river we begin to climb. People couldn't carry all their goods so they left them. In a short time they had very little and no food. We ate grass and things on the ground.

'When we were in the forest we could light fires from the wood. Beyond the forest and the snow there is no wood and no trees. People began to freeze to death. They died everywhere. Look, look how few old women! Babies die because mothers got no milk inside them.'

But they tramped all the way over the top of the mountains, 20,000 at a time, and they came through rain and storms when the wind chopped off slices of ice and threw them around like circular saws.

It was the same as crossing the Alps and must be one of the greatest mass escapes and feats of endurance ever known.

If Mr Bush could get out here and see it he would pick up the phone on his golf trolley and tell his air force commanders to bomb Saddam's army into metal dust.

The women got into vast groups when the Turkish Army stopped them in the village. They had nothing really. Rags. The rags had kept them warm.

A mountain track from the lowlands was a ribbon of bogged-down trucks from Turkish Kurds trying to get supplies to them. Men tried to push a 10-tonner uphill through a mud hole. The open back was full of fresh bread. Potatoes were in other lorries, spinach and cabbage in the rest.

An old man on a dirty white horse yelled the name of a relative from Iraq at a seethe of faces. No one came to him. He wept.

A place on the grass as big as 10 football pitches was solid with refugees. Children filled their mouths with uncooked noodles. Mothers held out cans to the soldiers and begged for fresh water. There was a laziness that comes from exhaustion.

Now a man with face burns came to a puddle and splashed the blisters. 'Saddam soldier put gasoline on him and set him on fire,' it was said.

The man even managed to grin through the blisters.

A woman they said spoke English was asked, 'Are you glad to be in Turkey?' She wiped her mouth with the end of a black scarf. A sentence began but she was too tired to finish it.

Mud was dry on her dress up to the waist. This was the depth of the last river she waded. Her child, a girl with red hair, tugged at the dress.

More people pressed in and sat on the ground. They had nothing, rags and pieces of blanket.

The mountains were a litter of pots and pans and mattresses thrown down when they could take the strain of carrying them no more.

One of the massive tragedies of the world begins to make pictures in the high mountains of Turkey. And still there are more people sliding through the stunted, leafless trees with fingers numbed from frostbite and bare feet showing a painful blue under long dresses.

Cold rain hosed down, making a swamp out of everything. The Kurds crouched under old plastic sacks and children stared out from the makeshift tents. Their eyes were like those of small animals staring out of holes.

John Edwards, reporting from the Zakho Mountains on the Turkey/Iraq border
The Daily Mail, April 6, 1991

On the Bottom

The journey did not last more than twenty minutes. Then the lorry stopped, and we saw a large door, and above it a sign, brightly illuminated (its memory still strikes me in my dreams): *Arbeit Macht Frei,* work gives freedom.

We climb down, they make us enter an enormous empty room that is poorly heated. We have a terrible thirst. The weak gurgle of the water in the radiators makes us ferocious; we have had nothing to drink for four days. But there is also a tap – and above it a card which says that it is forbidden to drink as the water is dirty. Nonsense. It seems obvious that the card is a joke, 'they' know that we are dying of thirst and they put us in a room, and there is a tap, and *Wassertrinken Verboten.* I drink and I incite my companions to do likewise, but I have to spit it out, the water is tepid and sweetish, with the smell of a swamp.

This is hell. Today, in our times, hell must be like this. A huge, empty room: we are tired, standing on our feet, with a tap which drips while we cannot drink the water, and we wait for something which will certainly be terrible, and nothing happens and nothing continues to happen. What can one think about? One cannot think any more, it is like being already dead. Someone sits down on the ground. The time passes drop by drop.

We are not dead. The door is opened and an SS man enters, smoking. He looks at us slowly and asks, *'Wer kann Deutsch?'* One of us whom I have never seen, named Flesch, moves forward; he will be our interpreter. The SS man makes a long calm speech; the interpreter translates. We have to form rows of five, with intervals of two yards between man and man; then we have to undress and make a bundle of the clothes in a special manner, the woollen garments on one side, all the rest on the other; we must take off our shoes but pay great attention that they are not stolen.

Stolen by whom? Why should our shoes be stolen? And what about our documents, the few things we have in our pockets, our watches? We all look at the interpreter, and the interpreter asks the German, and the German smokes and looks him through and through as if he were transparent, as if no one had spoken.

I had never seen old men naked. Mr Bergmann wore a truss and asked the interpreter if he should take it off, and the interpreter hesitated. But the German understood and spoke seriously to the interpreter pointing to someone. We saw the interpreter swallow and then he said: 'The officer says, take off the truss, and you will be given that of Mr Coen.' One could see the words coming bitterly out of Flesch's mouth; this was the German manner of laughing.

Now another German comes and tells us to put the shoes in a certain corner, and we put them there, because now it is all over and we feel outside this world and the only thing is to obey. Someone comes with a broom and sweeps away all the shoes, outside the door in a heap. He is crazy, he is mixing them all together, ninety-six pairs, they will be all unmatched. The outside door opens, a freezing wind enters and we are naked and cover ourselves up with our arms. The wind blows and slams the door; the German reopens it and stands watching with interest how we writhe to hide from the wind, one behind the other. Then he leaves and closes it.

Now the second act begins. Four men with razors, soapbrushes and clippers burst in; they have trousers and jackets with stripes, with a number sewn on the front; perhaps they are the same sort as those others of this evening (this evening or yesterday evening?); but these are robust and flourishing. We ask many questions but they catch hold of us and in a moment we find ourselves shaved and sheared. What comic faces we have without hair! The four speak a language which does not seem of this world. It is certainly not German, for I understand a little German.

Finally another door is opened: here we are, locked in, naked, sheared and standing, with our feet in water – it is a shower-room. We are alone. Slowly the astonishment dissolves, and we speak, and everyone asks questions and no one answers. If we are naked in a shower-room, it means that we will have a shower. If we have a shower it is because they are not going to kill us yet. But why then do they keep us standing, and give us nothing to drink, while nobody explains anything, and we have no shoes or clothes, but we are all naked with our feet in the water, and we have been travelling five days and cannot even sit down. And our women?

Mr Levi asks me if I think that our women are like us at this moment, and where they are, and if we will be able to see them again. I say yes, because he is married and has a daughter; certainly we will see them again. But by now my belief is that all this is a game to mock and sneer at us. Clearly they will kill us, whoever thinks he is going to live is mad, it means that he has swallowed the bait, but I have not; I have understood that it will soon all be over, perhaps in this same room, when they get bored of seeing us naked, dancing from foot to foot and trying every now and again to sit down on the floor. But there are two inches of cold water and we cannot sit down.

We walk up and down without sense, and we talk, everybody talks to everybody else, we make a great noise. The door opens, and a German enters; it is the officer of before. He speaks briefly, the interpreter translates. 'The officer says you must be quiet, because this is not a rabbinical school.' One sees the words which are not his, the bad words, twist his mouth as they come out, as if he was spitting out a foul taste. We beg him to ask what we are waiting for, how long we will stay here, about our women, everything; but he says no, that he does not want to ask. This Flesch, who is most unwilling to translate into Italian the hard cold German phrases and refuses to turn into German our questions because he knows that it is useless, is a German Jew of about fifty, who has a large scar on his face from a wound received fighting the Italians on the Piave. He is a closed, taciturn man, for whom I feel an instinctive respect as I feel that he has begun to suffer before us.

The German goes and we remain silent, although we are a little ashamed of our silence. It is still night and we wonder if the day will ever come. The door opens again, and someone else dressed in stripes comes in. He is different from the others, older, with glasses, a more civilized face, and much less robust. He speaks to us in Italian.

By now we are tired of being amazed. We seem to be watching some mad play, one of those plays in which the witches, the Holy Spirit and the devil appear. He speaks Italian badly, with a strong foreign accent. He makes a long speech, is very polite, and tries to reply to all our questions.

We are at Monowitz, near Auschwitz, in Upper Silesia, a region inhabited by both Poles and Germans. This camp is a work-camp, in German one says *Arbeitslager;* all the prisoners (there are about ten thousand) work in a factory which produces a type of rubber called Buna, so that the camp itself is called Buna.

We will be given shoes and clothes – no, not our own – other shoes, other clothes, like his. We are naked now because we are waiting for the shower and the disinfection, which will take place immediately after the reveille, because one cannot enter the camp without being disinfected.

Certainly there will be work to do, everyone must work here. But there is work and work: he, for example, acts as doctor. He is a Hungarian doctor who studied in Italy and he is the dentist of the Lager. He has been in the Lager for four and a half years (not in this one: Buna has only been open for a year and a half), but we can see that he is still quite well, not very thin. Why is he in the Lager? Is he Jewish like us? 'No,' he says simply, 'I am a criminal.'

We ask him many questions. He laughs, replies to some and not to others, and it is clear that he avoids certain subjects. He does not speak of the women: he says they are well, that we will see them again soon, but he does not say how or where. Instead he tells us other things, strange and crazy things, perhaps he too is playing with us. Perhaps he is mad – one goes mad in the Lager. He says that every Sunday there are concerts and football matches. He says that whoever boxes well can become cook. He says that whoever works well receives prize-coupons with which to buy tobacco and soap. He says that the water is really not drinkable, and that instead a coffee substitute is distributed every day, but generally nobody drinks it as the soup itself is sufficiently watery to quench thirst. We beg him to find us something to drink, but he says he cannot, that he has come to see us secretly, against SS orders, as we still have to be disinfected, and that he must leave at once; he has come because he has a liking for Italians, and because, he says, he 'has a little heart'. We ask him if there are other Italians in the camp and he says there are some, a few, he does not know how many; and he at once changes the subject. Meanwhile a bell rang and he immediately hurried off and left us stunned and disconcerted. Some feel refreshed but I do not. I still think that even this dentist, this incomprehensible person, wanted to amuse himself at our expense, and I do not want to believe a word of what he said.

At the sound of the bell, we can hear the still dark camp waking up. Unexpectedly the water gushes out boiling from the showers – five minutes of bliss; but immediately after, four men (perhaps they are the barbers) burst in yelling and shoving and drive us out, wet and steaming, into the adjoining room which is freezing; here other shouting people throw at us unrecognizable rags and thrust into our hands a pair of broken-down boots with wooden soles; we have no time to understand and we already find ourselves in the open, in the blue and icy snow of dawn, barefoot and naked, with all our clothing in our hands, with a hundred yards to run to the next hut. There we are finally allowed to get dressed.

When we finish, everyone remains in his own corner and we do not dare lift our eyes to look at one another. There is nowhere to look in a mirror, but our appearance stands in front of us, reflected in a hundred livid faces, in a hundred miserable and sordid puppets. We are transformed into the phantoms glimpsed yesterday evening.

Then for the first time we became aware that our language lacks words to express this offence, the demolition of a man. In a moment, with almost prophetic intuition, the reality was revealed to us: we had reached the bottom. It is not possible to sink lower than this; no human condition is more miserable than this, nor could it conceivably be so. Nothing belongs to us any more; they have taken away our clothes, our shoes, even our hair; if we speak, they will not listen to us, and if they listen, they will not understand. They will even take away our name: and if we want to keep it, we will have to find ourselves the strength to do so, to manage somehow so that behind the name something of us, of us as we were, still remains.

We know that we will have difficulty in being understood, and this is as it should be. But consider what value, what meaning is enclosed even in the smallest of our daily habits, in the hundred possessions which even the poorest beggar owns: a handkerchief, an old letter, the photo of a cherished prison. These things are part of us, almost like limbs of our body; nor is it conceivable that we can be deprived of them in our world, for we immediately find others to substitute the old ones, other objects which are ours in their personification and evocation of our memories.

Imagine now a man who is deprived of everyone he loves, and at the same time of his house, his habits, his clothes, in short, of everything he possesses: he will be a hollow man, reduced to suffering and needs, forgetful of dignity and restraint, for he who loses all often easily loses himself. He will be a man whose life or death can be lightly decided with no sense of human affinity, in the most fortunate of cases, on the basis of a pure judgement of utility. It is in this way that one can understand the double sense of the term 'extermination camp', and it is now clear what we seek to express with the phrase: 'to lie on the bottom'.

*Häftling**: I have learnt that I am Häftling. My number is 174517; we have been baptized, we will carry the tattoo on our left arm until we die.

The operation was slightly painful and extraordinarily rapid: they placed us all in a row, and one by one, according to the alphabetical order of our names, we filed past a skilful official, armed with a sort of pointed tool with a very short needle. It seems that this is the real, true initiation: only by 'showing one's number' can one get bread and soup. Several days passed, and not a few cuffs and punches, before we became used to showing our number promptly enough not to disorder the daily operation of food-distribution; weeks and months were needed to learn its sound in the German language. And for many days, while the habits of freedom still led me to look for the time on my wristwatch, my new name ironically appeared instead, a number tattooed in bluish characters under the skin.

Only much later, and slowly, a few of us learnt something of the funereal science of the numbers of Auschwitz, which epitomize the stages of destruction of European Judaism. To the old hands of the camp, the numbers told everything: the period of entry into the camp, the convoy of which one formed a part, and consequently the nationality. Everyone will treat with respect the numbers from 30,000 to 80,000 : there are only a few hundred left and they represented the few survivals from the Polish ghettos. It is as well to watch out in commercial dealings with a 116,000 or a 117,000 : they now number only about forty, but they represent the Greeks of Salonica, so take care they do not pull the wool over your eyes. As for the high numbers they carry an essentially comic air about them, like the words 'freshman' or 'conscript' in ordinary life. The typical high number is a corpulent, docile and stupid fellow: he can be convinced that leather shoes are distributed at the infirmary to all those with delicate feet, and can be persuaded to run there and leave his bowl of soup 'in your custody'; you can sell him a spoon for three rations of bread; you can send him to the most ferocious of the Kapos to ask him (as happened to me!) if it is true that his is the *kartoffelschalenkommando,* the 'Potato Peeling Command', and if one can be enrolled in it.

In fact, the whole process of introduction to what was for us a new order took place in a grotesque and sarcastic manner. When the tattooing operation was finished, they shut us in a vacant hut. The bunks are made, but we are severely forbidden to touch or sit on them: so we wander around aimlessly for half the day in the limited space available, still tormented by the parching thirst of the journey. Then the door opens and a boy in a striped suit comes in, with a fairly civilized air, small, thin and blond. He speaks French and we throng around him with a flood of questions which till now we had asked each other in vain.

But he does not speak willingly; no one here speaks willingly. We are new, we have nothing and we know nothing; why waste time on us? He reluctantly explains to us that all the others are out at work and will come back in the evening. He has come out of the infirmary this morning and is exempt from work for today. I asked him (with an ingenuousness that only a few days later already seemed incredible to me) if at least they would give us back our toothbrushes. He did not laugh, but with his face animated by fierce contempt, he threw at me, *'Vous n'êtes pas à la maison.'* And it is this refrain that we hear repeated by everyone: you are not at home, this is not a sanatorium, the only exit is by way of the Chimney. (What did it mean? Soon we were all to learn what it meant.)

And it was in fact so. Driven by thirst, I eyed a fine icicle outside the window, within hand's reach. I opened the window and broke off the icicle but at once a large, heavy guard prowling outside brutally snatched it away from me. *'Warum?'* I asked him in my poor German. *'Hier ist kein warum'* (there is no why here), he replied, pushing me inside with a shove.

The explanation is repugnant but simple: in this place everything is forbidden, not for hidden reasons, but because the camp has been created for that purpose. If one wants to live one must learn this quickly and well:

'No Sacred Face will help thee here! it's not
A Serchio bathing-party ...'

Hour after hour, this first long day of limbo draws to its end. While the sun sets in a tumult of fierce, blood-red clouds, they finally make us come out of the hut. Will they give us something to drink? No, they place us in line again, they lead us to a huge square which takes up the centre of the camp and they arrange us meticulously in squads. Then nothing happens for another hour: it seems that we are waiting for someone.

A band begins to play, next to the entrance of the camp: it plays *Rosamunda,* the well known sentimental song, and this seems so strange to us that we look sniggering at each other; we feel a shadow of relief, perhaps all these ceremonies are nothing but a colossal farce in Teutonic taste. But the band, on finishing *Rosamunda,* continues to play other marches, one after the other, and suddenly the squads of our comrades appear, returning from work. They walk in columns of five with a strange, unnatural hard gait, like stiff puppets made of jointless bones; but they walk scrupulously in time to the band.

They also arrange themselves like us in the huge square, according to a precise order; when the last squad has returned, they count and recount us for over an hour. Long checks are made which all seem to go to a man dressed in stripes, who accounts for them to a group of SS men in full battle dress.

Finally (it is dark by now, but the camp is brightly lit by headlamps and reflectors) one hears the shout *'Absperre!'* at which all the squads break up in a confused and turbulent movement. They no longer walk stiffly and erectly as before: each one drags himself along with obvious effort. I see that all of them carry in their hand or attached to their belt a steel bowl as large as a basin.

We new arrivals also wander among the crowd, searching for a voice, a friendly face or a guide. Against the wooden wall of a hut two boys are seated on the ground: they seem very young, sixteen years old at the outside, both with their face and hands dirty with soot. One of the two, as we are passing by, calls me and asks me in German some questions which I do not understand; then he asks where we come from. '*Italien,*' I reply; I want to ask him many things, but my German vocabulary is very limited.

'Are you a Jew?' I asked him.

'Yes, a Polish Jew.'

'How long have you been in the Lager?'

'Three years,' and he lifts up three fingers. He must have been a child when he entered, I think with horror; on the other hand this means that at least some manage to live here.

'What is your work?'

'*Schlosser,*' he replies. I do not understand. '*Eisen, Feuer*' (iron, fire), he insists, and makes a play with his hands of someone beating with a hammer on an anvil. So he is an ironsmith.

'*Ich Chemiker,*' I state; and he nods earnestly with his head, '*Chemiker gut.*' But all this has to do with the distant future: what torments me at the moment is my thirst.

'Drink, water. We no water,' I tell him.

He looks at me with a serious face, almost severe, and states clearly: 'Do not drink water, comrade,' and then other words that I do not understand.

'*Warum?*'

'*Geschwollen,*' he replies cryptically. I shake my head, I have not understood. '*Swollen,*' he makes me understand, blowing out his cheeks and sketching with his hands a monstrous tumefaction of the face and belly. '*Warten bis heute Abend.*'

'Wait until this evening,' I translate word by word.

Then he says: '*Ich Schlome. Du?*' I tell him my name, and he asks me: 'Where your mother?'

'In Italy.' Schlome is amazed: a Jew in Italy? 'Yes,' I explain as best I can, 'hidden, no one knows, run away, does not speak, no one sees her.' He has understood; he now gets up, approaches me and timidly embraces me. The adventure is over, and I feel filled with a serene sadness that is almost joy. I have never seen Schlome since, but I have not forgotten his serious and gentle face of a child, which welcomed me on the threshold of the house of the dead.

We have a great number of things to learn, but we have learnt many already. We already have a certain idea of the topography of the Lager; our Lager is a square of about six hundred yards in length, surrounded by two fences of barbed wire, the inner one carrying a high tension current. It consists of sixty wooden huts, which are called Blocks, ten of which are in construction. In addition, there is the body of the kitchens, which are in brick; an experimental farm, run by a detachment of privileged Häftlinge; the huts with the showers and the latrines, one for each group of six or eight Blocks. Besides these, certain Blocks are reserved for specific purposes. First of all, a group of eight, at the extreme eastern end of the camp, forms the infirmary and clinic; then there is Block 24 which is the *Krätzeblock,* reserved for infectious skin-diseases; Block 7, which no ordinary Häftling has ever entered, reserved for the '*Prominenz*', that is, the aristocracy, the internees holding the highest posts; Block 47, reserved for the *Reichsdeutsche* (the Aryan Germans, 'politicals' or criminals); Block 49, for the Kapos alone; Block 12, half of which, for use of the *Reichsdeutsche* and the Kapos, serves as canteen, that is, a distribution centre for tobacco, insect powder and occasionally other articles; Block 37, which formed the Quartermaster's office and the Office for Work; and finally, Block 29, which always has its windows closed as it is the *Frauenblock,* the camp brothel, served by Polish Häftling girls, and reserved for the *Reichsdeutsche.*

The ordinary living Blocks are divided into two parts. In one *Tagesraum* lives the head of the hut with his friends. There is a long table, seats, benches, and on all sides a heap of strange objects in bright colours, photographs, cuttings from magazines, sketches, imitation flowers, ornaments; on the walls, great sayings, proverbs and rhymes in praise of order, discipline and hygiene; in one corner, a shelf with the tools of the *Blockrisör* (official barber), the ladles to distribute the soup, and two rubber truncheons, one solid and one hollow, to enforce discipline should the proverbs prove insufficient. The other part is the dormitory: there are only one hundred and forty-eight bunks on three levels, fitted close to each other like the cells of a beehive, and divided by three corridors so as to utilize without wastage all the space in the room up to the roof. Here all the ordinary *Häftlinge* live, about two hundred to two hundred and fifty per hut. Consequently there are two men in most of the bunks, which are portable planks of wood, each covered by a thin straw sack and two blankets.

The corridors are so narrow that two people can barely pass together; the total area of the floor is so small that the inhabitants of the same Block cannot all stay there at the same time unless at least half are lying on their bunks. Hence the prohibition to enter a Block to which one does not belong.

In the middle of the Lager is the roll-call square, enormous, where we collect in the morning to form the work-squads and in the evening to be counted. Facing the roll call square there is a bed of grass, carefully mown, where the gallows are erected when necessary.

We had soon learnt that the guests of the Lager are divided into three categories: the criminals, the politicals and the Jews. All are clothed in stripes, all are Häftlinge, but the criminals wear a green triangle next to the number sewn on the jacket; the politicals wear a red triangle; and the Jews, who form the large majority, wear the Jewish star, red and yellow. SS men exist but are few and outside the camp, and are seen relatively infrequently. Our effective masters in practice are the green triangles, who have a free hand over us, as well as those of the other two categories who are ready to help them – and they are not few.

And we have learnt other things, more or less quickly, according to our intelligence: to reply *'Jawohl',* never to ask questions, always to pretend to understand. We have learnt the value of food; now we also diligently scrape the bottom of the bowl after the ration and we hold it under our chins when we eat bread so as not to lose the crumbs. We, too, know that it is not the same thing to be given a ladleful of soup from the top or from the bottom of the vat, and we are already able to judge, according to the capacity of the various vats, what is the most suitable place to try and reach in the queue when we line up.

We have learnt that everything is useful: the wire to tie up our shoes, the rags to wrap around our feet, waste paper to (illegally) pad out our jacket against the cold. We have learnt, on the other hand, that everything can be stolen, in fact is automatically stolen as soon as attention is relaxed; and to avoid this, we had to learn the art of sleeping with our head on a bundle made up of our jacket and containing all our belongings, from the bowl to the shoes.

We already know in good part the rules of the camp, which are incredibly complicated. The prohibitions are innumerable: to approach nearer to the barbed wire than two yards; to sleep with one's jacket, or without one's pants, or with one's cap on one's head; to use certain washrooms or latrines which are '*nur für Kapos*' or '*nur für Reichsdeutsche*'; not to go for the shower on the prescribed day, or to go there on a day not prescribed; to leave the hut with one's jacket unbuttoned, or with the collar raised; to carry paper or straw under one's clothes against the cold; to wash except stripped to the waist.

The rites to be carried out were infinite and senseless: every morning one had to make the 'bed' perfectly flat and smooth; smear one's muddy and repellent wooden shoes with the appropriate machine grease; scrape the mudstains off one's clothes (paint, grease and rust-stains were, however, permitted); in the evening one had to undergo the control for lice and the control of washing one's feet; on Saturday, have one's beard and hair shaved, mend or have mended one's rags; on Sunday, undergo the general control for skin diseases and the control of buttons on one's jacket, which had to be five.

In addition, there are innumerable circumstances, normally irrelevant, which here become problems. When one's nails grow long, they have to be shortened, which can only be done with one's teeth (for the toenails, the friction of the shoes is sufficient); if a button comes off, one has to tie it on with a piece of wire; if one goes to the latrine or the washroom, everything has to be carried along, always and everywhere, and while one washes one's face, the bundle of clothes has to be held tightly between one's knees: in any other manner it will be stolen in that second. If a shoe hurts, one has to go in the evening to the ceremony of the changing of the shoes: this tests the skill of the individual who, in the middle of the incredible crowd, has to be able to choose at an eye's glance one (not a pair, one) shoe, which fits. Because once the choice is made, there can be no second change.

And do not think that shoes form a factor of secondary importance in the life of the Lager. Death begins with the shoes; for most of us, they show themselves to be instruments of torture, which after a few hours of marching cause painful sores which become fatally infected. Whoever has them is forced to walk as if he was dragging a convict's chain (this explains the strange gait of the army which returns every evening on parade); he arrives last everywhere, and everywhere he receives blows. He cannot escape if they run after him; his feet swell and the more they swell, the more the friction with the wood and the cloth of the shoes becomes insupportable. Then only the hospital is left: but to enter the hospital with a diagnosis of '*dicke Füsse*' (swollen feet) is extremely dangerous, because it is well known to all, and especially to the SS, that here there is no cure for that complaint.

And in all this we have not yet mentioned the work, which in its turn is a Gordian knot of laws, taboos and problems.

We all work, except those who are ill (to be recognized as ill implies in itself an important equipment of knowledge and experience). Every morning we leave the camp in squads for the Buna; every evening, in squads, we return. As regards the work, we are divided into about two hundred *Kommandos,* each of which consists of between fifteen and one hundred and fifty men and is commanded by a Kapo. There are good and bad Kommandos: for the most part they are used as transport and the work is quite hard, especially in the winter, if for no other reason merely because it always takes place in the open. There are also skilled Kommandos (electricians, smiths, bricklayers, welders, mechanics, concrete-layers, etc.), each attached to a certain workshop or department of the Buna, and depending more directly on civilian foremen, mostly German and Polish. This naturally only applies to the hours of work; for the rest of the day the skilled workers (there are no more than three or four hundred in all) receive no different treatment from the ordinary workers. The detailing of individuals to the various Kommandos is organized by a special office of the Lager, the *Arbeitsdienst,* which is in continual touch with the civilian direction of the Buna. The *Arbeitsdienst* decides on the basis of unknown criteria, often openly on the basis of protection or corruption, so that if anyone manages to find enough to eat, he is practically certain to get a good post at Buna.

The hours of work vary with the season. All hours of light are working hours: so that from a minimum winter working day (8–12am and 12.30–4pm) one rises to a maximum summer one (6.30-12am and 1–6pm). Under no excuse are the Häftlinge allowed to be at work during the hours of darkness or when there is a thick fog, but they work regularly even if it rains or snows or (as occurs quite frequently) if the fierce wind of the Carpathians blows; the reason being that the darkness or fog might provide opportunities to escape.

One Sunday in every two is a regular working day; on the so-called holiday Sundays, instead of working at Buna, one works normally on the upkeep of the Lager, so that days of real rest are extremely rare.

Such will be our life. Every day, according to the established rhythm, *Ausrücken* and *Einrücken,* go out and come in; work, sleep and eat; fall ill, get better or die.

... And for how long? But the old ones laugh at this question: they recognize the new arrivals by this question. They laugh and they do not reply. For months and years, the problem of the remote future has grown pale to them and has lost all intensity in face of the far more urgent and concrete problems of the near future: how much one will eat today, if it will snow, if there will be coal to unload.

If we were logical, we would resign ourselves to the evidence that our fate is beyond knowledge, that every conjecture is arbitrary and demonstrably devoid of foundation. But men are rarely logical when their own fate is at stake; on every occasion, they prefer the extreme positions. According to our character, some of us are immediately convinced that all is lost, that one cannot live here, that the end is near and sure; others are convinced that however hard the present life may be, salvation is probable and not far off, and if we have faith and strength, we will see our houses and our dear ones again. The two classes of pessimists and optimists are not so clearly defined, however, not because there are many agnostics, but because the majority, without memory or coherence, drift between the two extremes, according to the moment and the mood of the person they happen to meet.

Here I am, then, on the bottom. One learns quickly enough to wipe out the past and the future when one is forced to. A fortnight after my arrival I already had the prescribed hunger, that chronic hunger unknown to free men, which makes one dream at night, and settles in all the limbs of one's body. I have already learnt not to let myself be robbed, and in fact if I find a spoon lying around, a piece of string, a button which I can acquire without danger of punishment, I pocket them and consider them mine by full right. On the back of my feet I already have those numb sores that will not heal. I push wagons, I work with a shovel, I turn rotten in the rain, I shiver in the wind; already my own body is no longer mine: my belly is swollen, my limbs emaciated, my face is thick in the morning, hollow in the evening; some of us have yellow skin, others grey. When we do not meet for a few days we hardly recognize each other.

We Italians had decided to meet every Sunday evening in a corner of the Lager, but we stopped it at once, because it was too sad to count our numbers and find fewer each time, and to see each other ever more deformed and more squalid. And it was so tiring to walk those few steps and then, meeting each other, to remember and to think. It was better not to think.

Primo Levi
If This Is A Man, 1958

2. A social worker's report

Imagine that you are a modern-day social worker, who has gone to pay a first visit to the couple, having been informed that they may be in need of help.

● In pairs, role-play the conversation that takes place between you and one of your colleagues back at the office, in which you describe what you have seen. You could write a brief memo to your boss, summarising the most important facts about the couple's situation and recommending action from Social Services.

2. Interview, description or comment?

● Analyse what Mayhew is doing in his account, using the headings below. Put a letter beside each paragraph, identifying what is happening in the text.

D = description
I = interview
C = comment
F = feelings about what he sees

● From your analysis, what can you say about how Mayhew reports on the street-sellers?

3. A modern Mayhew

● Imagine that, like Mayhew in his time, you want to bring to public attention some modern issue. You go out with your tape-recorder, with the aim of bringing back stories about someone's life, that you can use to make a statement. Choose one of these people, or one of your own, then switch on your imaginary tape-recorder and tell us what they say:

A nurse, sitting on night duty at a desk on a ward
A street beggar, sitting outside a supermarket
A doctor in a casualty department, at the end of a very long and busy shift
An English teacher, on the last day of term
A new age traveller, sitting by a campfire

Baghdad Under Fire

Marie Colvin was writing for *The Sunday Times* in January 1991, at a time when British troops had been sent to the Gulf to fight against the Iraqi forces of Saddam Hussein. Whilst journalists, newspapers and TV news programmes took their own different angles on the war, criticism of British and American actions in the war was rare. The general atmosphere was one in which criticism of the British and American forces was not seen to be acceptable and there was some censorship of the news by the Ministry of Defence in order to 'protect the national interest'. There was a strong emphasis on the new technology of the weaponry, the 'smart bombs' which supposedly hit military targets without taking civilian lives. The reality of life and death for the Iraqi people was rarely mentioned and towards the end of the war there were strong accusations that the press had been silenced and that the suffering of the civilian population had been suppressed. It is in this context that you should read Marie Colvin's article.

1. First thoughts

• While the article is being read to you, think about these issues:

Who does Colvin sympathise with?
What images of Baghdad remain with you by the end of the piece?
What do you think Colvin was trying to do in writing the piece?

2. Closer reading

In small groups, look closely at the article, trying to analyse in more detail what you think Colvin was trying to do.
• Look at the list of headings below. For each heading, skim through the piece and see whether you can find evidence of her doing what is listed. How much evidence can you find? Jot down page references or short quotes beside each heading.
• Next, order the headings in terms of their importance. For instance if you think that the most important thing about the article is the way in which it gives a 'flavour' of the place and its culture, put a number one beside it.

Reporting the news
Developing a narrative
Giving information about the country and its economy
Giving the 'flavour' of the place and its culture
Letting the Iraqi people speak for themselves
Describing the people
Conveying her own feelings and experiences
Expressing the Iraqi viewpoint
Putting across her own attitudes
Countering the view of Iraq presented in the Media
Making it interesting to read because of the human interest angle
Arguing a viewpoint

3. Readers' responses

Given the context of the war, the bombing of Baghdad and the pressure on British journalists to write pro-British articles, think about how different people might have responded to Marie Colvin's article.
• Write short statements by two of these people, giving their response to Marie Colvin's piece and the way she has reported on events:

Hussein, the Baghdad shopkeeper
A Conservative minister
A member of the family of a British soldier fighting in the Gulf
The editor of *The Sunday Times*, talking about the decision to publish this article
An official at the Ministry of Defence

4. A written commentary

• Develop the work you have done on this text into a piece of coursework by writing a commentary on it. What was it trying to achieve, in what context and with what results?

When the Wolves Stopped Howling

1. The title
● Talk about the title and what it makes you think of. Can you predict what kind of article this might be?

2. Sequencing sentences and close reading
● Before reading the article, look at these sentences taken from the opening. Read the sentences and try putting them into an order that works for you.

> 'And afterwards it was a human avalanche filling the mountainside'

> 'Then the columns of people joined up below the snowline at 6000 feet'

> 'Now thousands of them were stumbling in the lead-coloured water of violent little rivers, passing babies across fallen logs'

> 'When the wolves stopped howling, the people began to move again'

> 'These were the Kurds of Iraq, desperate in their search for sanctuary from the murderous pursuit of Saddam Hussein'

> 'Sometimes the infants fell and mothers screamed after them with snow squeezing through the toes of their bare feet'

> 'The valleys were full of snow and lightning and the babies stared cold and hungry through a wrap of wet blankets at the miserable sky'

> 'The sound of wailing and crying began as a small noise way up there and became something that covered the slopes with its awful sound'

● Think about what went into making your decision about the best order:
Did any words suggest that they had to come before or after something else?
Did some sentences seem to be summing up or introducing and therefore need to go at the beginning or the end?

What decisions did you make about what should go first: descriptions of people or the landscape, or who the people were or why they were there?

- Compare your order with that of another group. Read your openings aloud and explain your choices.
- Read the opening of the actual article and compare it with your opening, then read the rest of the article.
- Look closely at the last two paragraphs of the article. If you had to choose one sentence that sums up the point of this article, what would it be?

3. Whose voices?
- Make a list of all of the people you hear speaking in this article. Whose voices do you hear? Look closely at what they say.
- Pick some of the bits of dialogue to put together as a statement by the Kurds to be broadcast on western TV to explain their problems to the world. Do they say enough in the article to make this possible? Why do you think John Edwards has included so many bits of dialogue?

4. The writer's viewpoint
John Edwards doesn't always tell us his feelings directly but he does indicate his views in less obvious ways. Look at these extracts from the article and talk about what they reveal to the reader about the Kurds' plight. How does Edwards make his message clear?

> 'These were the Kurds of Iraq, desperate in their search for sanctuary from the murderous pursuit of Saddam Hussein'

> 'President Bush worries about his 8-iron golf shots pulling up short of the putting greens in Florida. But there is no golf in Isikveren. Just people falling into pits of mud and fighting with vanishing strength to live another day in the hell of the Zakho Mountains'

> 'But they tramped all the way over the mountains, 20,000 at a time, and they came through rain and storms when the wind chopped off slices of ice and threw them around like circular saws'

> 'It was the same as crossing the Alps and must be one of the greatest mass escapes and feats of endurance ever known.
>
> If Mr. Bush could get out here and see it he would pick up the phone on his golf trolley and tell his air force commanders to bomb Saddam's army into metal dust.'

5. Editing it down

Imagine that John Edwards has been told that there isn't enough space for his article as it stands and that he needs to edit it to down to half its length. Work with a partner to cut the article down, talking as you go about what you think it is essential to keep and what can go.

On the Bottom

1. Before reading

● Here are some sentences and phrases taken from the text you are about to read. In pairs, talk about them and think about the following:

What stories or ideas or historical events do they suggest to you?
What kind of writing might this be from e.g. a play, a press report, an autobiography, a conversation?
What could this be about?

> 'Today, in our times, hell must be like this'

> 'we wait for something which will certainly be terrible'

> 'One cannot think any more. It is like being already dead'

> 'We seem to be watching some mad play'

> 'we had reached the bottom'

● Look at this longer extract from the text. Talk about the additional information it gives you and what this adds to your view of what the text is about. What do you feel for the person describing this experience?

'Then for the first time we became aware that our language lacks words to express this offence, the demolition of a man. In a moment, with almost prophetic intuition, the reality was revealed to us: we had reached the bottom. It is not possible to sink lower than this; no human condition is more miserable than this, nor could it conceivably be so. Nothing belongs to us any more; they have taken away our clothes, our shoes, even our hair; if we speak, they will not listen to us, and if they listen, they will not understand. They will even take away our name: and if we want to keep it, we will have to find ourselves the strength to do so, to manage somehow so that behind the name something of us, of us as we were, still remains'

● Make a list for yourselves of any events in modern history or in today's world that this description could apply to.

2. Reading the text in stages: stage 1
● Listen to the text being read to you up to Page 134, finishing with the sentence, 'He makes a long speech, is very polite, and tries to reply to all our questions.'
● In pairs or small groups talk about your feelings and reactions on listening to this and any questions about this text that you need to have answered.

● As a whole class, pool your knowledge of the period of history being described and the extermination of a whole people which has come to be known as 'the Holocaust.' Either at this stage, or after reading the whole text, try to find out more, from books, from films (such as *Schindler's List*), from people you know whose relatives may have lived through it themselves, from adults who may have memories of their own of the war years.

3. Reading the text in stages: stage 2
● Listen to the text being read to you up to the beginning of the last paragraph on Page 141.
● Levi says, 'No human condition is more miserable than this'.

Look back through the text to discuss these issues:

What kinds of things does Levi describe that make you feel that this statement is true?
Were you shocked by what you read?
In saying, 'No human condition is more miserable than this,' Levi uses the present tense. Where else does he use it? How does this alter the power of the text?

● Levi is writing about his own experiences. Explore how he does this by picking one small section of the text you have read so far and looking closely at it. For instance, you could look at the arrival, or the meeting with Schlome, or the description of the branding of numbers on the prisoners' arms and what the numbers revealed about life in the camp.

Look closely at how much Levi tells us about what happened, describes his feelings, expresses outrage and anger, tries to analyse what was happening to him, urges the reader directly to feel sympathy for him.

4. Reading the text in stages: stage 3
● The last section of the text is just three paragraphs, in which Levi sums up the meaning of this experience of being in a concentration camp and what it does to a human being. Before reading it, talk about what kinds of things he *might* want to say to the reader and what kinds of feelings he *might* express.
● Read the very last section of the text, from the paragraph starting, 'If we were logical...' on Page 141 and talk about what Levi suggests about how a human being responds to such treatment and how s/he can survive it.
● Look closely at the last sentence of the text, 'It was better not to think.' Why do you think he says this?

5. The demolition of a man
● In small groups, look back at the whole text and talk about what Primo Levi is saying about the following:

What it is to be human
What demolishes or destroys a human being
How human beings survive being 'on the bottom'
What it is to be an oppressor, or destroyer of humanity

● Find short key quotes that for you sum up what Levi's thinking is about these issues.
● The title of the book from which this text is taken is *If This Is A Man*. Talk about why you think Levi chose this title.

6. Language and viewpoint
There are some indications that it is very hard for Levi to write what he is writing, that the horror of his experiences is sometimes too great to bear and that he struggles to say what is almost unsayable.
● Look for moments where you think Levi is either trying to say something that is almost unbearable to say, or is extremely complicated to explain. Look closely at what happens to the language at these moments. Are there any disruptions to the normal flow? You might look for some of these language changes:

A change of tense, from the past tense to the present, or vice versa
Repetition of something that is particularly painful or important to get across to the reader
Questions being asked rather than answered
Exclamations that suggest shock or dismay
Disruptions to the normal grammar of the sentence, that show him struggling to give voice to his feelings
A shift between matter-of-fact description of what happened and expression of powerful feelings
Understatement, a quiet voice that is not strident

7. A story that must be heard?

A very important text for all young people to read today.

Not really suitable for young people to read.

● In small groups, discuss the possible reasons for the opinions expressed above. What do you yourselves feel about this issue?

8. Primo Levi

Primo Levi was an Italian scientist, a chemist from Turin. As a young man he helped to form a resistance group, to try to fight against fascism. He was captured by the Italian fascist militia and sent to a detention camp in Italy. After a few weeks it was announced that all Jews in the camp would be sent to an unknown destination. It was only when they were on the train that they discovered that they were being taken to a place called Auschwitz, though they did not know at the time what that would mean. He was twenty five years old when he entered Auschwitz. The following year the camp was liberated and he was one of the few survivors who returned to Italy after the war. He resumed work as a chemist and went on to write many books including *If This Is A Man*, of which 'On the Bottom' is one chapter. In 1987, aged 68, Levi committed suicide.

● If you had been given the chance to talk to Primo Levi before his death, what would you have wanted to say to him and what questions would you have wanted to ask him?
● Look again at the last sentence of the text, 'It was better not to think.' Do you think that, writing this text thirteen years after being liberated, he still felt that? Why do you think he returned to his experiences and made his 'thinking' so public by publishing a book about them?
● Look at these comments written about Levi and talk about whether you agree with what they say about his writing:

'One of the few survivors of the Holocaust to speak of his experiences with a gentle voice.'
The Guardian

'Levi does not flinch from setting down the unbelievable details of that cruelty born of the 'mystique of barrenness', but then neither does he paint them in lurid colours to press his point home.The facts are surely enough.'
Paul Bailey, from the Introduction to *If This Is a Man* (Abacus)

9. Witnessing, experiencing and telling the world

In this section and in others in this book, there are examples of writing about human beings' inhumanity towards each other. John Edwards' account of the persecution and flight of the Kurds is an example of a paid reporter witnessing horrific events from a distance, rather than being a part of them.

● Look closely at 'When the Wolves Stopped Howling' alongside 'On the Bottom'. Think about these issues:

What differences do you notice in the writing?
Is the writing different because of a difference of viewpoint (observing and reporting as compared with experiencing and acting as witness)?
How different might each of the texts be if they were written by a different voice e.g. a Kurdish refugee telling her own story or an American news reporter describing the liberation of Auschwitz concentration camp?

Comparing Texts

1. Telling the world

● Compare 'When the Wolves Stopped Howling' and 'On the Bottom', as two pieces of writing on ethnic persecution and genocide. What difference does the stand-point of the writers make, Levi as someone who is involved and experiencing the horror, Edwards as a reporter witnessing it but not personally involved?

2. War reporting

● Compare 'When the Wolves Stopped Howling' and 'Baghdad under Fire', as two examples of war reporting. Build on your earlier work on the two texts to allow you to compare the attitudes of the writers, their voices, the use they make of other voices and the balance in the text between such features as dialogue, description, commentary, anecdote and so on. Write about your personal responses to each of the texts.

3. Choosing two texts to compare

● Choose two texts which seem to you to be very different examples of reportage. Write about what you found interesting about them and about the differences between them. Think about differences in subject matter, in each writer's viewpoint and voice, in their purposes and audiences and the style in which they are written.

Finding the Tollund Man

An early spring day – 8 May 1950. Evening was gathering over Tollund Fen in Bjaeldskov Dal (dale or valley). Momentarily, the sun burst in, bright and yet subdued, through a gate in blue thunder-clouds in the west, bringing everything mysteriously to life. The evening stillness was only broken, now and again, by the grating love-call of the snipe. The dead man, too, deep down in the umber-brown peat, seemed to have come alive. He lay on his damp bed as though asleep, resting on his side, the head inclined a little forward, arms and legs bent. His face wore a gentle expression – the eyes lightly closed, the lips softly pursed, as if in silent prayer. It was as though the dead man's soul had for a moment returned from another world, through the gate in the western sky.

The dead man who lay there was 2,000 years old. A few hours earlier he had been brought out from the sheltering peat by two men who, their spring sowing completed, had now to think of the cold winter days to come, and were occupied in cutting peat for the tile stove and kitchen range.

As they worked, they suddenly saw in the peat-layer a face so fresh that they could only suppose they had stumbled on a recent murder. They notified the police at Silkeborg, who came at once to the site. The police, however, also invited representatives of the local museum to accompany them, for well-preserved remains of Iron-Age men were not unknown in central Jutland. At the site the true context of the discovery was soon evident. A telephone call was put through straight away to Aarhus University, where at that moment I was lecturing to a group of students on archaeological problems. Some hours later – that same evening – I stood with my students, bent over the startling discovery, face to face with an Iron-Age man who, two millennia before, had been deposited in the bog as a sacrifice to the powers that ruled men's destinies.

The man lay on his right side in a natural attitude of sleep. The head was to the west, with the face turned to the south; the legs were to the east. He lay 50 yds out from firm ground, not far above the clean sand floor of the bog, and had been covered by 8 or 9 ft of peat, now dug away.

On his head he wore a pointed skin cap fastened securely under the chin by a hide thong. Round his waist there was a smooth hide belt. Otherwise he was

shrunken. An autopsy showed that the inner organs such as the heart, lungs and liver were very well preserved. So was the alimentary canal, which was removed by the palaeobotanist, Dr Hans Helbaek, with the object of determining the nature of the dead man's last meal. This was still contained in the stomach and in the larger and smaller intestines which, though somewhat flattened by the weight of the overlying peat, were otherwise intact.

These organs were carefully rinsed externally, to remove contamination from the surrounding peat. Their contents were then washed out and proved to consist of a blend of finely reduced plant remains and particles of seeds. The contents of the stomach and the smaller intestine were inconsiderable, occupying in volume barely 0.5 and 10 cubic centimetres respectively. The contents of the larger intestine, on the other hand, amounted to 260 cubic centimetres. All was of the same character. It was not possible to establish with certainty the proportions of the different ingredients because the plants had varied in their resistance to the digestive juices which had acted on them from the time the meal was eaten and for some while after death.

By the time it has been crushed in a hand-mill and between the teeth a meal of this kind, consisting largely of grains and seeds, is reduced to myriads of small particles. The basis of the investigation was a sample of 50 cubic centimetres taken from the larger intestine.

In collaboration with the anatomists, Drs Bjøvulf Vimtrop and Kay Schaurup, a point of great interest was established. Investigation showed that although the contents of the stomach consisted of vegetable remains of a gruel prepared from barley, linseed, 'gold-of-pleasure' *(camelina sativa)* and knotweed, with many different sorts of weeds that grow on ploughed land, it could not have contained any meat at the time of death, since recognizable traces of bone, sinew or muscular tissue would certainly have remained. It was further established, from the degree of digestion of the remains of the meal in the alimentary canal, that the Tollund man had lived for between 12 and 24 hours after eating his last meal.

In addition to the varieties of cultivated grain, it is worth noticing the unusual quantity of knotweed *(pale persicaria)* in the stomach. It must have been gathered deliberately and other plants represented may have been gathered along with it incidentally; for example, blue and green bristle-grass, dock, black bindweed, camomile and gold-of-pleasure. The gruel made from this mixture of cultivated and wild grains was no doubt the normal diet in the Early Iron Age, around the time of Christ, when the Tollund man was alive. Fish and meat were also eaten. Rich furnishings of bowls and dishes, with ribs of ox and sheep, and carving knives lying ready, are known in the graves of the time. But meat was certainly not the daily diet as it was in the time of the Stone-Age hunters. Milk and cheese, on the other hand, probably were, as the forms of the pottery vessels would seem to indicate.

It is not surprising that this 2,000 year-old 'recipe' for gruel from the Iron Age (consisting primarily of various cultivated grains together with the seeds of many types of weeds known at that time), should have been tried out in our own day, and in front of a big audience at that. Gruel made to this recipe was served up on an English television programme, in the summer of 1954, to two well-known archaeologists – Sir Mortimer Wheeler and Dr Glyn Daniel. Reports tell us that these gentlemen were not particularly smitten with the taste and had to wash it down with good Danish brandy, drunk from a cow-horn. Sir Mortimer finished up by saying that it would have been punishment enough for the Tollund man to have been compelled to eat this gruel for the rest of his life, however terrible his crime might have been. The Tollund man, though, would not have had brandy to help it down, as the archaeologists did. It was not until about a thousand years later that people learned to distil something stronger from fermented drinks. However, there was an alcoholic drink in the Iron Age, as has been revealed by analysis of sediments in bronze vessels of the period. It was half way between beer and a fruit wine. Barley and the wild plants cranberry and bog myrtle were used in its manufacture. The alcoholic content may have been increased by the addition of honey. This agrees with the account given in the Roman historian Tacitus' *Germania,* a work contemporary with Denmark's Early Iron Age. It says of the Germani that 'they drink a fluid made from wheat or barley, fermented so as to give it some resemblance to wine'.

When the exhaustive study of the Tollund man had been concluded, a decision was taken on preserving him for the future. Unfortunately it was only thought practicable to undertake the conservation of the splendid head. This was first of all placed for six months in a solution of water to which formalin and acetic acid had been added. The solution was then changed for one of 30 per cent alcohol, which was later replaced by one of 99 per cent alcohol to which toluol had been added. Finally, it was put into pure toluol progressively mixed with paraffin, for which wax heated to different temperatures was later substituted. After more than a year's treatment the head was sent to the Silkeborg Museum in central Jutland, a bare six miles from the spot where it had come to light in Tollund Fen. It can be seen there, alongside other discoveries of the Iron Age.

In the process of conservation the proportions of the head and the features of the face were happily completely retained, but the head as a whole had shrunk by about 12 per cent. In spite of this it has emerged as the best preserved head of an early man to have come down to us so far. The majestic head astonishes the beholder and rivets his attention. Standing in front of the glass case in which it is displayed, he finds himself face to face with an Iron-Age man. Dark in hue, the head is still full of life and more beautiful than the best portraits by the world's greatest artists, since it is the man himself we see.

P.V.Glob
The Bog People, 1965

The Tollund Man

I

Some day I will go to Aarhus
To see his peat-brown head,
The mild pods of his eye-lids,
His pointed skin cap.

In the flat country nearby
Where they dug him out,
His last gruel of winter seeds
Caked in his stomach,

Naked except for
The cap, noose and girdle,
I will stand a long time.
Bridegroom to the goddess,

She tightened her torc on him
And opened her fen,
Those dark juices working
Him to a saint's kept body,

Trove of the turfcutters'
Honeycombed workings.
Now his stained face
Reposes at Aarhus.

II

I could risk blasphemy,
Consecrate the cauldron bog
Our holy ground and pray
Him to make germinate

The scattered, ambushed
Flesh of labourers,
Stockinged corpses
Laid out in the farmyards,

Tell-tale skin and teeth
Flecking the sleepers
Of four young brothers, trailed
For miles along the lines.

III

Something of his sad freedom
As he rode the tumbril
Should come to me, driving,
Saying the names

Tollund, Grabaulle, Nebelgard,
Watching the pointing hands
Of country people,
Not knowing their tongue.

Out there in Jutland
In the old man-killing parishes
I will feel lost,
Unhappy and at home.

Seamus Heaney
Wintering Out, 1972

The Tollund Man

Tantrums

Frustration by his own body and size

When a toddler understands what objects are supposed to do, understands how to make them do it, but cannot manage because he is too little or too weak, then he needs help. There is no pleasure or learning in such a situation, only grief and giving up. Children do not need rooms full of expensive toys, either for their pleasure or for their development. But any equipment they do have must be tailored to them physically. The toddler may long to push his sister's doll's pram, but be too small to reach the handle. He may long to throw his brother's football but be too light to manage its weight. If he cannot have a toddle truck or a pram of his own, and an inflatable beach ball or plastic 'football', he is better off with none at all until he is bigger. We want him to feel as big and strong and competent to manage his world as possible. So we must keep at least his own possessions in scale with him.

You will not always manage to strike the right balance between the amount of frustration which is useful to your child's learning and the amount which is too much. When he is acutely frustrated the toddler is as liable to extremes of rage as to extremes of fear. Temper tantrums are the result of too much frustration just as phobias result from too much anxiety. More than half of all two year olds will have tantrums at least once a day while very few children will reach their third birthday without ever having experienced one. Toddlers who have a lot of tantrums are usually lively children who may be highly intelligent. They know what they want to do; they want to do a great many things and they mind a great deal when someone or something prevents them.

A tantrum is like an emotional blown fuse; it is not something which the toddler can prevent. The load of frustration builds up inside him until he is so full of tension that only an explosion can release it. While the tantrum lasts, the toddler is lost to the world, overwhelmed by his own internal rage and terrified by the violent feelings which he cannot control. However unpleasant your toddler's tantrums are for you, they are much worse for him.

Children's behaviour during a tantrum varies, but your particular child will probably behave similarly each time: he may rush around the room, wild and screaming. Remember that he is out of control so anything movable that happens to be in his path will be knocked flying. If you do not protect him he may bang into solid walls and heavy furniture. He may fling himself on the floor, writhing, kicking and screaming as if he were fighting with demons. He may scream and scream until he makes himself sick. He may scream and turn blue in the face because he has breathed out so far that, for the moment, he cannot breathe in again. Breath-holding tantrums are the most alarming of all for parents to watch. The child may go without breathing for so long that his face looks greyish and he almost loses consciousness. It is quite impossible for him actually to damage himself in this way. His body's reflexes will reassert themselves and force air back into his lungs long before he is in any danger.

Handling tantrums

You can prevent many tantrums by organising your toddler's life so that frustration stays within the limits of his tolerance most of the time. Tantrums do no positive good to either of you: when you must force your child to do something unpleasant or forbid something he enjoys, do it as tactfully as you can. There is no virtue in facing children with absolute 'dos' and 'don'ts' or in backing them into corners from which they can only explode in rage. Leave an escape route.

Prevent the child from getting hurt or hurting anyone or anything else. His overwhelming rage already terrifies him. If he comes out of a tantrum to discover that he has banged his head, scratched your face or broken a vase, he will see the damage as proof of his own horrible power, and evidence that when he cannot control himself you do not have the power to control him and keep him safe either.

It may be easiest to keep the toddler safe if you hold him, gently, on the floor. As he calms down he finds himself close to you and he finds, to his amazement, that everything is quite unchanged by the storm. Slowly he relaxes and cuddles into your arms. His screams subside into sobs; the furious monster becomes a pathetic baby who has screamed himself sick and frightened himself silly. It is comfort time.

A few toddlers cannot bear to be held while they are having tantrums. The physical restriction drives them to fresh heights of anger and makes the whole affair worse. If your child reacts like this, don't insist on overpowering him. Remove anything he is obviously going to break and try to fend him off from physically hurting himself.

Don't try to argue or remonstrate with the child. While the tantrum lasts, he is beyond reason.

Don't scream back if you can possibly help it. Anger is very infectious and you may well find yourself becoming angrier with every yell he utters, but try not to join in. If you do, you are likely to prolong the outburst because just as the toddler was about to calm down he will become aware of your angry voice and it will start him off again.

Don't ever let the child feel rewarded or punished for a tantrum. You want him to see that tantrums, which are horrible for him, change nothing either for or against him. If he threw the tantrum because you would not let him go out into the garden, don't change your mind and let him out now. Equally, if you had been going to take him for a walk before he had the tantrum, you should take him all the same as soon as he is calm again.

Don't let tantrums embarrass you into kid-glove handling in public. Many parents dread tantrums in public places but you must not let your toddler sense your concern. If you are reluctant to take him into the corner shop in case he throws a tantrum for sweets, or if you treat him with saccharine sweetness whenever visitors are present in case ordinary handling should provoke an outburst, he will soon realise what is going on. Once he realises that his genuinely uncontrollable tantrums are having an effect on your behaviour towards him, he is bound to learn to use them and to work himself up into the semi-deliberate tantrums which are typical of badly handled four year olds.

Assume that your child will not have a tantrum; behave as if you had never heard of the things and then treat them, when they occur, as unpleasant but completely irrelevant interludes in the day's ordinary events. It sounds easy, but it is not. I once visited a friend whose twenty month old boy asked her to take the cover off his sandpit. She said, 'Not now, nearly time for your bath', and returned to our conversation. The child tugged her arm to ask again but got no response. He then went to the sandpit and tried in vain to open it himself. He was tired and the frustration was too much for him. He exploded into a tantrum. When it was over and his mother had comforted him, she said to me, 'I do feel like a beast, I didn't know he wanted to play in the sand that badly.' And she took the cover off for him after all.

That mother's behaviour was easy to understand but also an excellent example of how not to handle tantrums! She said 'no' to the child when he first asked for help without giving any real thought to his request. The child's own efforts to uncover the sand did not show her how passionately he wanted to play there because she was not paying attention to him. Only when he threw a tantrum did she realise that he really did want that sand and that there was no very good reason for forbidding it. She meant to make it up to him by giving in after all but she had her second thoughts too late. Hasty or not, she should have stuck to her original 'no' because by changing it to 'yes' after the tantrum she must have made her child feel that his explosion had had a most desirable effect. It would have been better for both of them if she had taken a moment to listen and think when he asked for help rather than giving in when he screamed.

It is not easy being a toddler rocking wildly between those anxious and angry feelings. It is not easy being a toddler's parent either, striving to stay on the centre of that emotional see-saw and to hold it in equilibrium. But time is on your side. The worst of the emotional turbulence will be over by the time you discover that you now have a pre-school child.

He will get bigger, stronger and more competent. As he does so he will learn to manage things better so that he meets less extreme frustration in his everyday life. He will get to know and understand things better, too, so that his life contains fewer frightening novelties. As he becomes more fearless he will stop needing quite so much reassurance from you. Gradually he will learn to talk freely not only about the things that he can see in front of him but about things he is thinking and imagining. Once he can talk in this way he will sometimes be able to accept reassuring words in place of your continual physical comfort. With the help of language he will also learn to distinguish between fantasy and reality. Once he reaches this point he will at last be able to see both the unreality of most of his worst fears and the reasonableness of most of the demands and restrictions which you place on him. He will turn into a reasonable and communicative human being. Just give him time.

Penelope Leach
Baby and Child, 1988

The Facts About Drugs

Getting high throughout history

Drugs have been used as medicines, for pleasure and in religious ceremonies, but some remain strictly controlled.

Drugs of all kinds have been used since earliest recorded history. The value of the juice of the white opium poppy for inducing sleep and reducing pain was recorded in Sumerian more than 6,000 years ago. The cannabis plant was used in central Asia and China as early as 3000 BC.

Drugs are substances which significantly alter the physical or mental state of their user. People throughout history have used drugs for pleasure, as medicine or for religious purposes.

One way of assessing the strength of a drug is to measure the risk a user runs of becoming dependent. According to this definition, heroin – derived from opium – would be considered one of the strongest drugs because users quickly find they cannot do without it. Yet modern medicine also depends on drugs which, though legal, can lead to dependency. Doctors prescribe many drugs every day, including tranquillisers, which users sometimes find difficult or impossible to give up.

The outlawing of some drugs is a modern development. Until the late 19th century, opium could be bought in Britain as easily as cigarettes and alcohol can be bought today. Writers, artists and politicians used opium to increase their energy and creativity. Others, particularly the poor, used it as a way to treat illness without having to pay a doctor and instead of alcohol.

Britain's key involvement in the production and sale of drugs led to the Opium Wars (1839-42 and 1856-60) following an attempt by the Manchu government of China to get all foreign powers to surrender stocks of opium in order to discourage the drug's importation and use. China's eventual defeat allowed Britain to continue the importation of opium. Britain remained the main manufacturer and exporter of morphine, derived from opium, until the late 1930s.

Growing worries about the use of opium by the working classes and awareness by doctors of the dangers led to moves to restrict their legal availability by the 1890s. During the First World War (1914–18) opium and cocaine were made illegal amid fears about drug use among soldiers. The first international agreement to control the drugs trade was the International Opium Convention of 1912.

This century the United States has been the country most preoccupied with international drug control – partly because drugs are used by so many US citizens. In 1915 there were an estimated 150,000 opiate addicts in New York City alone. At that time attitudes to drugs in Britain were more relaxed. Heroin was prescribed to addicts by doctors until 1967. Until the early 1960s, the number of addicts was so small that the Home Office had personal contact with many of them.

But social concern about drugs intensified with the spread in the late 1950s and 1960s of 'youth culture' – the new-found identity of young people associated with changing attitudes and the development of popular music. Experimental drug use, particularly of cannabis and lysergic acid (LSD), a hallucinogen, is often associated with this period. A new Dangerous Drugs Act in 1964 outlawed the growing of cannabis. This was extended in 1966 to include LSD and mescaline. Under the Misuse of Drugs Act 1971, all drugs were categorised according to strength and danger. Drugs in Class A (the most dangerous) include cocaine and heroin. Drugs in Class B include cannabis and amphetamine.

Action against stronger, more physically addictive drugs has intensified in the last few years. In 1989 US President George Bush announced a $10.6 billion programme to wage 'war on drugs'. It aimed to break the links between drug producers and organised crime and improve education for school children on the dangers of drugs. Latin American governments – including Columbia, Peru and Bolivia – were offered $300 million to encourage them to take military action against drug producers.

Critics of this initiative argued that it did not attack the real problem of demand. Former Bolivian president Walter Guevara recently said: 'As long as there is someone ready to pay for cocaine, there will be someone in some part of the world ... willing to produce and market it.' Critics pointed out that the economies of countries such as Bolivia, Peru and Columbia, which need to export goods to earn money, have relied on the cultivation of drugs when the demand for exports dwindles: Bolivia earns an estimated $600 million annually from drugs.

In the last decade, drug use has risen in Britain. Official figures show that the number of opiate addicts rose between 1987 and 1990 from 10,716 to 17,755. The biggest rise was in young men under 25. Unofficial estimates by health workers suggest there could be up to 100,000 heroin addicts.

Cannabis, a far milder substance, remains the most widely used illegal drug. The Institute for the Study of Drug Dependence, a research body, estimates that at least a million people use the drug each year in Britain.

Experts also point out that as great a problem is posed to the nation's health by the widespread use of legal drugs. Alcohol Concern, a research and campaign organisation, estimates that 90 per cent of women and 93 per cent of men drink alcohol regularly, sometimes excessively. Up to one and a half million people regularly drink at levels that seriously damage their health.

Debate about drug use

A growth in the use of drugs such as cannabis has led to calls for changes in the laws designed to outlaw them.

There is continuing debate over the most effective way of reducing drug-taking. Some people have argued that one solution is to reduce the criminal penalties for those who are found in possession of drugs – particularly so-called 'softer' drugs, such as cannabis, which they argue cause less harm than other 'harder' drugs. At present about 80 per cent of recorded drug offences are for possession or use of cannabis.

Proposals for changes in the law have been raised increasingly in recent years as the recorded use of drugs has increased, particularly among young people. The number of drug addicts notified to the Home Office increased by 20 per cent to almost 18,000 between 1989 and 1990. Most addicts were men aged between 21 and 34. Known cannabis offenders doubled from 1986 to 1990.

Supporters of a change in the law come from a wide range of positions. Some argue for the legalisation of even the most dangerous drugs – and the creation of a free market in their production and use.

In 1989, Dr Vernon Coleman of the group Committee for a Free Britain, argued that if cannabis, cocaine and heroin were freely available through legal channels there would be few deaths from drug related activities. Many drug-related deaths, he said, were caused by criminals selling contaminated or poisoned drugs.

Others have argued that the huge drug profits made by organised crime could be channelled back to more socially useful ends.

The Standing Conference on Drug Abuse (SCODA) argues that the use of all drugs should be 'decriminalised' – in other words, that there should no longer be criminal penalties for their use. SCODA does not think that making it a crime helps to reduce drug taking. However, the group would like some legal controls to be kept – including bans on sales to those under 18 or on the use of drugs while using machinery or driving.

Supporters of a change in the law cite what they see as positive trends in the Netherlands. There cannabis is legally available in 250 licensed coffee houses where it can be bought and smoked. A recent survey showed that only 1.8 per cent of Dutch 18-year olds had used drugs in the past year. (A recent study of 13-16 year olds in Glasgow, Edinburgh and Dundee showed that one in five of 1,197 pupils had already taken illegal drugs once). Reformers argue that when border controls within Europe are relaxed in 1993 there will be nothing to stop the influx of cannabis from the Netherlands.

Although possession of cannabis remains illegal in Britain, in practice the police have been more tolerant of possession in recent years. They now often give people formal warnings – or 'caution' them – rather than prosecute them. In 1989, cautions were used in 39 per cent of cases of possession.

The government remains firmly opposed to any changes in the law. The then Home Secretary Kenneth Baker, argued in June 1990 that, even in small doses, cannabis use poses a risk to drivers and those using dangerous machinery at work or at home. He also argued that there is strong evidence that people progress from smoking cannabis to using heroin and cocaine.

Although all three main political parties support the increased use of cautions for minor drug offences, none supports further changes in the law.

The Labour Party says that the legalisation of dangerous drugs would be a disaster for Third World economies. The party's recent drugs consultation document said: 'Commercialisation of production would accelerate dangerous tendencies towards monocultivation (a dependence on growing a single crop) in producer countries'. This in turn would disrupt present patterns of mixed farming, by which food is produced for local markets.

The Liberal Democrats are also against legalising banned drugs. But a spokeswoman said: 'The system so far has failed to deal with the problem of drug addiction. That is something we believe should be looked at'.

Melissa Benn
The Education Guardian Sourcebook, 1992

Information Activities

Finding the Tollund Man

1. Reading the archaeologist's account
● Read the description of the discovery, retrieval and preservation of the Tollund man, which is an extract from the book *The Bog People* by P.V. Glob.

2. Picturing the scene
● You're P.V. Glob. You have just arrived at the scene of the discovery and in your notebook you do a quick sketch to remind yourself of exactly what you see. Use the descriptions on the first two pages of the text to mark the exact position of the body and any other details, the direction the head is pointing in, the clothing, anything found with him etc.

3. An archaeologist's handbook
On the second and following pages of the text, the writer gives us details about how the man was taken out of the peat bog, transported and preserved.
● Use the account to write a set of instructions for a trainee archaeologist on what to do if you find an Iron Age body in a peat bog. You could write it as a list of 'Do's and Don'ts'.

4. A factual account or the telling of a tale?
● In small groups, work on a photocopy of the text. Decide which bits of the text are giving the reader factual information and which bits are more concerned with telling a story or describing the events so as to make them come to life. Cut up the text and stick it down on a large sheet of paper, divided down the middle and headed 'Facts' and 'Story'.
● Choose one bit of 'Fact' and one bit of 'Story' to concentrate on. Look closely at the way in which language is used.
e.g.
Are the sentences different in any way (longer or shorter, with more or less clauses)?
Are the verbs active or passive? (e.g. 'a small lump of peat *was removed* from beside his head' is passive, whereas '*I removed* a small lump of peat' would be active.)
Are the kinds of words chosen different (poetic, scientific, geological, formal, conversational etc.)?

- Choose one sentence to re-write in a style different to Glob's.
e.g.

'This disclosed a rope, made of two leather thongs twisted together, which encircled the neck in a noose drawn tight into the throat and then coiled like a snake over the shoulder and down across the back.'

might be re-written as,

'I saw a snake-like coil of rope, twisting around his neck, like a constrictor squeezing the life out of him, before slipping over his shoulder and sliding away down his back.'

5. An entry in an encyclopaedia
- You have been asked to write 500 words on the Tollund man for a double page spread in a Children's Encyclopaedia. Decide:

What facts are essential
What would make interesting reading for 9-11 year olds
How you can break up the text with sub-headings, lists, information in boxes, diagrams, sketches, photographs etc.
Make sure that you keep within the word limit, so that your text will fit the space in the Encyclopaedia.

6. A poem about the Tollund man
- Try writing a poem based on your feelings and thoughts, having read the account of how the Tollund man was found. If you have ideas of your own, start to write it in your own way. If not, plunder the text itself for words and phrases that you might be able to use as they stand, or adapt or link together with your own words.

Seamus Heaney wrote a poem about wanting to see the Tollund man and his thoughts about him.

- Read Heaney's poem. Talk about what aspects of the Tollund man he is most interested in. If you only had the chance to read one of these texts, the account or the the poem, which would you choose? Why?

Tantrums

Penelope Leach's books about bringing up children are widely read by thousands of people who are struggling to cope with being parents and want advice from an 'expert'. In this section from her book, *Baby and Child*, she writes about toddlers' temper tantrums.

1. Reading the text
- Read the text or listen to it being read aloud.
- Look at these phrases which have been taken from the text. What do they tell you about:

The audience for the book (age, class, gender, state of mind?)
The way in which Leach is addressing her audience (with a voice of authority? hesitantly? trying to explain simply and clearly? patronisingly?)
The intentions behind the book (to give practical information, to give scientific background, to give advice, to make parents feel better and calm their fears?)
Whose side she is on, child or parent?

> 'A tantrum is like an emotional blown fuse'

> 'His body's reflexes will reassert themselves and force air back into his lungs long before he is in any danger'

> 'Prevent the child from getting hurt or hurting anyone or anything else'

> 'Don't scream back if you can possibly help it'

> 'It is not easy being a toddler rocking wildly between those anxious and angry feelings. It is not easy being a toddler's parent either, striving to stay on the centre of that emotional see-saw and to hold it in equilibrium'

2. Re-castings for different audiences and purposes
● Use the material about toddler tantrums and re-cast it in a different form, for a different audience and/or purpose. Choose one of the suggestions below:

A cartoon for parents in a magazine called 'Perfect Parenting'
A poster in the entrance of a pre-school nursery or creche, giving parents a list of Do's and Don'ts
Questions and answers in a problem page for the magazine, 'Perfect Parenting'
A drama script of a scene between a screaming toddler and a parent trying to follow Leach's advice
A drama script of a scene between a screaming toddler and a parent who ignores Leach's advice
A section in a book written 50 years ago, which presented the view that children should be seen and not heard and firmly disciplined.

3. The adolescent's guide to difficult parents
● Write one section in a guide for adolescents on dealing with difficult parents, using the same kind of style and approach as that used by Penelope Leach. (For instance, try to sound authoritative, re-assuring and scientific. Offer direct advice about strategies. Make it seem like you are the expert.)

Suggestions for sections
Dealing with parents' tantrums
What to do with a parent who says no
Handling the parent who worries too much
Coping with the embarrassing parent
Nagging and what to do about it
The musically ignorant parent

The Facts About Drugs

1. Skim reading the text
● Work in pairs or threes, each group being given one kind of information to look for in the text, from the list below:

The history of drugs
Drug use in America
Drugs and the law
Drug use in Britain
Cannabis
Heroin
Hallucinogenic drugs
Useful statistics on changing patterns of drug use
Arguments for de-criminalising drug use
Arguments against de-criminalising drug use
The policies of the political parties

● Skim read the text looking for any material that fits your heading and write brief notes that will allow you to report back to the rest of the group some of the key things that are being said.
● Listen to each other's reports, to familiarise yourselves with the whole text.

2. Fact or opinion?
● Make a list of all the people and organisations whose views are expressed in the article. What kind of balance is there between different kinds of views and different kinds of people and organisations?
● Put the people and organisations into three columns: supporters of relaxing the law, supporters of maintaining strong laws and those neutral on the issue of legalising drugs.
● Can you tell, from the way the article is written, what the writer thinks about drugs?

3. Boring old facts?
Factual writing can be very dry to read, however interesting the subject matter.
● If you were asked to present this material for a readership of your own age, what might you do to jazz it up and make it more lively? Talk about your own ideas, using the suggestions below as a starting-point for discussion:

Cartoons
Photographs
Charts and graphs
Maps
Time lines
Headings and sub-headings
Other ways of breaking up the print on the page (e.g. graphics, columns, boxes etc.)
Decide which bits of text might be better presented visually than in chunks of prose.

● Try doing a mock-up for a piece on drugs, which might be used in a PSE book for
schools or as a feature in *Just 17* magazine. In either case, do it as a double page
spread. Create a rough design for a lively looking piece. You don't need to write out
the text itself, just sketch out headings, graphics and a possible layout.
● Look at the way the material was actually presented for a secondary school age
readership in *The Education Guardian* (on Pages 174–175 of this book). Write a
detailed commentary on what has been done with the written text and how successful
it is in putting across information and ideas and reaching its target audience. You
could compare it with your own rough design.

Getting high throughout history

Drugs have been used as medicines, for pleasure and in religious ceremonies, but some remain strictly controlled.

DRUGS of all kinds have been used since earliest recorded history. The value of the juice of the white opium poppy for inducing sleep and reducing pain was recorded in Sumerian more than 6,000 years ago. The cannabis plant was used in central Asia and China as early as 3000BC.

Drugs are substances which significantly alter the physical or mental state of their user. People throughout history have used drugs for pleasure, as medicine or for religious purposes.

One way of assessing the strength of a drug is to measure the risk a user runs of becoming dependent. According to this definition, heroin — derived from opium — would be considered one of the strongest drugs because users quickly find they cannot do without it. Yet modern medicine also depends on drugs which, though legal, can lead to dependency. Doctors prescribe many drugs every day, including tranquillisers, which users sometimes find difficult or impossible to give up.

The outlawing of some drugs is a modern development. Until the late 19th century, opium could be bought in Britain as easily as cigarettes and alcohol can be bought today. Writers, artists and politicians used opium to increase their energy and creativity. Others, particularly the poor, used it as a way to treat illness without having to pay a doctor and instead of alcohol.

Britain's key involvement in the production and sale of drugs led to the Opium Wars (1839–42 and 1856–60) following an attempt by the Manchu government of China to get all foreign powers to surrender stocks of opium in order to discourage the drug's importation and use. China's eventual defeat allowed Britain to continue the importation of opium. Britain remained the main manufacturer and exporter of morphine, derived from opium, until the 1950s.

Growing worries about the use of

opium by the working classes and awareness by doctors of the dangers led to moves to restrict their legal availability by the 1890s. During the first world war (1914-18) opium and cocaine were made illegal amid fears about drug use among soldiers. The first international agreement to control the drugs trade was the International Opium Convention of 1912.

This century the United States has been the country most preoccupied with international drug control — partly because drugs are used by so many US citizens. In 1915 there were

Glossary

Dependence Experts avoid the word "addiction", which is generally limited to the body's physical need for a drug (being unable to do without it without suffering unpleasant physical feelings). Dependence also involves psychological need (being unable to do without the pleasurable effects of a drug or the routine of using it). Dependence can be physical or psychological or both or neither.

Amphetamine A manufactured drug which is a relatively cheap stimulant.

Hallucinogen A drug that makes people hallucinate — see objects in a distorted way.

Opiates Drugs derived from the opium poppy. Includes opium itself, prepared from the poppy's juice, and — developed from this — morphine and heroin.

an estimated 150,000 opiate addicts in New York City alone. At that time attitudes to drugs in Britain were more relaxed. Heroin was prescribed to addicts by doctors until 1967. Until the early 1960s, the number of addicts was so small that the Home Office had personal contact with many of them.

But social concern about drugs intensified with the spread in the late 1950s and 1960s of "youth culture" — the new-found identity of young people associated with changing attitudes and the development of popular music. Experimental drug use, particularly of cannabis and lysergic acid (LSD), a hallucinogen, is often associated with this period. A new Dangerous Drugs Act in 1964 outlawed the growing of cannabis. This was extended in 1966 to

include LSD and mescaline. Under the Misuse of Drugs Act 1971, all drugs were categorised according to strength and danger. Drugs in Class A (the most dangerous) include cocaine and heroin. Drugs in Class B include cannabis and amphetamine.

Action against stronger, more physically addictive drugs has intensified in the last few years. In 1989 US President George Bush announced a $10.6 billion programme to wage "war on drugs". It aimed to break the links between drug producers and organised crime and improve education for schoolchildren on the dangers of drugs. Latin American governments — including Columbia, Peru and Bolivia — were offered $300 million to encourage them to take military action against drug producers.

Critics of this initiative argued that it did not attack the real problem of demand. Former Bolivian president Walter Guevara recently said: "As long as there is someone ready to pay for cocaine, there will be someone in some part of the world . . . willing to produce and market it." Critics pointed out that the economies of countries such as Bolivia, Peru and Colombia, which need to export goods to earn money, have relied on the cultivation of drugs when the demand for exports dwindles: Bolivia earns an estimated $600 million annually from drugs.

In the last decade, drug use has risen in Britain. Official figures show that the number of opiate addicts rose between 1987 and 1990 from 10,716 to 17,755. The biggest rise was in young men under 25. Unofficial estimates by health workers suggest there could be up to 100,000 heroin addicts.

Cannabis, a far milder substance, remains the most widely used illegal drug. The Institute for the Study of Drug Dependence, a research body, estimates that at least a million people use the drug each year in Britain.

Experts also point out that as great a problem is posed to the nation's health by the widespread use of *legal* drugs. Alcohol Concern, a research and campaign organisation, estimates that 90 per cent of women and 93 per cent of men drink alcohol regularly, sometimes excessively. Up to one and half million people regularly drink at levels that seriously damage their health.

The Opium Wars between Britain and China in 1839–42 and Britain, France and China in 1856–60 took place after China tried to stop the illegal importation of opium from British India and restrict foreign trade MARY EVANS

Supply and demand

Cocaine comes from the leaves of the coca plant which grows mainly in Bolivia, Colombia and Peru. Local people have always chewed the leaves to ward off tiredness and hunger. The farmers grow coca plants because they and local businesses cannot afford to depend on other crops. The world price of other crops, textiles or raw materials may fall so there is a strong incentive to grow and trade coca.

PRICE Leaves to make 1 kilo of cocaine **$1,000**

Processing the leaves

1 The first stage of processing normally takes place in factories near the growing area. The leaves are soaked for four days in dilute sulphuric acid. The liquid is drained off and mixed with lime, petrol and other chemicals to make coca paste (unrefined cocaine). About half of this is smoked locally.

2 The remaining paste is normally taken to a laboratory, where the paste is refined into a crystalline powder, cocaine hydrochloride: cocaine proper. This is now ready for export.

Smuggling

PRICE 1 kilo of cocaine **$5,000**

"Mules" tape packets of cocaine to their bodies under their clothes, or hide packets in their luggage. Some swallow cocaine-filled condoms and wait for them to pass through the body when at their destination.

About 75% of exported cocaine goes to the US. Most of the rest comes to Europe mainly via Spain and Portugal. It is carried by couriers ('mules') on commercial flights or hidden on private aircraft or boats. A recent survey showed that most couriers were unaware of the stiff penalties they face if caught importing drugs. In 1990 there were 390 seizures of cocaine by British Customs and Excise.

MIAMI AIRPORT CUSTOMS FILES

Distribution

The cocaine is delivered to a pre-arranged site to await distribution. Distributors often work through 'front companies' that look like legal companies and through which the money is 'laundered' (profits declared to be from legal business).

Dealing

Dealers work alone or in networks. Some sell many drugs, others only one. Some use drugs, others only sell them. Some cocaine is converted into "crack": a substance that can be smoked. It has a faster effect than cocaine but lasts a shorter time.

PRICE 1 kilo of cocaine **$50,000**

The user

Cocaine is usually taken by sniffing it up the nostrils where it is absorbed into the bloodstream. The user experiences a stimulating effect and a lifted mood. It is very expensive (1g costs about £80 – £100) so many users have severe financial problems. Taking large doses can induce paranoia and panic and deep depression sets in between doses.

Experts agree that the main dangers from drug-taking are:

- Death from overdose after taking different drugs at the same time (eg alcohol with other depressants).
- Death or illness from taking too much.
- Accidents while intoxicated by any drug.
- Infection from sharing injection equipment without sterilising it.

PRICE 1 kilo of cocaine: street value **$170,000**

Source: Dr N Dorn, Institute for the Study of Drug Dependence; Howard League for Penal Reform GRAPHICS: PADDY ALLEN

Debate about drug use

A growth in the use of drugs such as cannabis has led to calls for changes in the laws designed to outlaw them.

THERE is continuing debate over the most effective way of reducing drug-taking. Some people have argued that one solution is to reduce the criminal penalties for those who are found in possession of drugs — particularly so-called "softer" drugs, such as cannabis, which they argue cause less harm than other "harder" drugs. At present about 80 per cent of recorded drug offences are for possession or use of cannabis.

Proposals for changes in the law have been raised increasingly in recent years as the recorded use of drugs has increased, particularly among young people. The number of drug addicts notified to the Home Office increased by 20 per cent to almost 18,000 between 1989 and 1990. Most addicts were men aged between 21 and 34. Known cannabis offenders doubled from 1986 to 1990.

Supporters of a change in the law come from a wide range of positions. Some argue for the legalisation of even the most dangerous drugs — and the creation of a free market in their production and use.

In 1989, Dr Vernon Coleman, of the group Committee for a Free Britain, argued that if cannabis, cocaine and heroin were freely available through legal channels there would be few deaths from drug-related activities. Many drug-related deaths, he said, were caused by criminals selling contaminated or poisoned drugs.

Others have argued that the huge drug profits made by organised crime could be channelled back to more socially useful ends.

The Standing Conference on Drug Abuse (SCODA) argues that the use of all drugs should be "decriminalised" — in other words, that there should no longer be criminal penalties for their use. SCODA does not think that making it a crime helps to reduce drug-taking. However, the group would like some legal controls to be kept — including bans on sales to those under 18 or on the use of drugs while using machinery or driving.

Supporters of a change in the law cite what they see as positive trends in the Netherlands. There cannabis is legally available in 250 licensed coffee houses where it can be bought and smoked. A recent survey showed that only 1.8 per cent of Dutch 18-year-olds had used drugs in the past year. (A recent study of 13- to 16-year-olds in Glasgow, Edinburgh and Dundee showed that one in five of 1,197 pupils had already taken illegal drugs once.) Reformers argue that when border controls within Europe are relaxed in 1993 there will be nothing to stop the influx of cannabis from the Netherlands.

Although possession of cannabis remains illegal in Britain, in practice the police have been more tolerant of possession in recent years. They now often give people formal warnings — or "caution" them — rather than prosecute them. In 1989, cautions were used in 39 per cent of cases of possession.

The Government remains firmly opposed to any changes in the law. The then Home Secretary, Kenneth Baker, argued in June 1990 that, even in small doses, cannabis use poses a risk to drivers and those using dangerous machinery at work or at home. He also argued that there is strong evidence that people progress from smoking cannabis to using heroin and cocaine.

Although all three main political parties support the increased use of cautions for minor drug offences, none supports further changes in the law.

The Labour Party says that the legalisation of dangerous drugs would be a disaster for Third-World economies. The party's recent drugs consultation document said: "Commercialisation of production would accelerate dangerous tendencies towards monocultivation [a dependence on growing a single crop] in producer countries." This, in turn, would disrupt present patterns of mixed farming, by which food is produced for local markets.

The Liberal Democrats are also against legalising banned drugs. But a spokeswoman said: "The system so far has failed to deal with the problem of drug addiction. That is something we believe should be looked at."

Members of a Peruvian anti-drug police unit patrol the waters of the Alto Huallaga River in search of traffickers based in this jungle region

The Trial of Craig and Bentley

First Day, Tuesday 9th December 1952

The Clerk of the Court: Christopher Craig, Derek William Bentley, you are charged that on the 2nd day of November last you murdered Sidney George Miles. Christopher Craig, are you guilty or not guilty?

The Prisoner Craig: Not guilty.

The Clerk of the Court: Derek William Bentley, are you guilty or not guilty?

The Prisoner Bentley: Not guilty.

The Lord Chief Justice: Craig may sit down.

(A jury was empanelled and sworn.)

The Clerk of the Court: Members of the jury, the prisoners at the Bar, Christopher Craig and Derek William Bentley, are charged with the murder of Sidney George Miles on the 2nd November last. To this indictment they have severally pleaded not guilty, and it is your charge to say, having heard the evidence, whether they or either of them be guilty or not.

Opening Speech for the Prosecution

Mr Humphreys:

May it please you, my lord. Gentlemen of the jury, in this case I am instructed for the Crown with my friend Mr John Bass. The accused Christopher Craig, who is 16 years of age, is represented by my friend Mr Parris; the accused Derek Bentley, further from you, who is 19, is represented by my friend Mr Frank Cassels. The charge against these two youths is that on the night of 2nd November last they together murdered a police officer, Sidney George Miles.

You may have read something of this case in the Press; you may have read how these two young men were found on the roof of a building in Croydon, that there was what was described as a gun battle, as result of which one police constable was killed and another wounded, and of a spectacular jump or dive by the boy Craig from the roof of that building, as a result of which he was injured and had to appear at the Magistrates' Court on a stretcher, and of alleged confessions by Bentley that he knew Craig had a gun. On behalf of the Prosecution I ask you to forget everything you have read about this case up to the moment. This case will be tried, as cases are in every English Court, upon the evidence before you and on that alone.

The case for the Prosecution is this: that Craig deliberately and wilfully murdered that police constable, and thereafter gloried in the murder; that Bentley incited Craig to begin the shooting and, although technically under arrest at the actual time of the killing of Miles, was party to that murder and equally responsible in law.

The story can only be made intelligible to you if you will be good enough to look at a plan and some photographs which have been prepared; and with his lordship's leave I will ask that you now be given copies of these photographs and the plan. You will see, if you hold it a little sideways so that the writing is the right way up, Tamworth Road at the bottom, and at the bottom right-hand corner is No. 74 Tamworth Road, from which a witness will come and say what she saw. Straight opposite No. 74 is a large block shown grey, which is the premises of Barlow & Parker, wholesale confectioners. What you are looking at now is a flat roof, and in the middle of the roof the blue hatched oblongs are skylights. On the left of that block you will see marked 'B' the head of the stairway which comes up through the building and on to the flat roof. Further up the plan, marked 'A', is the head of the lift shaft, which is a large concrete building on the flat roof. The points 'A' and 'B' will be the important ones for you to understand the shooting which followed later on this night.

Now, if that is clear to you I can proceed with my story. You must appreciate, however, that those photographs were taken in daylight and this fight and this murder took place at night. I think one witness will say there was a moon, but it was generally obscured by clouds, and for most of the time the police were using torches; and, therefore, what took place on this flat roof took place at night in circumstances in which, for most of the time, there was either a fitful gleam of moon or darkness. The whole of the gun fight seems to have taken from 20 to 25 minutes.

Now, the story is this. You will come back to your plan to No. 74 Tamworth Road. At 9.15 p.m. on this night, the 2nd November, a lady looking out of her window there saw two men climbing a gate, and the gate is the one at the bottom left-hand corner of the grey part of the plan. She sent for the police. At 9.25 two lots of police arrived simultaneously: a police van with Detective-Constable Fairfax, and Police-Constable Harrison, both of whom will be called before you, and a wireless car with Police-Constable Miles, who was later killed, and Police-Constable McDonald, who also gives evidence. These four men will be the four principal witnesses of what happened on the roof, except that one of them is now dead – Miles.

The leader of the attack upon the men upon the roof was Sergeant Fairfax. He went over that gate at the bottom left-hand corner of the grey part of your plan and climbed up a drain-pipe. He climbed up on that flat roof as a result of what he had been told of two men being seen there. When he got on to the flat roof he saw the two accused men; they were over to the left towards the stack marked 'A' upon your plan. He went straight up to them; he went up to within six feet of them in the dark. He said, 'I am a police officer. Come out from behind that stack,' and the answer was in a voice which will be recognised and described as Craig's voice: 'If you want us, f——g well come and get us.' I am not going to trouble you with the language, it does not assist one way or the other; I am giving you the substance of the repy. The reply to that by the officer (who was, of course, unarmed) was, 'All right,' and he charged in and grabbed Bentley. With him in custody he turned and pursued Craig round the stack; but Bentley got away and shouted an observation, heard by three separate officers in the darkness in three separate places, which may be, in your view, the most important observation that Bentley made that night: 'Let him have it, Chris' – and the name of the other accused is Christopher Craig – 'Let him have it Chris.' The immediate reply to that comment by Bentley was a loud report, and Fairfax was hit on the shoulder with what turned out to be a bullet from the gun which Craig held. That observation was not only heard by Sergeant Fairfax grappling with two men in the dark on the roof, but by another officer, McDonald, who was at that moment climbing up the same stack-pipe, and by another officer who had arrived from an entirely different direction and who was further away to the right of your plan on the flat roof, P.C. Harrison. All three heard it, and all three heard the shot which followed immediately upon it. That statement, in the submission of the Prosecution, was a deliberate incitement to Craig to murder Sergeant Fairfax. It was spoken to a man whom he, Bentley, clearly knew had a gun. That shot began a gun fight in the course of which Miles was killed; that incitement, in the submission of the Prosecution, covered the whole of the shooting thereafter; even though at the time of the actual shot which killed P.C. Miles, Bentley was in custody and under arrest.

Fairfax, although hit in the shoulder with a bullet which glanced across and only cut his skin, got up and knocked Bentley down. There was another shot which missed. Fairfax then dragged Bentley behind one of the roof lights and rapidly felt him for weapons. Even at that moment in the darkness, arresting one man with the other man shooting at him, he had time to feel Bentley quickly over and find in his breast pocket a substantial knife and also a knuckle-duster (you know what that means). This shows that at the time Bentley was himself armed to that extent and, therefore, prepared to use violence in the course of the common purpose the two men had that night, which was, as they later admit, housebreaking, to break into that building and steal what they could.

Sergeant Fairfax told Bentley that he was proposed to work round to the doorway, which is upon your plan, where both of them could get cover from the shooting which was still coming from the direction of the lift. Bentley's reply to that statement of what the sergeant was going to do with him was, 'He'll shoot you.' Nevertheless, they reached the staircase head in safety, and both took cover behind it.

So far Fairfax has been alone upon the roof with the two men, one of whom he now holds and the other is shooting at them; but just about that moment P.C. McDonald arrives up the drain-pipe. Apparently he is a big and heavy man, and had difficulty in getting up the last few feet, and Fairfax went and helped him up. So now there are two officers on the roof and the two men. Fairfax said to McDonald, 'He got me in the shoulder'; Bentley, who, you will remember, is under arrest with Fairfax at the time, said, 'I told the silly bugger not to use it'. That means, you may think, that Bentley knew quite well that Craig had a gun, and that he knew that Craig at least meant to use it. But that statement, of course, is completely contradicted by Bentley's earlier statement, heard by three police officers. 'Let him have it, Chris'.

Fairfax, now with the reinforcement of McDonald, shouted to Craig, 'Drop your gun'. Craig's reply was 'Come and get it' and another shot was fired. It seems to have missed everything; but that shot was probably at P.C. Harrison who had climbed from the ground up to the roof of No. 25 and from where he got on to the sloping roof of Barlow and Parker's warehouse. P.C. Harrison, although he heard these shots being fired, crept along the gutter towards Craig. To do so he was lying on his back with his feet in the gutter, and was completely helpless. Presenting a sitting target, he could do nothing whatsoever to avoid such shots as were fired towards him as he lay or crawled or crept along. Craig saw him and deliberately fired at him, certainly once, probably twice. Harrison, realising that it was suicide to attempt to go further, crawled back, got down, raced round to the door of the main building and with the other officers, shortly came up that staircase, (the one leading to the roof) when a key had been obtained, and joined in the fight on the roof.

Meanwhile, to come back to what was happening on the roof, McDonald asked Fairfax, after these shots had been fired at Harrison, 'What sort of gun has he got?' Bentley, still under arrest, cut in and said, 'He's got a .45 Colt and plenty of ammunition for it too.'

Down below, the police, as I have stated, had found somebody with the keys, had got the door open at the foot and came racing up the stairs. They were led by P.C. Miles. Miles, when he got to the head of the staircase, went straight out onto the roof. Craig fired again. Miles fell dead with a bullet straight between the eyes. Craig then came from behind the stack holding the gun in both hands and fired again at the stairs.

P.C. Harrison was next out of the doorway. Stepping over Miles' body, he threw at Craig all he had to throw, his truncheon, a bottle he had picked up somewhere and a block of wood. The reply by Craig was quite clear: 'I am Craig. You have just given my brother twelve years. Come on, you coppers. I'm only sixteen,' and another shot was fired.

Bentley, at that moment technically under arrest and with men who were being shot at, said, 'You want to look out; he'll blow your heads off.' At that moment they began to take him downstairs, and he shouted 'Look out, Chris; they're taking me down'. The reply from Craig was another burst of firing. You, gentlemen of the jury, will have to interpret all the evidence in this case, and you will have to interpret that further observation by Bentley, made although he is technically under arrest, while he is still on the roof where the fight is going on and, to all intent and purposes, in the presence of Craig. He is being taken down by the police officers and he calls out. 'Look out Chris; they're taking me down.' Was that a further invitation? Cry for help? Challenge? What was it? The result was clear: a further burst of firing by Craig.

Then P.C. Jaggs arrived. He came up the drainpipe and came round at the head of the stairs. Fairfax had gone down with Bentley, and at the foot of the stairs he was given a gun. That shows how long this fight had been going on, for the police, hearing the firing had had time to send to the police station and get firearms from the proper authorised supply, and return. Fairfax was given a gun with which to return to the fight. As he got to the top of the stairs, now for the first time armed, he shouted out to Craig, 'Drop your gun, I also have a gun,' and he ran straight at him in the darkness in a semi-circle, firing twice. He missed. Down below in the garden was P.C. Lowe, because the police reinforcements were such that the whole building was now surrounded, and he from his position in the garden looked up and saw Craig outlined against the sky on a railing which is close to the top of the lift shaft or stack. Craig above at the railing was heard by several officers to make a little speech; various officers heard part of it, but Lowe seems to have heard most of it completely. The answer to Fairfax coming out with a gun and shouting to Craig 'Drop your gun, I also have a gun,' was this: 'Yes it's a Colt ·45. Are you hiding behind a shield? Is it bullet proof? Are we going to have a shooting match? It's just what I like. Have they hurt you, Derek?' Now that is Derek Bentley, who at the moment was being taken down the stairs by police officers after he had called out, 'Look out, Chris; they're taking me down'.

Officers then heard four clicks, clicks as of a gun the trigger of which had been pulled but for some reason has not fired, and then a shot. You will remember this is a revolver and each time that the trigger is pulled the gun moves round so that a different cartridge is presented at the breach for firing, and if there is a cartridge which does not fire at the moment, then the gun moves round until the next cartridge is ready for firing, and if that is live and in good order it will fire. They heard four clicks and then a shot, and then a cry from Craig, 'There; it's empty,' and then he dived from the roof, into the darkness below, which is 20 to 25 feet. He seems to have fallen beyond the glass of the greenhouse, that is to say he jumped just short of the greenhouse. As he jumps he throws his revolver; the revolver goes through the glass and makes that hole in the roof, and is later found in the greenhouse. He falls short and in some way breaks his wrist, hurts his back and the middle of his chest or breastbone, and there lies injured. As he jumps he calls out, 'Give my love to ...'. It sounded like a girl's name. I do not know what; but when he arrived below, a police officer, not knowing, of course, whether he was still armed or not, or how injured he was or was not, jumped at him, and as he holds him down, Craig says 'I wish I was f...... dead. I hope I've killed the f...... lot'. You will bear that in mind if any question arises as to the intent with which he was shooting at the police officers on this night.

On him was found a different kind of sheath-knife. So he had a knife as well as a gun, and Bentley had a knife as well as a knuckle-duster. The gun fight, if such as it was, was at the end. Constable Fairfax was taken to hospital, so was Craig, and P.C. Miles to the mortuary.

Later observations by the two men in different places may be very valuable to you, gentlemen of the jury, in deciding the intent in their minds when they were present at incidents which had taken place during the previous half hour. Bentley, who was quite uninjured, was handed over at the foot of the stairs to Sergeant Roberts. He was told he would be taken to the police station concerning the shooting of P.C. Miles, and he then said, 'I didn't have the gun; Chris shot him.' Then he said in the police car on the way to the police station, 'I knew he had a gun; but I didn't think he would use it. He has done one of your blokes in.' At the police station he was seen by Detective Chief Inspector Smith, and he said, 'I didn't kill him, guv'nor; Chris did it.' He was then asked if he wanted to make a statement, and he made a statement under caution; which means he was told he need not say anything if he did not want to, but if he did it would be taken down in writing and might be given in evidence. That statement will be at a later stage read to you in full; at the moment I am only going to to read such parts of it as I put before you as being particularly pertinent to the case for the Crown. At a later stage it will be read in full, and if you wish you shall in due course have copies of it. He said: 'I have known Craig since I went to school. We were stopped by our parents going out together, but we still continued going out with each other – I mean we have not gone out together until tonight.' You can make what you like of that contradiction. Then he goes on to say that on this night he and Craig had got together and then caught a bus to Croydon. 'We got off at West Croydon and then walked down the road where the toilets are – I think it is Tamworth Road. When we came to the place where you found me, Chris looked in the window. There was a little iron gate at the side'- that is the gate marked on the plan. 'Chris then jumped over and I followed. Chris then climbed up the drain-pipe to the roof and I followed. Up to then Chris had not said anything. We both got out on to the flat roof at the top. Then someone in a garden on the opposite side shone a torch up towards us. Chris said, 'It's a copper; hide behind here.' We hid behind a shelter arrangement on the roof.' That, members of the jury, sounds as if it was the stack. 'We were there waiting for about ten minutes. I did not know he was going to use the gun. A plain-clothes man climbed up the drain-pipe and on to the roof.' Members of the jury, that would obviously be Fairfax. 'The man said, ' I am a police officer – the place is surrounded.' The importance of that might be, as a matter of law, that they are agreeing that they are told before there is any shooting that it is the police who are approaching them, and for a lawful purpose. He goes on to say: 'He caught hold of me and as we walked away Chris fired. There was nobody else there at the time. The policeman and I then went round a corner by a door. A little later the door opened and a policeman in uniform came out. Chris fired again then and this policeman fell down. I could see that he was hurt as a lot of blood came from his forehead just above his nose. The policeman dragged him round the corner behind the brickwork entrance to the door. I remember I shouted something, but forget what it was. I could not see Chris when I shouted to him – he was behind a wall. I heard some more policemen behind the door and the policeman with me said, 'I don't think he has any more bullets.' Chris shouted, 'Oh yes I have,' and he fired again. I think I heard him fire three times altogether. The policemen then pushed me down the stairs and I did not see any more. I knew we were going to break into the place; I did not know what we were going to get – just anything that was going. I did not have a gun and I did not know Chris had one until he shot. I now know that the policeman in uniform that was shot is dead.' That is all I read at the moment, and it is all that is of importance to the case against Bentley.

May I say at once, of course, that that statement made by Bentley is in no sense any evidence against Craig; because their concerted action to break and enter these premises and steal what they could, and to resist their lawful apprehension by such violence as they might think necessary, was over, and the moment they are arrested, what they severally say is not evidence against each other.

Craig was taken to hospital. He was found to be injured. He was given drugs to relieve his pain; he was given an anaesthetic on two separate occasions when his wrist was set. Inquiries have been made at the hospital to find out precisely when and what drugs Craig received in order that no evidence may be put before you of what he said at the hospital which he might be saying at a time when he was not fully aware of what he was saying, being under the influence of drugs. Of the observations he made to various police officers at various times my friend defending, Mr Parris, has asked me for the moment to omit two, as he will ask his lordship's ruling at a later stage as to whether they are admissible. Therefore I only read those statements he made when in hospital which are not disputed. The first he made was at 11 at night just after he arrived in hospital: 'I had six in the gun. I fired at a policeman. I had six tommy-gun bullets.' He was promptly cautioned, and thereafter these police officers will say that they cautioned him again and again, so that he knows perfectly well that anything he said might be given in evidence. 'Is the copper dead? How about the others? We ought to have shot them all.' Then at about 11.45 that night Chief Inspector Smith came to see him, as the officer in charge of the case, and said, 'I have just seen the dead body of P.C. Miles at Mayday

Mortuary. I charge you, as a result of enquiries I have made, with being concerned with Bentley in murdering him.' He again cautioned Craig, and Craig said, 'He's dead is he? What about the others?' At 2.30 a.m. on the 3rd November, he said to another officer who was by his bedside, P.C.Ross, 'Did I really kill a policeman? I got the gun from a house in Purley. There are plenty more where that came from.' At 6.30 am, four hours later, he said to a P.C. Denholm, 'Is he dead?' 'Who?' said the officer. 'That copper. I shot him in the head and he fell down like a ton of bricks.' That night he made an observation to a P.C. Smith which I will not now mention (your lordship will find it at page 23 of the depositions). On the 5th November, this is three days after the injuires were received by Craig, he said to another officer at 2 o'clock in the afternoon, 'Is the policeman I shot in the shoulder still in hospital? I know the one I shot in the head is dead.' And later that afternoon he said, 'What do you get for carrying a knuckle-duster? Bentley had mine.' You will bear that observation in mind, members of the jury. This is Craig speaking, and evidence against Craig alone. He is asking about the knuckle-duster and saying, 'Bentley had mine.' That is of interest to you as showing the association between the two, and the arming of the two men before they go out on this common enterprise. Then he went on to say: 'Did you see the gun I had? It was all on the wobble, so I took it to work and sawed two inches off the barrel.' In fact, the piece of sawn-off barrel was under a floorboard in the attic at Craig's home, and also a vast array of ammunition. Then on the 6th November he made an observation to another police constable which I am asked to omit – your lordship will find it in P.C. Brown's deposition on page 22.

The scene of the shooting was examined. Bullets, where they could be found, were collected; empty cases, where they could be found, were collected and the whole were examined; and, subject to any point raised by the Defence, I make no point of how many shots were fired except to say this, that it would seem that at least nine shots were fired. The importance of that fact is this, that the revolver only holds six, and that means that at some period, or periods, during the fight Craig, who alone had the ammunition, was reloading. The importance of that to you is to show a deliberate purpose in his mind, as distinct from a foolish boy who happened to have a loaded gun and in fear, or losing his head, whatever it may be, pulls the trigger. He was from time to time reloading.

Later the two men were formally charged. Bentley, on the morning of the 3rd November a few hours after the shooting, when he was formally charged with the murder of Miles, said, 'Craig shot him. I had not got a gun. He was with me on the roof and shot him between the eyes.' It is rather interesting to note, therefore, that both men knew not only that Miles was killed with a shot in the face, but that the shot was between the eyes – and it was. Craig was charged formally with the murder at 9.30 in the morning and said, 'I've nothing to say.'

Members of the jury, that is the case for the Crown. Any criminal charge made in any English Court of law must be proved to the satisfaction of the jury. If you fail to find the charge proved against either man, you will acquit. It is only if you are satisfied that the Prosecution do prove that charge that you will convict.

The case for the Crown is this and nothing less, that Craig deliberately murdered P.C. Miles and, as I have said, thereafter gloried in the murder and only regretted he had not shot more. Bentley incited Craig to begin the shooting, and although he was technically under arrest at the time of the actual murder of P.C. Miles, was nevertheless still mentally supporting Craig in all that Craig continued to do; and in English law, and you may think in common sense, was in every sense party to that murder.

Now with the assistance of my friend I will call the evidence before you.

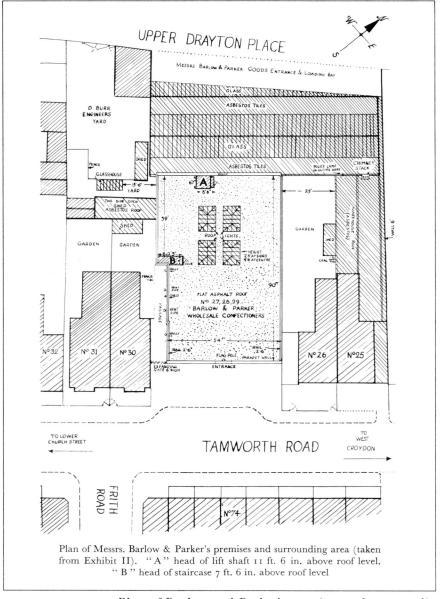

Plan of Messrs. Barlow & Parker's premises and surrounding area (taken from Exhibit II). "A" head of lift shaft 11 ft. 6 in. above roof level. "B" head of staircase 7 ft. 6 in. above roof level

Plan of Barlow and Parker's premises and surrounding area

Evidence for the Prosecution, P.C. McDonald Examined

Mr Bass: At about that time did you hear somebody shout something?

P.C. Mcdonald: I did. I heard someone shout, 'Let him have it, Chris.'

By The Lord Chief Justice

The Lord Chief Justice: Were you then on the ground, or were you still on the pipe?

P.C. Mcdonald: I was practically level with the roof, my lord, but I could not get up the last six feet.

The Lord Chief Justice: It was while you were still clinging to the pipe that you heard it?

P.C. McDonald: Yes.

Mr Bass: You heard someone shout, 'Let him have it, Chris.' I do not suppose you knew the voice at that time did you?

P.C. McDonald: I could not say for certain.

Mr Bass: Did you then come down the pipe?

P.C. McDonald: Yes.

Mr Bass: And did you hear something?

P.C. McDonald: Yes; I had reached the ground and I heard two or three shots fired from the direction of the roof.

Mr Bass: Did you then get up the pipe again?

P.C. McDonald: I did.

Cross-examination by Mr Parris

Mr Parris: Now let us see what your recollection is like. How may shots do you say were fired before the fatal one?

P.C. McDonald: Six.

Mr Parris: Six?

P.C. McDonald: Yes

Mr Parris: And you were up on the roof, I think, the whole time?

P.C. McDonald: No.

Mr Parris: How long did you go down for?

P.C. McDonald: There were two or three shots when I was not on the roof.

Mr Parris: Well, you were within hearing distance the whole time; is that right?

P.C. McDonald: Yes; I think I was within hearing distance of all shots.

Mr Parris: How many shots in all do you say there were?

P.C. McDonald: Ten or eleven.

By The Lord Chief Justice

The Lord Chief Justice: I wonder how anybody could be expected to be accurate on a matter like this, on a night like this when these men are being fired at, in fear of their lives, and now they are being asked weeks afterwards to count how many shots were fired.

Examination continued

Mr Parris: As his lordship says, it is rather unnerving to hear shots on a roof top?

P.C. McDonald: It is sir.

Mr Parris: It rather disturbs one's recollection of what happened?

P.C. McDonald: I do not know about that.

Cross-examined by Mr Cassels

Mr Cassells: Officer, I want to get from you just this: where do you say you were when you heard, 'Let him have it, Chris'?

P.C. McDonald: I was just below the roof. I had been trying to struggle up the last six feet of the pipe and I was then just trying to get down again.

Mr Cassells: You were starting to go down, were you?

P.C. McDonald: I was trying to get my footing to go down.

Mr Cassells: Were you wearing police boots?

P.C. McDonald: Yes.

Mr Cassells: Leather soles and steel tips?

P.C. McDonald: No, they had rubber soles.

Mr Cassells: Did you hear anything else said on the roof apart from this remark?

P.C. McDonald: I could not make out any more of the conversation; there was conversation, but I could not make out what it was.

Mr Cassells: You just did hear this particular remark?

P.C. McDonald: Yes.

Mr Cassells: I am suggesting you never heard that remark used by Bentley, or used by anybody else?

P.C. McDonald: I could not say whether it was Bentley who used it or not.

By The Lord Chief Justice

The Lord Chief Justice: Well, did you hear the word 'Chris' used?

P.C. McDonald: I did.

The Lord Chief Justice: So far as you know, there were three people on the roof?

P.C. McDonald: Yes.

The Lord Chief Justice: There was Sergeant Fairfax and the two men?

P.C. McDonald: Yes.

The Lord Chief Justice: And you heard: 'Let him have it, Chris'; is that right?

P.C. McDonald: That is right, my lord.

The Lord Chief Justice: Very good.

Cross-examination continued

Mr Cassells: Now, after you had heard that remark you heard some shots?

P.C. McDonald: Some little time. I was on the ground before I heard the shots.

Mr Cassells: There was sufficient time between that remark and the first shot for you to have climbed down the drain-pipe and have reached the ground; is that right?

P.C. McDonald: That is right.

Mr Cassells: Did you at any time while you were on the roof either yourself say or hear Sergeant Fairfax say to Bentley, 'What's his name?' ?

P.C. McDonald: No I did not hear that.

Mr Cassells: Did anybody ask Bentley what the name of the other man was?

P.C. McDonald: I cannot recollect anyone asking that.

Re-examined by Mr Bass

Mr Bass: Can you give me some idea as to how long it took you to get down the drain-pipe after you had heard the remark, 'Let him have it, Chris', before you heard the shot?

P.C. McDonald: Not very long.

Mr Bass: Was it minutes or seconds?

P.C. McDonald: Minutes.

By The Lord Chief Justice

The Lord Chief Justice: Minutes?

P.C. McDonald: Well, a minute, my lord.

The Lord Chief Justice: What had you got to do?

P.C. McDonald: I had to find my foothold as I went down; but it was not long.

The Lord Chief Justice: Do you think you could have counted to sixty?

P.C. McDonald: I am not sure that I could.

The Lord Chief Justice: People can always say minutes when they mean seconds in these cases.

Evidence for the Defence, Craig examined

Mr Parris: What was your ambition in life?

Craig: To be a gunsmith.

Mr Parris: Now, when you left school, did you ever take a gun with you to work?

Craig: Yes.

Mr Parris: Once, or more than once?

Craig: I used to take them nearly every day, sir.

Mr Parris: Now, the weapon in this case has the barrel sawn off?

Craig: Yes.

Mr Parris: Why was the barrel sawn off?

Craig: So that I could carry it – take it to work.

Mr Parris: Why did you want to do that?

Craig: It was smaller. You could put it in your pocket.

Mr Parris: Why did you want to take a gun to work?

Craig: It just made me feel big.

Mr Parris: It just made you feel big?

Craig: Yes sir.

Mr Parris: Did people ever say anything to you about not being able to read properly?

Craig: Yes they used to take the mickey out of me.

Mr Parris: What does that mean? Does it mean they used to mock you?

Craig: Yes.

Mr Parris: Taunt you?

Craig: Yes.

Mr Parris: Had that got anything to do with carrying a gun?

Craig: I do not think so.

Mr Parris: Now, because you could not read, did you go to the picutures?

Craig: Yes, a lot sir.

Mr Parris: How often?

Craig: A lot of times; three or four times a week.

Mr Parris: Three or four times a week. What sort of films used you to see?

Craig: Gangster films.

Mr Parris: Did you like that sort?

Craig: Yes.

Mr Parris: Coming to this Sunday. You and Bentley were up on the roof-top?

Craig: Yes.

Mr Parris: For the purpose of trying to get into this sweetshop?

Craig: Yes.

Mr Parris: How long were you up there before any police officer arrived?

Craig: A couple of minutes.

Mr Parris: Where was it that you first saw the officer Fairfax?

Craig: I saw him at the iron gate down below.

Mr Parris: When he got up on the roof, where were you?

Craig: Behind the stack, the lift shaft.

Mr Parris: Just look at the plan. Is that the stack marked 'A' that you refer to?

Craig: Yes.

Mr Parris: Now, I want you to tell us in your own words what happened after that. First, did he come towards you?

Craig: He came from the drain-pipe, one of the drain-pipes by the letter 'B', that stack thing sir, and he came round and grabbed Bentley.

Mr Parris: Where was Bentley when he was grabbed?

Craig: Well, I was on the west side behind the 'A', and Bentley was over the east side, standing in the gutter-way, the gulley.

Mr Parris: When he grabbed Bentley, where did the officer go?

Craig: He took him round behind the thing marked 'B'.

Mr Parris: That is the staircase head?

Craig: Yes.

Mr Parris: Which way did they go?

Craig: I could not be sure, because I was behind, but they went round those glass things.

Mr Parris: You could not be sure because you were behind the stack?

Craig: Yes.

Mr Parris: What was the next thing that the officer Fairfax did?

Craig: He left Bentley, sir, and came back for me.

Mr Parris: Now, the officer has said that some time at that stage of the proceedings Bentley said, 'Let him have it, Chris.' Did you hear any words like that?

Craig: No, sir.

Mr Parris: When was the first shot fired?

Craig: He was level with the first glass thing, had just come round it -

Mr Parris: Do not go too fast. He was level with the first glass thing?

Craig: Yes.

Mr Parris: Which side?

Craig: On the west side.

Mr Parris: That is, on the left *here*, on the west ?

Craig: Yes.

Mr Parris: Was he level with the front end of that roof line or the back end of it?

Craig: He was between the door at the letter 'B' and the glass thing.

Mr Parris: In between the glass and the door?

Craig: Yes.

Mr Parris: Where did you fire the shot?

Craig: Down at the ground.

Mr Parris: Down at the ground?

Craig: Yes; about 6 feet in front, maybe less.

Mr Parris: How far in front of you?

Craig: A few feet in front of me.

Mr Parris: What happened to the officer when you fired that shot?

Craig: He ducked to the ground.

Mr Parris: Did you fire another shot?

Craig: Not then, sir; just a little while later he got up and rushed at Bentley, or something, and I tried to frighten him off and I fired another one over *this* side.

Evidence for the Defence, Bentley examined

Mr Cassells: It is alleged by two of the officers in the car that you said, 'I knew he had got a gun, but I didn't think he would use it'?

Bentley: I did not say that, sir.

Mr Cassells: Did you say that?

Bentley: No.

Mr Cassells: When you got to the police station, and after you had been there for something like six hours, did you make the statement as it is written down?

Bentley: No, sir.

Mr Cassells: Do you know what dictation means?

Bentley: Yes.

Mr Cassells: Did you dictate it?

Bentley: No, sir.

Mr Cassells: How was it taken from you?

Bentley: In questions.

Mr Cassells: Who was asking you questions?

Bentley: These two officers *there* (indicating).

Mr Cassells: And were you answering them as best you could?

Bentley: Yes.

Mr Cassells: I only want to ask you about one matter in the statement. It is recorded in the statement that you said, 'I didn't know he was going to use the gun'?

Bentley: I did not say that, sir.

Mr Cassells: How did that come about?

Bentley: I do not know.

Mr Cassells: Were you asked any questions about the gun?

Bentley: I cannot remember.

Mr Cassells: Now, Bentley, although you knew you were going to try and break into this warehouse, you did not know until the first shot was fired that Craig was armed?

Bentley: No, sir.

By The Lord Chief Justice

The Lord Chief Justice: When did you first know you were going to break into the warehouse – because you have told the jury that you made no arrangement about breaking in, and that all you knew was that Craig got over the gate and you followed him?

Bentley: Yes, that is right sir; that is the first I knew of it.

The Lord Chief Justice: Had you not planned to break in?

Bentley: No, sir.

The Lord Chief Justice: Then why did you follow him?

Bentley: That I cannot answer.

The Lord Chief Justice: You cannot answer it?

Bentley: No, sir.

The Lord Chief Justice: But you intended to break in?

Bentley: When I was over the gate, we were already trespassing then.

Examination continued

Mr Cassells: Did you at any time tell Craig to use the gun or to use violence towards the police?

Bentley: No, sir.

Mr Cassells: Did you yourself at any time use any violence towards any of the police officers?

Bentley: No, sir.

Cross examined by Mr Humphreys

Mr Humphreys: How long did you say you have known Craig?

Bentley: At school, sir.

Mr Humphreys: How long is that?

Bentley: I cannot say for certain.

Mr Humphreys: Months or years?

Bentley: Years.

Mr Humphreys: You know of his love of firearms?

Bentley: No, sir.

Mr Humphreys: What?

Bentley: No, sir.

Mr Humphreys: He has told us he came to school with a gun every time, that he swapped guns, and four or five other boys at school had guns, and so on. You knew nothing about it?

Bentley: I was leaving just as he came, sir.

Mr Humphreys: All the years you have known him you knew nothing about his mania for firearms?

Bentley: I knew nothing, sir.

Mr Humphreys: But you knew this night, before ever a shot was fired, that he had a gun upon him, did you not?

Bentley: No, sir.

Mr Humphreys: Then what he has told the jury is a lie, is it?

Bentley: I think so.

Mr Humphreys: You heard it, did you not?

Bentley: I did, sir.

Mr Humphreys: That is untrue?

Bentley: That is untrue.

Mr Humphreys: And all that the police officers have said about your showing your knowledge of that gun is untrue?

Bentley: All untrue, sir.

Mr Humphreys: As between Craig and all those police officers on the one hand and you on the other, what you are saying is right, and what Craig and the police officers is saying is untrue. Is that right?

Bentley: Craig may have put something in the way of that answer. I do not know. He may have got muddled up.

Mr Humphreys: Well let us see what the police officers say. The police officers say, first, that you said on the roof while you were being detained, 'I told the silly bugger not to use it'?

Bentley: I did not say that, sir.

Mr Humphreys: Just to remind you, that was said after P.C. McDonald had arrived on the roof to assist Sergeant Fairfax, and he and Sergeant Fairfax were discussing the matter, and Sergeant Fairfax says, 'He's got me in the shoulder', and then you butt in and say, 'I told the silly bugger not to use it'?

Bentley: I never said that, sir.

Mr Humphreys: That is quite untrue?

Bentley: That is quite untrue, sir.

Mr Humphreys: Then later on, when McDonald again says to Sergeant Fairfax, 'What sort of gun has he got?', referring to Craig, you again butt in and say, 'He's got a ·45 Colt and plenty of ammunition for it too.'?

Bentley: That is untrue.

Mr Humphreys: You did not say it?

Bentley: No, sir.

Mr Humphreys: But it was true was it not?

Bentley: I do not know.

Mr Humphreys: You knew perfectly well that he had a .45 gun and plenty of ammunition?

Bentley: No, sir.

Verdict and Sentences

The Clerk of the Court: Members of the jury, are you agreed upon your verdict?

The Foreman of the Jury: We are.

The Clerk of the Court: Do you find the prisoner Christopher Craig guilty or not guilty of murder?

The Foreman of the Jury: Guilty.

The Clerk of the Court: Do you find the prisoner Derek William Bentley guilty or not guilty of murder?

The Foreman of the Jury: Guilty, with a recommendation to mercy.

The Clerk of the Court: You find both prisoners guilty, and that is the verdict of you all?

The Foreman of the Jury: It is.

The Clerk of the Court: Christopher Craig you stand convicted of murder, have you anything to say why sentence should not be passed according to law? Derek William Bentley, you stand convicted of murder, have you anything to say why sentence of death should not be passed according to law?

(The prisoners made no answer.)

The Lord Chief Justice:

Derek William Bentley, you are 19 years of age; it is my duty to pass upon you the only sentence which the law can pass for the crime of wilful murder. The sentence of the Court upon you is that you be taken from this place to a lawful prison, and thence to a place of execution, and there you suffer death by hanging, and that your body be buried within the precincts of the prison in which you shall have been last confined before your execution; and may the Lord have mercy upon your soul. Take him down.

Christopher Craig, you are under 19, but in my judgement and evidently in the judgement of the jury you are the more guilty of the two. Your heart was filled with hate, and you murdered a policeman without thought of his wife, his family, or himself; and never once have you expressed a word of sorrow for what you have done. I can only sentence you to be detained until Her Majesty's pleasure be known. I shall tell the Secretary of State when forwarding the recommendation of the jury in Bentley's case that in my opinion you are one of the most dangerous young criminals who has ever stood in that dock.

While the jury were out considering their verdict in this case, I had to deal with another case in which you were concerned with another boy whom you led into it in holding up an elderly couple at the point of revolvers and stealing from them; and it is quite obvious that the people in this country will not be safe if you are out of prison. I shall recommend the time which I suggest to the

Secretary of State that you shall be kept in confinement. The sentence upon you is that you be kept in strict custody until the pleasure of Her Majesty be known. Take him down.

Transcripts from the trial of Craig and Bentley, The Chief Clerk of the Court
The Crown v. Craig and Bentley, Central Criminal Court, Old Bailey, 1952

The Day of Execution

As the day fixed for Bentley's execution drew nearer the fever of excitement mounted. Crowds demonstrated in the streets of London and presented numerous petitions to Cabinet Ministers. Once the crowd tried to break the police barrier outside the home of Mr Anthony Eden. Editors of national newspapers were deluged with a vast flow of indignant letters. But the judicial process was by then at an end. The Home Secretary had made his final decision and could not be deflected by a wave of mob hysteria. The course of justice moved inevitably towards its sordid climax.

Bentley was due to be hanged at Wandsworth Jail at 9.a.m. on Wednesday, 28th January, 1953. At dawn that morning a crowd began to gather outside the main gates of the prison. The first comers were mostly young people – youths draped in jackets and girls in brightly coloured jeans. They huddled together in the cold, whispering and watching the newspaper reporters and the press photographers standing on the other side of the avenue.

As the minutes passed more and more people arrived to stand silently in little groups waiting.

At half-past eight a Post Office despatch rider drew up at the prison gates holding a telegram in his hand. A few people started to cheer, doubtless under the impression that he was carrying an eleventh-hour reprieve. Ten minutes later a Rolls-Royce arrived bringing Mrs Van Der Elst, the ardent campaigner against capital punishment. That was the signal for the crowd, which by then numbered some five hundred people, to begin a noisy demonstration. They surged round Mrs Van Der Elst yelling, cheering and waving.

Mrs Van Der Elst walked up to the prison gates and knocked loudly on the entrance door, shouting: 'This boy is being murdered and two hundred M.P.s could not stop it – I want to see the Governor.'

Others all round her took up the cry: 'Murder.'

Four police constables with arms outstretched moved between the crowd and the prison gates. By this time the shouting was growing in intensity. Some were chanting 'Reprieve Bentley. Reprieve Bentley.'

Then it was nine o'clock.

A man called for silence. Hats were removed and a large group near the main gate started to sing 'Abide with me' and others 'The Lord is my Shepherd.'

A short time later the iron gates could be heard clanging inside the prison. The shouting increased in volume and several men forced their way past the flimsy police barrier and started to hammer on the massive green-painted gates.

Then the gates swung open and a prison officer emerged holding a notice board above his head.

The crowd roared, and as the prison officer attempted to suspend the notice board on the hooks outside the prison gates angry demonstrators fought their way forward, seized the board from his grasp, and dashed it against the door.

Broken glass showered around them and a yelling mob surged into the entrance of the prison. For a moment it seemed as though the police would be carried away by the rush, but then the great gates were slowly forced into position and the key was turned in the lock.

There were more shouts and cries and then the mob began to disperse.

Half an hour later a prison officer was sweeping up the broken glass and the litter from the prison entrance watched by about twenty silent onlookers. The notice board hung crookedly from one hook. The two printed notices, torn and partly obliterated, proclaimed to the public:-

'We the undersigned, hereby declare that judgement of death was this day executed on Derek William Bentley in Her Majesty's Prison of Wandsworth in our presence. The 28th January 1953.'

The lower notice read:

'I (the name which followed was undecipherable owing to broken glass), the surgeon of Her Majesty's Prison of Wandsworth, hereby certify, that I this day examined the body of Derek William Bentley, on whom judgement of death was this day executed in the prison and that on examination I found the said Derek William Bentley was dead.'

Montgomery Hyde
Trial of Craig and Bentley, 1954

The People's Charter
A Petition to Parliament
1942

To the Honourable the Commons of Great Britain and Ireland, in Parliament assembled

The Petition of the undersigned people of the United Kingdom, Showeth That Government originated from, was designed to protect the freedom and promote the happiness of, and ought to be responsible to, the whole people...

That the only authority on which any body of men can make laws and govern society, is delegation from the people.

That as Government was designed for the benefit and protection of, and must be obeyed and supported by all, therefore all should be equally represented...

That your honourable House, as at present constituted, has not been elected by, and acts irresponsibly of, the people; and hitherto has only represented parties, and benefitted the few, regardless of the miseries, grievances, and petitions of the many. Your honourable House has enacted laws contrary to the expressed wishes of the people, and by unconstitutional means enforced obedience to them, thereby creating an unbeatable despotism on the one hand, and degrading slavery on the other...

That your petitioners instance, in proof of their assertion, that your honourable House has not been elected by the people; that the population of Great Britain and Ireland is at the present time about twenty six millions of persons; and that yet, out of this number, little more than nine hundred thousand have been permitted to vote in the recent election of representatives to make laws to govern the whole.

That the existing state of representation is not only extremely limited and unjust, but unequally divided, and gives preponderating influence to the landed and monied interests to the utter ruin of small-trading and labouring classes.

That the borough of Guildford, with a population of 3,920 returns to Parliament as many members as the Tower Hamlets, with a population of 300,000; Evesham, with a population of 3,998 elects as many representatives as Manchester, with a population of 200,000 ...

That bribery, intimidation, corruption, perjury and riot, prevail at all parliamentary elections, to an extent best understood by the Members of your honourable House.

That your petitioners complain that they are enormously taxed to pay the interest of what is termed the national debt, a debt amounting at present to £800,000,000, being only a portion of the enormous amount expended in cruel and expensive wars for the suppression of all liberty, by men not authorised by the people, and who, consequently, had no right to tax posterity for the outrages committed by them upon mankind. And your petitioners loudly complain of the augmentation of that debt, after twenty-six years of almost uninterrupted peace, and whilst poverty and discontent rage over the land.

That taxation, both general and local, is at this time too enormous to be borne; and in the opinion of your petitioners is contrary to the spirit of the Bill of Rights, wherein it is clearly expressed that no subject shall be compelled to contribute to any tax, tallage, or aid, unless imposed by common consent in Parliament.

That in England, Ireland, Scotland, and Wales thousands of people are dying from actual want; and your petitioners, whilst sensible that poverty is the great exciting cause of crime, view with mingled astonishment and alarm the ill provision made for the poor, the aged, and infirm; and likewise perceive, with feelings of indignation, the determination of your honourable House to continue the Poor-law Bill in operation, notwithstanding the many proofs which have been afforded by sad experience of the unconstitutional principle of that bill, of its unchristian character, and of the cruel and murderous effects produced upon the wages of working men, and the lives of the subjects of this realm.

That your petitioners conceive that bill to be contrary to all previous statutes, opposed to the spirit of the constitution, and an actual violation of the precepts of the Christian religion; and, therefore, your petitioners look with apprehension to the results which may flow from its continuance.

That your petitioners would direct the attention of your honourable House to the great disparity existing between the wages of the producing millions, and the salaries of those whose comparative usefulness ought to be questioned, where riches and luxury prevail amongst the rulers, and poverty and starvation amongst the ruled.

That your petitioners, with all due respect and loyalty, would compare the daily income of the Sovereign Majesty with that of thousands of the working men of this nation; and whilst your petitioners have learned that her Majesty receives daily for her private use the sum of £164 17*s*. 10*d*., they have also ascertained that many thousands of the families of the labourers are only in the receipt of 33/4*d*. per head per day ...

That notwithstanding the wretched and unparalleled condition of the people, your honourable House has manifested no disposition to curtail the expenses of the State, to diminish taxation, or promote general prosperity.

That unless immediate remedial measures be adopted, your petitioners fear the increasing distress of the people will lead to results fearful to contemplate; because your petitioners can produce evidence of the gradual decline of wages, at the same time that the constant increase of the national burdens must be apparent to all.

That your petitioners know that it is the undoubted constitutional right of the people, to meet freely, when, how and where they choose, in public places, peaceably, in the day, to discuss their grievances, and political or other subjects, or for the purpose of framing, discussing, or passing any vote, petition, or remonstrance upon any subject whatsoever.

That your petitioners complain that the right has unconstitutionally been infringed; and five hundred well-disposed persons have been arrested, excessive bail demanded, tried by packed juries, sentenced to imprisonment, and treated as felons of the worst description.

That an unconstitutional police force is distributed all over the country, at enormous cost, to prevent the due exercise of the people's rights. And your petitioners are of opinion that the Poor-law Bastiles and the police stations, being co-existent, have originated from the same curse, viz. the increased desire on the part of the irresponsible few to oppress and starve the many.

That a vast and unconstitutional army is upheld at the public expense, for the purpose of repressing public opinion in the three kingdoms, and likewise to intimidate the millions in the due exercise of those rights and privileges which ought to belong to them.

That your petitioners complain that the hours of labour, particularly of the factory workers, are protracted beyond the limits of human endurance, and that the wages earned, after unnatural application to toil in heated and unhealthy workshops, are inadequate to sustain the bodily strength, and supply those comforts which are so imperative after an excessive waste of physical energy.

That your petitioners also direct the attention of your honourable House to the starvation wages of the agricultural labourer, and view with horror and indignation the paltry income of those whose toil gives being to the staple food of this people.

That your petitioners deeply deplore the existence of any kind of monopoly in this nation, and whilst they unequivocally condemn the levying of any tax upon the necessaries of life, and upon those articles principally required by the labouring classes, they are also sensible that the abolition of any one monopoly will never unshackle labour from its misery until the people possess that power under which all monopoly and oppression must cease; and your petitioners respectfully mention the existing monopolies of the suffrage, of paper money, of machinery, of land, of the public press, of religious privileges, of the means of travelling and transit, and of a host of other evils too numerous to mention, all arising from class legislation, but which your honourable House has always consistently endeavoured to increase instead of diminish.

That your petitioners are sensible, from the numerous petitions presented to your honourable House, that your honourable House is fully acquainted with the grievances of the working men; and your petitioners pray that the rights and wrongs of labour may be considered, with a view to the protection of the one, and to the removal of the other; because your petitioners are of opinion that it is the worst species of legislation which leaves the grievances of society to be removed only by violence or revolution, both of which may be apprehended if complaints are unattended to and petitions despised.

That your petitioners complain that upwards of nine millions of pounds per annum are unjustly abstracted from them to maintain a church establishment, from which they principally dissent ... Your petitioners complain that it is unjust, and not in accordance with the Christian religion, to enforce compulsory support of religious creeds, and expensive church establishments, with which the people do not agree.

That your petitioners believe all men have a right to worship God as may appear best to their consciences, and that no legislative enactments should interfere between man and his Creator.

That your petitioners direct the attention of your honourable House to the enormous revenue annually swallowed up by the bishops and the clergy, and entreat you to contrast their deeds with the conduct of the founder of the Christian religion, who denounced worshippers of Mammon, and taught charity, meekness, and brotherly love ...

That your petitioners maintain that it is the inherent, indubitable and constitutional right, founded upon the ancient practice of the realm of England, and supported by well approved statutes, of every male inhabitant of the United Kingdom, he being of age and of sound mind, nonconvict of crime, and not confined under any judicial process, to exercise the elective franchise in the choice of Members to serve in the Commons House of Parliament.

That your petitioners can prove, that by the ancient customs and statutes of this realm, Parliament should be held once in each year.

That your petitioners maintain that Members elected to serve in Parliament ought to be the servants of the people, and should, at short and stated intervals, return to their constituencies, to ascertain if their conduct is approved of, and to give the people power to reject all who have not acted honestly and justly.

That your petitioners complain that possession of property is made the test of men's qualification to sit in Parliament.

That your petitioners can give proof that such qualification is irrational, unnecessary and not in accordance with the ancient usages of England.

That your petitioners complain, that by influence, patronage and intimidation, there is at present no purity of election; and your petitioners contend for the right of voting by ballot.

That your petitioners complain that seats in your honourable House are sought for at a most extravagant rate of expense; which proves an enormous degree of fraud and corruption.

That your petitioners, therefore, contend, that to put an end to secret political traffic, all representatives should be paid a limited amount for their services.

That your petitioners complain of the many grievances borne by the people of Ireland, and contend that they are fully entitled to a repeal of the legislative union.

That your petitioners have viewed with great indignation the partiality shown to the aristocracy in the courts of justice, and the cruelty of that system of law which deprived Frost, Williams and Jones of the benefit of their objections offered by Sir Frederick Pollock during the trial at Monmouth, and which was approved of by a large majority of the judges.

That your petitioners beg to assure your honourable House that they cannot, within the limits of this their petition, set forth even a tithe of the many grievances of which they may justly complain; but should your honourable House be pleased to grant your petitioners a hearing by representatives at the Bar of your honourable House, your petitioners will be enabled to unfold a tale of wrong and suffering – of intolerable injustice – which will create utter astonishment in the minds of all benevolent and good men, that the people of Great Britain and Ireland have so long quietly endured their wretched condition, brought upon them as it has been by unjust exclusion from political authority, and by the manifold corruption of class-legislation.

That your petitioners, therefore, exercising their just constitutional right, demand that your honourable House do remedy the many gross and manifest evils of which your petitioners complain, do immediately, without alteration, deduction, or addition, pass into a law the document entitled 'The People's Charter' ...

And that your petitioners, desiring to promote the peace of the United Kingdom, security of property, and prosperity of commerce, seriously and earnestly press this, their petition, on the attention of your honourable House.

(And your petitioners, etc.)

The Chartist Petition, 3 May 1842

Criminal Justice and Public Order Act 1994

Powers in relation to raves

Section 63 – Powers to remove persons attending or preparing for a rave

(1) This section applies to a gathering on land in the open air of 100 or more persons (whether or not trespassers) at which amplified music is played during the night (with or without intermissions) and is such as, by reason of its loudness and duration and the time at which it is played, is likely to cause serious distress to the inhabitants of the locality; and for this purpose—

   (a) such a gathering continues during intermissions in the music and, where the gathering extends over several days, throughout the period during which amplified music is played at night (with or without intermissions); and

   (b) 'music' includes sounds wholly or predominantly characterised by the emission of a succession of repetitive beats.

(2) If, as respects any land in the open air, a police officer of at least the rank of superintendent reasonably believes that—

   (a) two or more persons are making preparations for the holding there of a gathering to which this section applies,

   (b) ten or more persons are waiting for such a gathering to begin there, or

   (c) ten or more persons are attending such a gathering which is in progress, he may give a direction that those persons and any other persons who come to prepare or wait for or to attend the gathering are to leave the land and remove any vehicles or other property which they have with them on the land.

(3) A direction under subsection (2) above, if not communicated to the persons referred to in subsection (2) by the police officer giving the direction, may be communicated to them by any constable at the scene.

(4) Persons shall be treated as having had a direction under subsection (2) above communicated to them if reasonable steps have been taken to bring it to their attention.

(5) A direction under subsection (2) above does not apply to an exempt person.

(6) If a person knowing that a direction has been given which applies to him—

(a) fails to leave the land as soon as reasonably practicable, or

(b) having left again enters the land within the period of 7 days beginningwith the day on which the direction was given,

he commits an offence and is liable on summary conviction to imprisonment for a term not exceeding three months or a fine not exceeding level 4 on the standard scale, or both.

(7) In proceedings for an offence under this section it is a defence for the accused to show that he had a reasonable excuse for failing to leave the land as soon as reasonably practicable or, as the case may be, for again entering the land.

(8) A constable in uniform who reasonably suspects that a person is committing an offence under this section may arrest him without a warrant.

(9) This section does not apply

(a) in England and Wales, to a gathering licensed by an entertainment licence; or

(b) in Scotland, to a gathering in premises which, by virtue of section 41 of the Civic Government (Scotland) Act 1982, are licensed to be used as a place of public entertainment.

(10) In this section—

'entertainment licence' means a licence granted by a local authority under—

(a) Schedule 12 to the London Government Act 1963;

(b) section 3 of the Private Places of Entertainment (Licensing) Act 1967; or

(c) Schedule 1 to the Local Government (Miscellaneous Provisions) Act 1982;

'exempt person', in relation to land (or any gathering on land), means the occupier, any member of his family and any employee or agent of his and any person whose home is situated on the land;

'land in the open air' includes a place partly open to the air;

'local authority' means—

(a) in Greater London, a London borough council or the Common Council of the City of London;

(b) in England outside Greater London, a district council or the council of the Isles of Scilly;

(c) in Wales, a county council or county borough council; and 'occupier', 'trespasser' and 'vehicle' have the same meaning as in section 61.

(11) Until 1st April 1996, in this section 'local authority' means, in Wales, a district council.

Section 64 – Supplementary powers of entry and seizure

(1) If a police officer of at least the rank of superintendent reasonably believes that circumstances exist in relation to any land which would justify the giving of a direction under section 63 in relation to a gathering to which that section applies he may authorise any constable to enter the land for any of the purposes specified in subsection (2) below.

(2) Those purposes are—

(a) to ascertain whether such circumstances exist; and

(b) to exercise any power conferred on a constable by section 63 or subsection (4) below.

(3) A constable who is so authorised to enter land for any purpose may enter the land without a warrant.

(4) If a direction has been given under section 63 and a constable reasonably suspects that any person to whom the direction applies has, without reasonable excuse—

(a) failed to remove any vehicle or sound equipment on the land which appears to the constable to belong to him or to be in his possession or under his control; or

(b) entered the land as a trespasser with a vehicle or sound equipment within the period of 7 days beginning with the day on which the direction was given,

the constable may seize and remove that vehicle or sound equipment.

(5) Subsection (4) above does not authorise the seizure of any vehicle or sound equipment of an exempt person.

(6) In this section—

'exempt person' has the same meaning as in section 63; 'sound equipment' means equipment designed or adapted for amplifying music and any equipment suitable for use in connection with such equipment, and 'music' has the same meaning as in section 63; and

'vehicle' has the same meaning as in section 61.

Section 65 – Raves: power to stop persons from proceeding.

(1) If a constable in uniform reasonably believes that a person is on his way to a gathering to which section 63 applies in relation to which a direction under section 63(2) is in force, he may, subject to subsections (2) and (3) below—

(a) stop that person, and

(b) direct him not to proceed in the direction of the gathering.

(2) The power conferred by subsection (1) above may only be exercised at a place within 5 miles of the boundary of the site of the gathering.

(3) No direction may be given under subsection (1) above to an exempt person.

(4) If a person knowing that a direction under subsection (1) above has been given to him fails to comply with that direction, he commits an offence and is liable on summary conviction to a fine not exceeding level 3 on the standard scale.

(5) A constable in uniform who reasonably suspects that a person is committing an offence under this section may arrest him without a warrant.

(6) In this section, 'exempt person' has the same meaning as in section 63.

Section 66 – Power of court to forfeit sound equipment

(1) Where a person is convicted of an offence under section 63 in relation to a gathering to which that section applies and the court is satisfied that any sound equipment which has been seized from him under section 64(4), or which was in his possession or under his control at the relevant time, has been used at the gathering the court may make an order for forfeiture under this subsection in respect of that property.

(2) The court may make an order under subsection (1) above whether or not it also deals with the offender in respect of the offence in any other way and without regard to any restrictions on forfeiture in any enactment.

(3) In considering whether to make an order under subsection (1) above in respect of any property a court shall have regard—

(a) to the value of the property; and

(b) to the likely financial and other effects on the offender of the making of the order (taken together with any other order that the court contemplates making).

(4) An order under subsection (1) above shall operate to deprive the offender of his rights, if any, in the property to which it relates, and the property shall (if not already in their possession) be taken into the possession of the police.

(5) Except in a case to which subsection (6) below applies, where any property has been forfeited under subsection (1) above, a magistrates' court may, on application by a claimant of the property, other than the offender from whom it was forfeited under subsection (1) above, make an order for delivery of the property to the applicant if it appears to the court that he is the owner of the property.

(6) In a case where forfeiture under subsection (1) above has been by order of a Scottish court, a claimant such as is mentioned in subsection (5) above may, in such manner as may be prescribed by act of adjournal, apply to that court for an order for the return of the property in question.

(7) No application shall be made under subsection (5), or by virtue of subsection (6) above by any claimant of the property after the expiration of 6

months from the date on which an order under subsection (1) above was made in respect of the property.

(8) No such application shall succeed unless the claimant satisfies the court either that he had not consented to the offender having possession of the property or that he did not know, and had no reason to suspect, that the property was likely to be used at a gathering to which section 63 applies.

(9) An order under subsection (5), or by virtue of subsection (6) above shall not affect the right of any person to take, within the period of 6 months from the date of an order under subsection (5), or as the case may be by virtue of subsection (6) above, proceedings for the recovery of the property from the person in possession of it in pursuance of the order, but on the expiration of that period the right shall cease.

(10) The Secretary of State may make regulations for the disposal of property, and for the application of the proceeds of sale of property, forfeited under subsection (1) above where no application by a claimant of the property under subsection (5), or by virtue of subsection (6) above has been made within the period specified in subsection (7) above or no such application has succeeded.

(11) The regulations may also provide for the investment of money and for the audit of accounts.

(12) The power to make regulations under subsection (10) above shall be exercisable by statutory instrument which shall be subject to annulment in pursuance of a resolution of either House of Parliament.

(13) In this section—

'relevant time', in relation to a person—

(a) convicted in England and Wales of an offence under section 63, means the time of his arrest for the offence or of the issue of a summons in respect of it;

(b) so convicted in Scotland, means the time of his arrest for, or of his being cited as an accused in respect of, the offence;

'sound equipment' has the same meaning as in section 64.

Criminal Justice and Public Order Act 1994

Political and Legal Documents Activities

The Trial of Craig and Bentley

1. Capital punishment – for or against?
● Before reading the text, in small groups talk about the statements below. Spend about three minutes on each talking through one another's views.

A.
> Capital punishment should be used only in particularly vicious murder cases

B.
> Capital punishment does not act as a deterrent as crime levels in the USA demonstrate

C.
> Capital punishment is a way of solving the problem of over-crowded prisons

D.
> The power of life and death over a citizen should not be handed to any government

E.
> Capital punishment makes the executioner no better than the killer

F.
> Capital punishment should never be allowed because of the risk of executing an innocent person

G.
> Ordinary people need capital punishment to satisfy their desire for revenge against murderers

Three areas of the classroom should be labelled with Agree, Don't Know and Disagree signs.

● Your teacher will read out a few of the statements one at a time. Each time you should go and stand in the part of the room that best reflects your views on that statement.

● Next listen to and respond to some arguments from different parts of the room. If at any point you feel you have been persuaded to change your position, move to another part of the room.

2. Opening speech for the prosecution – 'Let him have it, Chris.'

You are going to put yourselves in the position of jurors at the trial. You will each need a copy of the plan and a notebook and pen.

● Listen while your teacher reads aloud the beginning of the opening speech for the Prosecution. S/he will stop at the phrase 'Let him have it, Chris' on Page 178.

● In pairs, spend three or four minutes repeating the words 'Let him have it, Chris' out loud. How many different interpretations can you come up with? Share your ideas and discuss what Derek Bentley could have meant when he said these words.

3. Weighing up the evidence

● Listen to the rest of the speech for the Prosecution making a note as you do so of any points that seem important and any questions you want answered. Feedback initial responses in groups.

Mr Humphrey's job is to try to convict Craig and Bentley of the charge of murder. But his opening speech is not evidence, that comes later when witnesses and the accused are examined. What then is his opening speech trying to do and how?

● In pairs find phrases from the speech to illustrate each of the statements below.

Craig deliberately fired at a police officer

Bentley encouraged Craig to fire his gun

The police were courageous

When Bentley went with Craig that night he knew Craig had a gun

The spoken word carries great importance in a trial

Bentley is stupid and unreliable

Craig hated the police

4. Evidence for the prosecution: P. C. McDonald examined

Five people should prepare a reading of this extract and perform it for the rest of the class.

● When you have watched and listened to this extract, study the transcript in small groups and make a note of anything important that was revealed. Try completing the following sentences to help you focus on the language used:

It is obvious that the Lord Chief Justice is on the side of the police when he...

Mr Parris, Craig's Defence lawyer, makes P.C. McDonald seem uncertain of the facts when he says...

Mr Cassells, Bentley's Defence lawyer suggests that it is surprising P.C. McDonald could have heard the words 'Let him have it, Chris' when he says...

Mr Cassells, Bentley's Defence lawyer makes it clear a police officer can sometimes be wrong when he says...

Mr Cassells is trying to suggest that a police officer said 'Let him have it, Chris' when he says...

Mr Cassells is trying to destroy the Prosecution's case that 'Let him have it, Chris' was Bentley's incitement to Craig to fire when he shows that...

● Be ready to share your ideas and observations in a whole class feedback.

5. Evidence for the defence – Craig examined

● In small groups read the transcript of this extract from the trial and annotate it to show the impression of Craig that his lawyer intends to give the jury. To help you get started try looking for points in the examination when Craig is being portrayed as:

Someone to be pitied
Still a child
Intending to frighten the police officers not murder them
A wayward youth out of his depth

6. Evidence for the defence – Bentley examined

Four people should prepare a reading of this extract from the trial and then present it to the rest of the class.
● In small groups, talk about your first reactions to Bentley's examination at this point in the trial. List three important points or observations to report back to the rest of the class. Consider the following:

The answers he gives
The sorts of questions asked
His performance compared to Craig
The intentions and attitudes of the questioners

● In pairs, your teacher will assign you one of the roles and imaginary situations listed below. Improvise a short conversation that takes place in private immediately after this point in the trial.

Mr Cassells and Mr Parris
The Lord Chief Justice debates with himself
Mr Humphreys talks to Mr Cass (also acting for the Prosecution)
Bentley talks to his mother

7. Verdict and sentences

● In small groups read aloud the verdict and sentences and talk about whether you feel that justice has been done. Are there areas of uncertainty in the case which would leave you feeling uncomfortable about carrying out the sentence?

Some of the considerations a Home Secretary must weigh up when considering the prerogative of mercy:

The motive
The degree of premeditation or deliberation
The amount of provocation
The state of mind of the prisoner
His physical condition
His character, background and history
The recommendation or absence of recommendation from the jury

● In small groups discuss each of the above in relation to Bentley. Draw up a list of points in Bentley's favour which should ensure the Home Secretary uses the prerogative of mercy and Bentley avoids the death penalty.
● Imagine that you are Bentley's mother or father. Have a look at his sister Iris' letter and write another letter of appeal to the Home Secretary.

Sir David Maxwell Patrick Fyfe

I plead with you as Derek Bentley's sister to reconsider your decision. If you could have been able to see Derek yesterday I am sure those words he said to my Mother 'I am not afraid to die because I am innocent – Mum' would have moved you as they did us. I ask are these the words of a boy who has a life in his conscience.
Please I beseech you save my brother's life – time is short but we are hopeful.

Miss Iris Bentley

8. Final Assignments

Read the description of 'The Day of Execution' and use it to help you with one of the following assignments:

Journal
● Read 'The Day of Execution' on Page 196 and write the journal or diary of one of the crowd at the prison gates that morning.

Talk Radio
● Write the script of two callers to Talk Radio giving opposing views on the death penalty.

Press report
● Read 'The Day of Execution' on Page 196 and write a press report describing the scene outside the prison gates that morning. Decide first whether the paper you work for is for or against hanging and slant your write-up of the events of that morning to satisfy your editor and readers.

Speech for the defence
● Imagine that you are Bentley's defence lawyer. Prepare part of your final speech on his behalf and present it to others in the group.

Video Nation
● Prepare and record a 60 second piece to camera for inclusion in BBC2's *Video Nation* programme where ordinary people get to appear on televsion speaking on issues about which they feel strongly.

Song, poem or rap
Elvis Costello has recorded a song 'Let Him Dangle' in which his anger and disgust about this case is powerfully conveyed. Write your feelings and views on any aspect of this case in the form of a song, poem or rap.

Summary of people and events

1933 Derek Bentley born.

1936 Christopher Craig born.

1952

November 2 Craig and Bentley break into warehouse in Croydon.
Craig shoots P.C. Miles dead.
Craig and Bentley arrested.

December 9 Trial of Craig and Bentley opens at Central Criminal Court beforeLord Goddard, Lord Chief Justice of England.

December 11 Conclusion of trial. Both prisoners found guilty. Craig sentenced to be detained during her Majesty's pleasure. Bentley sentenced to death.

1953

January 13 Bentley appeals to Court of Criminal Appeal. Appeal dismissed.

January 26 Home Secretary (Sir David Maxwell Fyfe) announces that he is unable to recommend that Bentley should be reprieved.
Mr Paget Q.C., M.P. said in the House of Commons:
'A three-quarter witted boy is to be hung for a murder he did not commit, which was committed fifteen minutes after he was arrested. Can we be made to keep silent when a thing as horrible and as shocking as this is to happen?'

January 27 A Motion was placed upon the Order Paper in the House of Commons signed by 200 Members:
'That this House respectfully dissents from the opinion of the Home Secretary, that there are not sufficient grounds on which to advise the exercise of Her Majesty's mercy in the case of Derek Bentley and urges him to reconsider the matter so as to give effect to the jury's recommendation and to the expressed view of the Lord Chief Justice that Bentley's guilt was less than that of Christopher Craig.'
The Speaker ruled that the House might discuss the execution of Derek Bentley after he had been hung but not before.

January 28 Bentley executed in Wandsworth Prison. Iris Bentley begins the campaign to have his name cleared.

1993

July The Home Secretary Michael Howard issued the following statement: '19 year old epileptic Derek Bentley should not have been hanged'. A full pardon was refused.

1995 Iris Bentley given permission to provide Derek's grave at Croydon Crematorium with a headstone. On it is inscribed: 'Derek Bentley, Victim of British Justice'.

June Iris Bentley's campaign for a full pardon for her brother continues.

The trial was held in the Central Criminal Court, Old Bailey, London in December 1952

Judge: The Lord Chief Justice of England, The Right Honourable Lord Goddard.

Prosecuting Lawyers: Mr Christmas Humphreys and Mr Bass.

Craig's Defence Lawyer: Mr Parris.

Bentley's Defence Lawyer: Mr Cassells.

The People's Charter
A Petition to Parliament 1842

1. Preparing to read it aloud
Distribute sections of the petition around the class. In pairs you are going to prepare and then read aloud one or two sections from this document which was delivered to the House of Commons 150 years ago.
- Look closely at your section(s) and talk about what they mean. Individually, write a one sentence summary of each section in everyday English.
- Read them to each other and agree on one which sums up that section the best.
- Think about changes in tone and pace during different parts of the reading.
- Practise reading each section in a way which best suits the content and the method of persuasion being used. This might be:

fast, slow, angry, subservient, mocking, pleading, outraged, disbelieving, calm, wild, quiet, very loud...etc.

2. Performing the petition
You are going to read your section aloud as part of a whole class reading of the petition.
- As a whole class talk about how you should perform this reading. You could have everyone standing up to begin with and then sitting down once they've read their bit. Once seated, they could assume the role of MPs listening to the speech and make MP-like comments in response to what they are listening to.

3. What does the petition tell us?
- In sixes or eights, hear each pair's summary. Look through the whole document and talk about your reactions to the petition. Think about:

What you have learned of the lives of the people who signed this petition
What picture of Britain 150 years ago it gives you

- Agree a list of the three most important or interesting points about life in the UK in the 1840s that the petition brings to your attention. Report back to the rest of the class.

4. Them and us
This was the second petition from the Chartist campaigners and it was rejected by the House. Read the press extract, 'Destitution and Defiance in Northern Lancashire' on Page 216. Lord Macaulay saw the campaigners as a serious threat. Commenting on the petition you have just read he said it was:
'an attack on property and thus utterly incompatible with the very existence of civilization.'

Destitution and Defiance in North Lancashire

... Mr Beesley then detailed the alarming destitution and misery which prevailed in North Lancashire. They were compelled to lie on shavings; they had no covering for the night save the rags which they wore during the day, and were compelled to have their shirts washed on a Saturday night to appear decent on Sunday; and were destitute of food during a considerable portion of the week. In some places the authorities had done all that laid in their power to put Chartism down; they had threatened to stop the relief of all who were Chartists; one individual who was in the receipt of 3s. 6d. per week from the authorities, was informed by them that they had heard he had subscribed to the Chartist fund; if he continued this they would give him no more relief; but he boldly told them that he would support the Charter until they had gained their rights as Englishmen, and if they stopped his relief, they should take him and wife and five children into the workhouse. This showed the determined spirit evinced by the men of North Lancashire.

Anonymous
Report in the *Northern Star,* 23rd April, 1842

Role plays
The class will be divided in two. Half of you are going to be MPs and the other half are going to be campaigners.
● In your role groups, spend ten minutes brainstorming onto paper the following:

Your reactions to this petition and the response to it by parliament
Your views of the other role group in the room
The things that are most important to you in your life
The things that you fear the most
Three questions about the petition that you would like the other group to answer

● As a whole class, use the list of questions from each group to role play a 'Questions and Answers' session between the campaigners and the MPs.
Choose one of the following situations to explore their differences further. You could then write the role play up as a script.
● In threes or fours work out a short scene in which either an MP or a campaigner returns home and tells their family about what has happened.
● In fives or sixes, imagine that you are either a small group of campaigners or a small group of MPs talking about the petition and its reception in the House. It is later that day, in the alehouse.
● An MP and a campaigner meet on the street outside. Devise a short scene to show what happens and what they say to each other.

5. Your own petition or charter
● In small groups, prepare and later read aloud, your own petition on a subject that is important to you. Use the same structure as the document you have been reading (i.e. it takes the form of a series of complaints, it begins very formally – 'We the undersigned' etc.) but use today's language and issues. Here are some ideas:

The rights of animals
The rights of young people
The rights of girls and young women
The rights of boys and young men
The rights of black people people in Britain

Criminal Justice and Public Order Act 1994

Section 63 – 66 Powers in relation to raves

1. Before reading – Who said this?
● Read the following quotes and discuss who might have said them.

> ❝'music' includes sounds wholly or predominantly characterised by the emission of a succession of repetitive beats.❞

a) A visitor from another planet
b) An anthropologist studying a little known tribe
c) The National Curriculum document
d) Any other ideas?

> ❝two or more persons are making preparations for the holding there of a gathering❞

a) A character in a religious story
b) The voice-over on a television documentary about rituals
c) Lenny from *Of Mice and Men*
d) Any other ideas?

2. Skim reading
Everyone in the class will be given one of the following references:
section 63, 64, 65 or 66.
● When your teacher says so, your task is to turn to your section as quickly as you can and skim-read for 30 seconds only.
● Get into groups with other readers of your section and spend 10 minutes brainstorming onto paper everything about it that you managed to grasp.
● Hear all the groups report back on their findings.

3. Raves and ravers
● Decide which of the following could be defined as a rave. Back up your answers with detailed reference to *The Criminal Justice and Public Order Act 1994*.

A summer wedding party held in the grounds of a pub with a marquee
A dinner dance on the deck of a luxury cruise liner

Dancing in Trafalgar Square on New Year's Eve
A Greenham Common Peace Camp Commemorative Weekend Concert
Pavarotti in the Park
A queue of people at a bus stop outside a night club

4. Closer reading
● Return to the text to help you prepare for one of the following improvised scenes in which you argue through the legal details of 'Powers in relation to raves'.

Police Constable Plod is in a cow field at 6am attempting to arrest several people whom he reasonably believes are attending a rave. Police Constable Plod has however, unaccountably lost his helmet. The group of people who are in the field have a sound deck, tapes and vinyls, a generator but have lost the speakers. It so happens that one of the group has studied the *Criminal Justice and Public Order Act 1994*, especially Part V, 'Powers in relation to raves'.

Zak Grunge is on a boat moored off Margate with several friends. He has a large cassette player and tapes. It is 11pm and he is keen to hold a party. The police are seen making their way over the boat. His friends panic but Zak tries to explain to them that they are within their rights.

Sir Crispin Peckitt is in a police car having been removed for attending a rave. Several hundred other elderly men and women have also been arrested. He is outraged and exclaims that the VE Day Celebrations in Hyde Park can in no way be defined as a rave. Newly promoted Superintendent Norbert No-nothing does not agree and proceeds to explain to him the letter of the law.

5. Legal definitions
What does the language used in the Act's definitions reveal about the intentions and attitudes behind the Act?
● Compare these two definitions of music. The first is from The Criminal Justice Act and the second is from a dictionary. Talk about their differences and the possible reasons for them.

❛'music' includes sounds wholly or predominantly characterised by the emission of a succession of repetitive beats❜

❛an art form consisting of sequences of sound in time, especially tones of definite pitch organized melodically, harmonically, rhythmically and according to tone colour; an art form characteristic of a particular people, culture or tradition; any sequence of sounds perceived as pleasing or harmonious❜

Here is the Act's definition of sound equipment:

> ' 'sound equipment' means equipment designed or adapted for amplifying music and any equipment suitable for use in connection with such equipment '

● Try writing definitions of the following, imitating the style and language used in the document:

A kiss
A conversation
A book
Crossing the road

6. The language
● Talk about the language used to write this document. Discuss whether you agree or disagree with the following suggestions. Adding a few of your own may help you get started. Legalistic language is:
impersonal
precise
vague
abnormal
old fashioned
formal
off-putting
clever
interesting

How to Write a Letter

We shy persons need to write a letter now and then, or else we'll dry up and blow away. It's true. And I speak as one who loves to reach for the phone, dial the number, and talk. I say, 'Big Bopper here – what's shakin', babes?' The telephone is to shyness what Hawaii is to February, it's a way out of the woods, *and yet:* a letter is better.

Such a sweet gift – a piece of handmade writing, in an envelope that is not a bill, sitting in our friend's path when she trudges home from a long day spent among wahoos and savages, a day our words will help repair. They don't need to be immortal, just sincere. She can read them twice and again tomorrow: *You're someone I care about, Corinne, and think of often and every time I do you make me smile.*

We need to write, otherwise nobody will know who we are. They will have only a vague impression of us as A Nice Person, because, frankly, we don't shine at conversation, we lack the confidence to thrust our faces forward and say, 'Hi, I'm Heather Hooten; let me tell you about my week. 'Mostly we say 'Uh-huh' and 'Oh, really.' People smile and look over our shoulder, looking for someone else to meet.

So a shy person sits down and writes a letter. To be known by another person – to meet and talk freely on the page – to be close despite distance. To escape from anonymity and be our own sweet selves and express the music of our souls.

Same thing that moves a giant rock star to sing his heart out in front of 123,000 people moves us to take ballpoint in hand and write a few lines to our dear Aunt Eleanor. *We want to be known.* We want her to know that we have fallen in love, that we quit our job, that we're moving to New York, and we want to say a few things that might not get said in casual conversation: *Thank you for what you've meant to me, I am very happy right now.*

The first step in writing letters is to get over the guilt of *not* writing. You don't 'owe' anybody a letter. Letters are a gift. The burning shame you feel when you see unanswered mail makes it harder to pick up a pen and makes for a cheerless letter when you finally do. *I feel bad about not writing, but I've been so busy,* etc. Skip this. Few letters are obligatory, and they are *Thanks for the wonderful gift* and *I am terribly sorry to hear about George's death* and *Yes, you're welcome to stay with us next month,* and not many more than that. Write those promptly if you want to keep your friends. Don't worry about the others, except love letters, of course. When your true love writes, *Dear Light of My Life, Joy of My Heart, O Lovely Pulsating Core of My Sensate Life,* some response is called for.

Some of the best letters are tossed off in a burst of inspiration, so keep your writing stuff in one place where you can sit down for a few minutes and *(Dear Roy, I am in the middle of a book entitled* We Are Still Married *but thought I'd drop you a line. Hi to your sweetie, too.)* dash off a note to a pal. Envelopes, stamps, address book, everything in a drawer so you can write fast when the pen is hot.

A blank white eight-by-eleven sheet can look as big as Montana if the pen's not so hot – try a smaller page and write boldly. Or use a note card with a piece of fine art on the front; if your letter ain't good, at least they get the Matisse. Get a pen that makes a sensuous line, get a comfortable typewriter, a friendly word processor – whichever feels easy to the hand.

Sit for a few minutes with the blank sheet in front of you, and meditate on the person you will write to, let your friend come to mind until you can almost see her or him in the room with you. Remember the last time you saw each other and how your friend looked and what you said and what perhaps was unsaid between you, and when your friend becomes real to you, start to write.

Write the salutation – *Dear* You – and take a deep breath and plunge in. A simple declarative sentence will do, followed by another and another and another. Tell us what you're doing and tell it like you were talking to us. Don't think about grammar, don't think about lit'ry style, don't try to write dramatically, just give us your news. Where did you go, who did you see, what did they say, what do you think?

If you don't know where to begin, start with the present moment: *I'm sitting at the kitchen table on a rainy Saturday morning. Everyone is gone and the house is quiet.* Let your simple description of the present moment lead to something else, let the letter drift gently along.

The toughest letter to crank out is one that is meant to impress, as we all know from writing job applications; if it's hard work to slip off a letter to a friend, maybe you're trying too hard to be terrific. A letter is only a report to someone who already likes you for reasons other than your brilliance. Take it easy.

Don't worry about form. It's not a term paper. When you come to the end of one episode, just start a new paragraph. You can go from a few lines about the sad state of pro football to the fight with your mother to your fond memories of Mexico to your cat's urinary-tract infection to a few thoughts on personal indebtedness and on to the kitchen sink and what's in it. The more you write, the easier it gets, and when you have a True True Friend to write to, a *compadre,* a soul sibling, then it's like driving a car down a country road, you just get behind the keyboard and press on the gas.

Don't tear up the page and start over when you write a bad line – try to write your way out of it. Make mistakes and plunge on. Let the letter cook along and let yourself be bold. Outrage, confusion, love – whatever is in your mind, let it find a way to the page. Writing is a means of discovery, always, and when you come to the end and write *Yours ever* or *Hugs and kisses,* you'll know something you didn't when you wrote *Dear Pal.*

Probably your friend will put your letter away, and it'll be read again a few years from now – and it will improve with age. And forty years from now, your friend's grandkids will dig it out of the attic and read it, a sweet and precious relic of the ancient eighties that gives them a sudden clear glimpse of you and her and the world we old-timers knew. You will then have created an object of art. Your simple lines about where you went, who you saw, what they said, will speak to those children and they will feel in their hearts the humanity of our times.

You can't pick up a phone and call the future and tell them about our times. You have to pick up a piece of paper.

Garrison Keillor
We Are Still Married, 1989

A Last Letter

You shall receave, deare wief, my last words in these my last lynes. My love I send you, that you may keepe it when I am dead; and my councell, that you may remember it when I am noe more. I would not, with my last Will, present you with sorrowes, deare Besse. Lett them goe to the grave with me, and be buried in the dust. And, seeing it is not the will of God that ever I shall see you in this lief, beare my destruccion gentlie and with a hart like yourself.

First I send you all the thanks my hart cann conceive, or my penn expresse, for your many troubles and cares taken for me, which – though they have not taken effect as you wished – yet my debt is to you never the lesse; but pay it I never shall in this world.

Secondlie, I beseich you, for the love you bare me living, that you doe not hide yourself many dayes, but by your travell seeke to helpe your miserable fortunes, and the right of your poore childe. Your mourning cannot avayle me that am but dust.

You shall understand that my lands were conveyed to my child, bona fide. The wrightings were drawn at Midsummer was twelvemonethes, as divers can wittnesse. My honest cosen Brett can testifie so much, and Dalberie, too, cann remember somewhat therein. And I trust my bloud will quench their malice that desire my slaughter; and that they will not alsoe seeke to kill you and yours with extreame poverty. To what frind to direct thee I knowe not, for all mine have left mee in the true tyme of triall: and I plainly perceive that my death was determyned from the first day. Most sorry I am (as God knoweth) that, being thus surprised with death, I can leave you noe better estate. I meant you all myne office of wynes, or that I could purchase by selling it; half my stuffe, the jewells, but some few, for my boy. But God hath prevented all my determinations; the great God that worketh all in all. If you can live free from want, care for no more; for the rest is but vanity. Love God, and beginne betymes to repose yourself on Him; therein shall you find true and lastinge ritches, and endles comfort. For the rest, when you have travelled and wearied your thoughts on all sorts of worldly cogitations, you shall sit downe by Sorrow in the end. Teach your sonne alsoe to serve and feare God, while he is young;

that the feare of God may grow upp in him. Then will God be a husband unto you, and a father unto him; a husband and a father which can never be taken from you.

Bayly oweth me two hundred pounds and Adrion six hundred pounds. In Gersey, alsoe, I have much owinge me. The arrearages of the wynes will pay my debts. And, howsoever, for my soul's healthe, I beseech you pay all poore men. When I am gonne, no doubt you shalbe sought unto by many, for the world thinks that I was very ritch; but take heed of the pretences of men and of their affections; for they laste but in honest and worthy men. And no greater misery cann befall you in this life then to become a pray, and after to be despised. I speak it (God knowes) not to disswad you from marriage – for that willbe best for you – both in respect of God and the world. As for me, I am no more your's, nor you myne. Death hath cutt us asunder; and God hath devided me from the world, and you from me.

Remember your poore childe for his father's sake, that comforted you and loved you in his happiest tymes.

Gett those letters (if it bee possible) which I writt to the Lords, wherein I sued for my lief, but God knoweth that itt was for you and yours that I desired it, but itt is true that I disdaine myself for begging itt. And know itt (deare wief) that your sonne is the childe of a true man, and who, in his own respect, despiseth Death, and all his misshapen and ouglie formes.

I cannot wright much. God knowes howe hardlie I stole this tyme, when all sleep; and it is tyme to separate my thoughts from the world. Begg my dead body, which living was denyed you; and either lay itt att Sherborne if the land continue, or in Exiter church, by my father and mother. I can wright noe more. Tyme and Death call me awaye.

The everlasting, infinite powerfull, and inscrutable God, that Almightie God that is goodnes itself, mercy itself, the true lief and light, keep and yours, and have mercy on me, and teach me to forgeve my persecutors and false accusers; and send us to meete in His glorious kingdome. My true wief, farewell. Blesse my poore boye; pray for me. My true God hold you both in His armes.

Written with the dyeing hand of sometyme thy husband, but now (alasse!) overthrowne.

Your's that was; but nowe not my owne,

W. Ralegh

Sir Walter Ralegh,
December 1603

A Love Letter

Broadway Central Hotel,
New York
Saturday, 31st May
6–7p.m.

We got into dock at 8.30 this morning, and then there was a lot of loitering about the luggage: and finally I got here. And it's a beastly hotel: and I'm in a beastly room over a cobbled street where there's the Hell of a noise; and I've been tramping this damned city all day, and riding in its cars (when they weren't too full) and it's hot; and I'm very tired and cross; and my pyjamas haven't come; and my letters of introduction, which I left behind *en masse*, haven't come; and nothing's come; and I don't know a soul in New York; and I'm *very* tired; and I don't like the food; and I don't like the people's faces; and I don't like the newspapers; and I haven't a friend in the world; and nobody loves me; and I'm going to be extraordinarily miserable these six months; and I want to die.

There!

Oh, it's Saturday evening, and if I were in England I might be lying on the sofa in Kensington, or on the floor in Gray's Inn, and my head in your lap, and your face bent down over mine, and your hands about my head, and my eyes shut, and I only feeling your hands going to and fro in my hair and your kind lips wandering over my face. And I'm here in a dirty room and lonely and tired and ill, and this won't get to you for ten days.

I'm crying. I want you. I don't want to be alone.

Rupert

Rupert Brooke
To Cathleen Nesbitt, actress, 31 May 1913

A Sister to a Brother

I trust my dearest Love, that this is the last letter we shall have to send to you further than Kendal, for at Kendal we will meet you with one – God be thanked we are all well. Mary looks better today, and seems pretty strong and dear Sara for these two days has had no tickling cough and is in other respects without cause of complaint. But we have been, and the whole vale – since Monday afternoon in the greatest consternation. If you did not leave before Saturday you must have heard the cause of it from Coleridge for I have recounted to him the melancholy history. George Green and his wife, our Sally's Father and Mother, went to Langdale on Saturday to a Sale, the morning was very cold and about noon it began to snow, though not heavily but enough to cover the ground. They left Langdale between 5 and 6 o'clock in the evening and made their way right up the Fells, intending to drop down just above their own cottage, in Easedale – (Blenkrigg Gill under Miles Holmes's Intack). They came to the highest ridge of the hill that can be seen from Langdale in good time, for they were seen there by some people in Langdale: but alas! they never reached home. They were probably bewildered by a mist before daylight was gone, and may have either fallen down a precipice or perished with cold – six children had been left in the house, all younger than Sally, and the youngest an infant at the breast. Poor things they sate up till 11 o'clock on Saturday night, expecting their parents, and then went to bed, satisfied that they had stopped all night in Langdale on account of the bad weather; the next day they felt no alarm; but stayed in the house quietly and saw none of the neighbours, therefore it was not known that their Father and Mother had not come back till Monday noon, when that pretty little Girl, the eldest of the household (whom you will remember, having admired the exquisite simplicity and beauty of her Figure one day when you were walking with Mary in Easedale) – this Girl went to George Rowlandson's to borrow a cloak. They asked why, and she told them she was going to lait their folk who were not come home. George Rowlandson immediately concluded that they were lost and many men went out to search upon the Fells. Yesterday between 50 and 60 were out, and to-day almost as many, but all in vain. It is very unfortunate that there should be so much snow on the Fells. Mary and I have been up at the house this morning, two of the elder daughters are come home, and all wait with trembling and fear, yet with most earnest wishes, the time when the poor creatures may be brought home and carried to their graves. It is a heart – rending sight – so many little, *little* creatures. The Infant was sleeping in the cradle, a delicate creature the image of Sara Coleridge. Poor Sally is in great distress. We have told her that we will keep her till we can find a nice place for her, and in the mean time instruct her in reading, sewing etc. We hope she will continue to be a good girl.

We do not intend her to have anything to do with the children after our new servant comes. We have hired little Mary, the young woman who lived at Mrs Havill's and who has been so long desirous to come to us. This very moment three, nay four of the poor orphans (for Sally was with them) have left the room, The three had been at Mrs North's who has sent them home with a basket of provisions, and will visit them herself with clothes for all the younger, being very ragged. That sweet Girl looks so interesting, has such an intelligent, yet so innocent a countenance that she would win any heart. She is a far nicer Girl than Sally and one that we could not but have more pleasure from; but poor Sally has fallen to us, and we cannot cast her off for her Sister; but we hope that Mrs North will take *her,* or a least send her to school.

Old Molly's legs are much swoln and she grows daily weaker. I hope her sufferings will soon be at an end. She talks with chearfulness of dying except when she turns to poor John's desolate condition. I really think I have nothing more to say for I have not heart to talk of our own little concerns, all being well with us. We have been strangely unsettled for these three days. Pray bring Sally a new Testament – you can buy it at Kendal. The children are at School. I hope you will think Thomas looks better than when you went away – he is very healthy.

Remember me affectionately to Mr De Quincey and tell him that we hope to hear that he intends coming into the North this summer. We had a letter from Coleridge on Monday, written just after you set off for Dunmow. We were much disappointed that there was no letter from you. We hope for one from Dunmow tonight.

God bless thee my dearest William and grant that we may see thee again in good health and soon – thine evermore.

Dorothy Wordsworth

I open my letter to tell you that we are at ease – the poor lost creatures are found. John Fisher has called at the window to tell us – he says they had rolled a great way – and were found just above Benson's, Where that is I cannot tell; but it must have been low down. She was near a wall – and he lying a little above her.

Dorothy Wordsworth
To William Wordsworth
Grasmere, Wednesday March 23 1808

Mira's Letters Home

18 October 1960

Respected Ma,

I realize I let two weeks pass before writing you. Hope you are not too worried. I sent a post-card to baba *[Mira's father]* from London which you must have received. It took me a while to get settled. I already started my classes and I am finding out that life here is going to be quite busy. Imagine my spending all my day and even evenings doing either studies or housework. I shop twice a week, but I may have to do it only once. Fortunately the fridge is big enough. Yes, three of us girls share an apartment, and so far I like my house-mates. They are both American and around my age ... The university campus is just beautiful. I enjoy walking everyday from building to building and hear students chat or birds make funny noises. People here are very friendly and open. They even smile before they know you! I have already been invited by two students (both girls) and I enjoyed meeting their parents. But, ma, food here is really tasteless. I miss your cooking and grandma's mango pickle and Choto mashi's special spinach. Oh, well, I guess I shall get used to it all. I cook for myself only over the week-ends. There is hardly any time during the week ... Classes have been very interesting so far and I am getting used to the American system bit by bit. I like the way the professors treat the students ... There is so much I could tell you but I must make it brief and perhaps, write another letter next week. Please do not worry about me. I am taking care of myself and I feel very well. The cool air of autumn seems to suit me well, after the heat in Calcutta. Please show this to baba and tell him that I would write him separately telling him all about my courses and the professors, etc., later ... Please, please do not worry if my letters take a while to arrive. Remember, I am a big girl now and if I could travel around half of the world to be here I can also take care of myself.

How is your health, and baba's? Please give my respect to grandma, mashimas and pishimas. How is Uma? I think of you all and wonder how you all are. Ma, the life here is so different that sometimes I have to talk to myself in Bengali to think about Calcutta and you all. I miss you a lot. But, time seems to fly very quickly here. With respect and love,

Yours,
Miru

10 December 1960

My affectionate Miru,

You must have received all my letters by now. We have had only three letters from you in the last month and a half. I know you are busy, but I worry if I do not hear from you. Have you received the parcel I sent by sea-mail? I put some pickles and other 'goodies' together and requested your uncle next door to mail it for me. I did not want to let your baba know about this. You know how much fuss he makes over food parcels. He always gives me big lectures that food in America is a thousand times better and more nutritious. As if that is enough! ... Uma's wedding date is now firmed up and it would be some time in February. Please plan to be here and do not tell your father that I suggested it. Everyone would be very upset if you miss this first wedding of the family. The future groom seems like a good boy and Uma and he met a couple of times when the two families went to the movies together. I think she liked him ... Your Ghosh mashima asked me the other day if I was expecting an American son-in-law. Imagine her guts! I retorted, 'Of course not. Our Miru is as she was before and she would not do such a thing. She went to America to study, not to catch a husband.' ... Have you made some friends? How do you spend your week-ends and evenings? Surely, you do not study all the time.

I have to end this letter and get back to the invitation lists. Mejo mashi and I have been digging out all the names of relatives to make a good list and not to leave out anyone. Most of our shoppings is complete except the jewelry. We do not want to pick them up until just before the wedding. It's not safe. Oh, Mira, you should have seen the diamond and ruby necklace! It is just beautiful! Write soon and remember the wedding date.

Your mother

This is the letter which Mira wished she could write to her mother in reply:

My dear ma,

With every letter from you I have an increasing feeling of a distance between us. I cannot explain it even to myself. On the one hand, I know why you are worried about my health, about my life and about my safety. Yet, I thought I had gone ten thousand miles to get away from this protective love which makes me feel suffocated sometimes. It breaks my heart to tell you this and I can never bring myself to say so. What a strange dilemma! I read between the lines of your letters and sometimes I feel like screaming with frustration and anger. What are you fantasizing about my life here? In case I fall in love with an American or whoever, be sure I will do what I wish to do. If you think that you can dictate my life from such a distance, you are under some illusions. But, you know that it's not so easy for me to act the way I would like to. I do not know why. Even when some young men ask me out, your face and the rest (aunts, neighbours, all) appear in front of my eyes. What is this inner restriction? I cannot talk about it to anyone here and I cannot talk about it, least of all, with you. It's not just being free to mix with American men, in different things I feel a tug from behind. I wish I had some power to tear away from this tug and pull ... I also wish I could do everything a good daughter is supposed to do, the way you brought me up. Believe me, it would be so very satisfying to be your good daughter who does not tarnish the name of the family or the wish of her parents, especially her mother. While I am in this interminable conflict, I seem to have no choice but to remain in this tension and confusion. I shall continue to try to please you as much as I can until some part of me gives way. I like my life here and yet I miss India, the family and most of all *you* so intensely sometimes. Sometimes, I feel I am walking in my sleep and this is a big dream after all. Is it really possible for me to close my eyes and finish my studies and be back exactly the way I came and everything would be just fine for ever. Oh, God, I wish I had some idea how to deal with these problems ... I must sleep; there is a 8.30 class tomorrow. I am so tired.

Your loving and confused daughter

This is the letter Mira really wrote:

January 1961

Respected Ma,

It was nice to hear from you and get all the news. I am happy to know that Uma's wedding date is firmed. February is a difficult month for me. The classes would be in full session and it would be a loss of nearly three to four weeks of my work here. This break will really be hard for me and I am not so sure I really want to be there only for a wedding between two people who do not even know each other well. No, don't worry. I am not talking about my choosing my own husband or anything like that. But, it seems strange to me when I tell my American friends the way marriages take place in our families. I seem to feel a bit embarrassed about it all. Perhaps, I am not making myself very clear. There are things I feel more and more strange about our customs and it's no point telling you all this. I know you will begin to see mountains out of mole hills. Perhaps, baba and I could talk about these things a bit better. At any rate, I shall try.

Thanks so much for sending the food parcel. No, I won't tell baba a word. I am waiting eagerly for it. The pickles! Even the idea makes my mouth water! By the way, please tell Ghosh mashima that Miru has not changed that much yet. And, suppose I do marry an American, is it really the end of the world, ma? I thought you liked fair-skinned tall men! (Well, I am joking.) Is Uma really happy about this match? I guess I should not say things like this at this point. Forgive me. This letter has been a bit confused and please don't read between lines now. I must stop and shall write a longer one perhaps, this week-end. I must rush. *Pranam* to you and baba and greetings to all.

Your Miru

A week later:

January 1961

Ma,

This is a quick note to tell you that I am making plans to come in February. If I can finish some of my term-ending papers beforehand I may be able to come without feeling too guilty. It would be wonderful to see you all again. It would be good for me to be back in the family and taste all the good cookings of a wedding. Do you think I should bring a separate gift for Uma from here? Something she might like? Do ask her and let me know. I am terribly busy, but well. I take a glass of milk every night and feel wonderful every morning! The parcel is not here yet. How are you and baba? I wrote him a long letter giving all the details of our university and life here. Has he received it yet? Please take care of yourself and don't go out everyday on errands. How is everyone? My *pranam* and love,

Miru

A year later:

4 January 1962

My respected ma and baba,

I am writing this very important letter to ask your permission to marry John – John Cohn whom I met nearly 6 months ago. John is two years senior to me and already has a part-position in his department which is biology. He comes from a good family; his father is a professor of biochemistry and he has one sister who is in music school. I met his family over the last Christmas and we got along very well. John is very interested in India and would like to come and visit you all as soon as the summer vacation begins. But I would like to come as his wife. It would be easier. We talked and discussed the matter over many hours, and this seems like the best way to do it. Please send your blessings. We would have a civil marriage and, perhaps, a Hindu one when we come, if you so wish. I know how disappointed ma would be otherwise ... Please ma, try to understand that time has changed and perhaps, I have changed too. I love John and it is important that I marry him and it would be easier and more convenient for both of us to continue our studies when we are married. It's also less expensive to share the same living space ...I am sorry that I had to break the news like this. I did not know how to do it any other way. Both of you gave me enough independence to allow me to think for myself for my life and this is a very important decision for me to make. Ma, I realize this is going to shock you. But, as I said, you do try to understand and I know that neither you nor baba would stand in the way of my happiness. Please write soon and let me know if you want to know anything more about John ... We do not plan to get married until April or May just before the summer holidays.

Please accept my *pranam* and love.

Yours,
Miru

This was the reply from her mother after a week:

Mira,

Both your father and I are astounded by your letter. So Ghosh mashima was not so wrong after all! How can you do such a thing to us? We suggest that you come home as soon as you can and we will discuss the matter face to face. Your baba is sending you enough money for your trip. If marriage is what is in your mind, I don't see any point of your remaining in America. We could arrange a marriage for you here in no time. It's pity that all the effort and expenses for your trip abroad came to this. At any rate, I always told your baba that a woman's higher education comes to little. But, who listens to me? Now, he could learn some lessons. Please drop a line as soon as you get the money and get your air-ticket.

Affectionately yours,

ma

My respected parents,

John and I got married last week-end and used the money you sent me for a small reception we gave. I felt good that something arrived from my family for this important occasion of my life. I have to get married without your verbal blessings, but I considered the token money as your blessings. We still hope to visit you in summer and I would like to know if you so wish. My address will change from next week and I give it below. Hope your health is good and everyone in the house is fine.

With *pranam,*

Miru

This is the letter which Mira wished she had written:

Dear baba and ma,

I am even more astounded by your lack of understanding. I know you have feelings and hopes for me. How can you not be flexible enough to realize that I am not in your generation? You show no sympathy for my inner struggle before I decided to take this step. Perhaps, in your time it was not important to love a man or woman to marry. You loved later and loved slowly (or did not love, perhaps). I am in America, not India, and I am influenced by the atmosphere here. I take the responsibility of my marriage. If I make a mistake (I know it is always possible), at least *I* make it, not you. Marriage now-a-days does not have to be for ever. I love John and I am happy with him. If I have occasional doubts, these are my own. The security I lost when I made the step to come here is not going to offer me the security you had to protect your marriage. There are many others around you. I am alone here, so is John and many others. Unfortunately this is true and this situation makes us bold and perhaps, even, daring. I don't believe I could ever make you see this. Sometimes, I feel as if I am split in the middle. Please let me live the other half, at least now. My life and learning here go well with this step. I know many other Indian girls would not do this. Their love and concern for their parents and families would be paramount and they will sacrifice their desire to live a new life, to experiment perhaps. Even if it turns out to be nothing but only an experiment, let me go through it myself. I am a big girl now ... Oh, God, I wish I could be freer to be happy right now. Yet the same nagging tag continues. May be, I should stay here for ever to erase this nagging pull from behind. Perhaps, John can help me do so. But he is so eager to go to India. I suppose I am alone after all, in this. Please try to understand the struggle within me and be with me. I need you for myself.

Love,

Your daughter

Twenty years later Mira's own daughter wrote to Mira:

June 1981

Dear Mummy,

This last trip to India with you has brought home to me a few hard facts – facts that I wanted to avoid seeing for some time. As you well know, you and I have had a few arguments and several days of tensions during the trip. As I approach my seventeenth year I suddenly ask myself where do I belong. I know this is the usual teen-age identity crisis, etc., etc. You came to this country when you were slightly older than I am now and married my father and admired the American lifestyle and tried to be an American as much as you could. I am born of you who is Indian and my father who is American. Of course, I am American. Except for a few trips to India I have little to do with India outwardly. But, I feel how much you would like me to become Indian sometimes. I cannot explain it with examples. But I feel it in my bones. The India that you never quite shook off your system comes back to you now and you want to see your daughter live it, at least partly.

Yes, mummy I know I am wrapped up in many superficial things, things my friends and peers indulge in and I can understand your need to protect me. But, I am part of them and in order for me to be accepted by my friends sometimes I do things which do not always please me either. I need their approval and I want to be like them sometimes. But, your good intentions to teach me those good Indian things then clash. Although I dislike the superficiality of my friends, I cannot move back to your life-style just because it is better (for you) or more ancient or deep. Let me live the life I am surrounded by and reject and suffer as I wish and as many of my friends are going through ... While I understand your point, I must admit sometimes I really do not know how to communicate to you what I really feel. Words seem to fail on both sides.

That's why I am writing this letter. Perhaps it will be a bit easier. Dad does not seem to be the problem in this regard. When I argue with him or reject something he wants me to do, I do not feel such ambivalence as I do when the same thing happens with you. Isn't it strange! Perhaps, I am a bit Indian under my skin after all. Although every time I visit India after the first two weeks of love and food, I begin to weary of all the slow sloth and all the rest. I ache to come back to my superficial friends with whom I do not always need to use even language. It's the communication that I feel is at stake between you and me and between India and me. Mummy, you did not have to grow up in America; you grew up in India and could keep a lot of nostalgia and good memories when you decided to reject India. When you criticize me, you never think that we were born in two different worlds and that makes a big difference between us even though I am your flesh and blood as you often point out, rightly.

My dearest mother, I cannot be protected by you. Forgive me if I remind you of something you related to me many times. You could not be protected by my grandparents (your parents) when you decided to embrace this culture along with my father. Nor can you protect me despite the fact that we are not separated by physical distance. Perhaps, we are separated by something else and I suspect, that is India.

I have never written a letter like this before in my short life. I feel good about writing this and I would like to hear what you have to say. Ma, perhaps, you and I still can be friends in this way that you and your mother could not be. Let's try. I love you.

Yours,

Rita

from *Between Ourselves, Letters between Mothers and Daughters*, 1994

Prison Policy: Letters to a Newspaper

From Mr Michael Howard, MP

Sir: The most interesting thing about Polly Toynbee's long article about crime and punishment ('Listen, minister; prison doesn't work', 31 May) is that she made no mention of victims. The success of prison as a punishment cannot be measured solely by how it compares with community sentences in terms of reconviction rates of offenders.

But the latest figures suggest that recidivism for those who are subject to a community sentence (55 per cent) is actually marginally higher than for those sentenced to imprisonment (54 per cent). It must also be remembered that it is the more serious offenders who are sentenced to prison.

Research suggests that a burglar in prison for 12 months rather than serving a community sentence may be prevented from committing between three and 13 other offences.

Police officers all over the country tell me that a disproportionately large number of offences are committed by a few persistent offenders. When these offenders are not at liberty, the crime rate in their areas tends to drop, sometimes dramatically. If the courts decide that such criminals should be deprived of their liberty, their victims, actual and potential, are likely to rejoice. And it may not be entirely fortuitous that the recent increase in the number of criminals imprisoned has coincided with the biggest fall in recorded crime in 40 years.

Yours faithfully,

MICHAEL HOWARD
Home Secretary
Home Office
London, SW1
1 June, 1995

From Mr Peter Coad

Sir: Contrary to Polly Toynbee's claim, Home Office Research Finding No 12 states, 'There was no firm evidence that community penalties out-performed custody or vice versa in preventing re-offending'. In fact, probation orders with a probation centre requirement have a reconviction rate 12 per cent higher than offenders discharged from prison.

It is naive of Ms Toynbee to make the simplistic comparison of the cost of keeping an offender in prison at £1,900 a month and a probation order at £105. Reconviction rates of those on probation are as high as 62 per cent; with very low detection rates, the re-offending rate will be much higher. Crime costs the UK over £20bn a year. Two teenage criminals were estimated to have cost the taxpayer £1m during the course of a year. For persistent offenders, the cost of imprisonment is a bargain.

During the 1980s, the prison population fell, but at the same time the crime rate rocketed. The recent increase in the use of custodial sentences has resulted in a fall in the crime rate. Draconian sentencing policies have stabilised property crime for a decade in the United States.

A British version of 'three strikes and you're out' should be seriously considered. The cost of crime in emotional, physical and material terms is incalculable. The protection of society must take precedence over the welfare of offenders, particularly persistent ones.

Yours faithfully,

PETER COAD
Bristol, 1 June, 1995

From Mr Stephen Shaw

Sir: Polly Toynbee raises the issue of whether it was lawful for the Home Secretary to withdraw home leave from prisoners.

Until the new criteria were introduced, a large number of prisoners up and down the country enjoyed home leave and temporary release as part of a 'compact' between them and the prison authorities. It is arguable that, under such arrangements, home leave constituted a prisoner's legitimate expectation, the unilateral withdrawal of which could be struck out by the courts. I understand that legal challenges on these grounds are now being prepared on behalf of several prisoners who have been adversely affected.

When the cutbacks were announced, the Home Secretary predicted that the effect would be to reduce home leave and temporary release by 40 per cent. Reports that have reached the Prison Reform Trust suggest that the actual reduction has been far greater.

Yours faithfully,

STEPHEN SHAW
Director, Prison Reform Trust, London, EC1, 2 June, 1995

The Independent, 3rd June 1995

Letters Activities

How to Write a Letter

1. The title
• Talk about the title. What does it lead you to expect from the piece?

2. Advice on letter writing
• In pairs, write your own list of advice to letter writers, then compare your list with that of another pair.
• Now read Garrison Keillor's piece.

3. Keillor's advice
• Go through the text carefully, finding at least two different things that Keillor says under each of these headings:

Why letters need to be written
Why letters are better than telephones or conversations
Getting ready to write
Getting going
What to do once you're writing

4. Writing a letter of your own
• Follow Keillor's instructions yourself, as far as you can. Choose someone who you would like to write to and work through his strategies for writing a good letter.

A Last Letter

1. Looking for clues about the context
• Read the letter aloud or listen to it being read to you.
• In small groups, ask yourselves these questions, to see how much you can discover about the context of this letter, just by reading closely and finding clues in the text.

Who?
What?
When?
Why?

• Share your findings as a whole group, then listen to the brief account of the story behind the letter, which appears on Page 239.

2. The letter arrives
• In pairs, role-play the scene when Elizabeth and her son receive the letter. The person role-playing Elizabeth reads the letter aloud. The son interrupts with thoughts and feelings, to which Elizabeth responds.

e.g. **Elizabeth:** Sit down beside me and I'll read you the letter that your father has just written to us. I hope it's good news.
Son: When can I see him again, mother? We haven't been allowed to visit him for so long.
Elizabeth: Perhaps his letter will tell us when he's likely to be released. He says, 'You shall receave, dear wief, my....' Oh my God, no!'
etc.

3. Charting the writer's concerns
This letter is a man's last testimony, written in dangerous times, and wanting to express the last things he will ever be able to say to his wife. Perhaps it is also his last statement, for himself, about feelings and ideas he holds dear.
• Make a chart for yourself like the one below. Find examples from the letter of the writer showing each of the concerns listed.

Practical arrangements	Feelings about his death	Feelings about his family	Concern about his family's future	Feelings about God	Thoughts about his enemies

• What thoughts do you have about what concerns him most? Are you surprised by the emphasis he gives to any of them? What do his concerns tell you about life for a man like him in those times?

4. Charting the emotional temperature of the letter
• Give each of the paragraphs a number. For each paragraph, choose which of these descriptions seems to best match the emotional state of the writer:

Matter of fact
Full of grief
Cracking up
Concerned
Afraid
Angry
Regretful
Calm
Purposeful
Self-pitying
Confessional

5. Who's the letter for?

You could say that the letter was written to Ralegh's wife Elizabeth. But you could also make a case for saying that it was written for Ralegh himself, that it was written to God, or even that it was written to be seen by his jailors and those close to the King, to make them more sympathetic to him.

● Go back to the letter, looking for evidence of the different possible audiences for the letter. Decide which you think is most important, then share your conclusions with another group, or with the class as a whole.

6. Letters, responses and replies

● Write one of these letters, responses or replies to Sir Walter Ralegh's letter:

Elizabeth (or her son) writes a letter to the King, begging for a reprieve for Ralegh.

The jailor reads the letter before passing it on to Elizabeth. He writes a report for the King on the state of mind of the prisoner.

The King, having seen the letter, discusses with a trusted companion what he should do about Ralegh.

On 11 December, after his reprieve, Ralegh writes another letter to Elizabeth and his son.

The story of Sir Walter Ralegh

Ralegh lived from 1554-1618. He was a poet, historian, colonist, soldier and courtier. He became the favourite of Queen Elizabeth I and was rewarded with estates in Ireland and England, positions of power and importance and a knighthood. He secretly married Elizabeth Throckmorton, one of the Queen's attendants. When the marriage became public in 1592 because of the birth of their son, Ralegh was briefly imprisoned in the Tower of London. In 1595 he led an expedition up the Orinoco and in 1596 took part in a raid on Cadiz with the Earl of Essex. As the Queen's favourite Ralegh had not been popular and he gained many enemies who accused him of pride and extravagance.

When James I came to the throne in 1603, Ralegh fell out of favour and was arrested on suspicion of plotting to dethrone the king. He was sentenced to be executed on 11 December. He was reprieved on 10 December, after having written this letter of farewell to his wife. He lived imprisoned in the Tower with his wife until 1616 when he was released to undertake an expedition to the Orinoco in search of gold. The expedition failed and on his return he was arrested again and finally executed in 1618.

A Love Letter

1. A close look at language
This letter is a short text but it has a very strong and distinctive style.
- Read the text out loud.
- What do you notice about the grammar of the sentences in the first paragraph? What effect does this have on you as a reader?
- Mark on the text any moments when the mood changes or there is a change of gear. Look closely at these moments to see how the writer makes a shift in tone of voice.

How does he use sentence structure differently?
How does he address the reader differently?
How does he create different kinds of images?
How does he use contrast?

2. A telephone call
- Imagine Rupert Brooke telephoning Cathleen Nesbitt from New York. Write a script of the conversation between them, drawing on what you know about Brooke's feelings and tone from reading his letter.

3. A reply
- Write Cathleen's reply to Rupert. Decide for yourself what her feelings might be for him and how she might react to his letter. She might respond by replying in a similar tone and and style, or alternatively, you could indicate her different personality and approach to life by giving her a different kind of voice.

A Sister to a Brother

1. Reading it aloud
- Working in pairs, first read the letter aloud to each other, sharing the reading.
- Now read it aloud again, choosing a tone of voice from the list below:

Sad but able to cope
Full of grief and uncertainty about what to do for the best
Matter of fact, given that, living in the early nineteenth century, death is something that occurs quite frequently
Perfectly cheerful

Which tone seemed to you to suit the text best?

2. Faxes and phonecalls
Dorothy Wordsworth was writing at a time when there were no telephones or fax machines. How differently might she have communicated her thoughts, feelings and news if this modern technology had been available to her?

- Write a fax from Dorothy to William. Decide what kinds of things might be left out. For instance, would she give her feelings? Would she describe things in as much detail? Would any bits of news or information be more important than others? Would the style be any different?
- Role-play a telephone conversation between Dorothy and William, in which Dorothy conveys her news and William responds. If possible tape record it so that you can listen back to it.
- Listen back to your tape, then look at the text again. Look at what kinds of things were left out of your telephone conversation. (e.g. was it feelings, or descriptions, or details of the main events?) What difference did it make to have someone responding?

3. Telling a story

Dorothy Wordsworth's letter tells the story of what has happened to the parents of her servant girl, Sally.

- Look closely at the telling of the story. It is told not as a story to excite or entertain the reader but rather as a series of events that the reader (William) will want to know about, given that he knows all the people involved.
- Try re-writing the story of Sally's family as a ballad, to be handed down to future generations as a tragic tale.

4. The social historian's view

Letters are a very good source of information about the past and are often used by historians researching a particular period or event. Letters can give insights into people's lives, their housing, work, standard of living, health and social relationships. Social historians are particularly interested in how society was organised and the details of life for ordinary people.

- If a social historian were reading Dorothy Wordsworth's letter, what would there be to interest him/her? Look through the letter and pick out any phrases which give you information or ideas about any of these areas of life:

Health and life expectancy
The poor and what support was provided for them
Media and communications
Work and employment rights
Childhood
Life in the countryside
Transport
Religion
Sense of community
Gender roles
Families and family life

Mira's Letters Home

1. Mira's first letter
- Read Mira's letter written on 18 October 1960, then try writing the first paragraph of Ma's reply to her. Now read Ma's actual reply.

2. What Mira wanted to say
- Read what Mira would have liked to write to her mother, in response to her letter of 10 December 1960.
- Imagine what Mira wrote to her mother, then read Mira's actual reply.

3. Changing attitudes
- Read Mira's next letter written in January 1961.
- Mira wrote again on 4th January 1962. Predict what kinds of things she might say to her parents in this letter.

4. Conflict of identity
- Read all of the other letters, except the last one.
- Look closely at the letter Mira wished she had written. Talk about the conflicts experienced by Mira. Is she entirely happy? What does she feel about India, America and her parents?

5. Mira's daughter
Mira and her American husband stay in America and have a daughter. At seventeen. she writes a letter to her mother. Talk about what Mira's daughter might write to her.
- Now read Mira's daughter's letter.

6. Ma and Babu
- Choose one of Mira's letters. Role-play the conversation between Ma and Babu, as they receive the letter.

7. Other voices
- Choose one of the people mentioned in the letters whose voice is not heard e.g. Babu, John Cohn or Uma. Write a letter from that person to Mira, or the letter they would like to send to her.

8. A story told in letters
Mira's letters and her parents' replies tell the story of a girl's journey to a new country, the clash of cultures she experiences, her marriage and relationship with her daughter. It is not fiction. These are actual letters written by real people.
In fiction, writers sometimes use the letter form to tell stories. Alice Walker's novel *The Color Purple*, for instance, is written entirely in letters.
- Try writing a story of your own, in which the characters, plot and issues are entirely revealed through letters. The titles below give some suggestions for the kinds of storylines or subject matter that might lend themselves to being told in letters.

The Old Man's Will	The Evacuee
The Prisoner	The Holiday Romance

Prison Policy: Letters to a Newspaper

1. What the article might have said
● Read the three letters that were published by *The Independent* newspaper as readers' responses to an article written by Polly Toynbee, called 'Listen, minister; prison doesn't work'.
● Note down any words or phrases you don't understand. Talk about them as a whole class, using dictionaries, your teacher and each other to sort out difficulties.
● From reading the letters carefully, can you work out what Polly Toynbee's article must have been arguing? Make a list of all the things you can tell about the article from reading the responses.

2. Telegrams
● Work in small groups, with each group just concentrating on one of the three letters.
Try to summarise the main points the writer is trying to make, in telegram form.

3. The language of letters to the newspaper
● Work with someone else. Look at each of these rather difficult phrases drawn from the letters. Try to re-phrase them in simpler language. Really struggle to make sense of the language, which has been used in rather special ways. The first one has been done for you.

A.
> 'It is arguable that, under such arrangements, home leave constituted a prisoner's legitimate expectation, the unilateral withdrawal of which could be struck out by the courts.'

One could argue that before, prisoners felt that they had a right to home leave and if they weren't given it they could go to court to get it back again.

B.
> 'Draconian sentencing policies have stabilised property crime for a decade in the United States.'

C.
> 'Contrary to Polly Toynbee's claim, Home Office Reasearch Finding No 12 states, 'There was no firm evidence that community penalties out-performed custody or vice versa in preventing re-offending.'

D.
> 'The success of prison as a punishment cannot be measured solely by how it compares with community sentences in terms of reconviction rates by offenders.'

E.

> ❛The protection of society must take precedence over the welfare of offenders, particularly persistent ones.❜

● Try to find something to say about each of them, using the headings on the chart below.

Phrase	Sentences	Vocabulary	Use of Evidence	Connecting Words	Tone
A.					

4. Same issue, different context

● Try re-presenting some of the arguments in these letters, in a different context. Adapt your language to fit the new context but feel free to use any of the arguments presented in the letters. Choose one idea from this list:

A phone-call to a radio phone-in programme on Capital FM
A conversation between two first-time offenders in a prison for young offenders
A letter to a tabloid newspaper, like *The Daily Mirror* or *The Sun*.
A press release produced by The Prison Reform Trust.
A Breakfast TV show invites two experts from each side of the argument to present their case during an item called 'Are our prisons a waste of money?'

Sources

Klondyke Kate, Liza Cody, *The Independent* , 25th July 1992, reprinted in *Heroes and Villains,* Victor Gollancz, 1994.

Boring, Boring Arsenal, Nick Hornby, from *Fever Pitch,* Victor Gollancz, 1992.

Sole Mate Strides On, Simon Caulkin, *The Guardian.*

Alone Again Naturally, John Pareles, *New York Times,* reprinted in *The Guardian* ,1st November 1994.

Madonna's Diary, Craig Brown, from *Rear Columns, Collected Diaries of the Famous, Private Eye,* 1992.

Dr Johnson's Journey to the Western Isles, Samuel Johnson, from *A Journey to the Western Isles of Scotland,* Oxford University Press, 1970.

Boswell's Journey to the Western Isles, James Boswell, from *The Journal of a Tour to the Hebrides,* Everyman.

Des Moines, Bill Bryson, from *The Lost Continent,* Abacus, 1992.

Tokyo Pastoral, Angela Carter, *New Society,* reprinted in *Nothing Sacred,* Virago, 1992.

On a Train, Paul Theroux, from *The Great Railway Bazaar,* Hamish Hamilton, 1977.

First Train Journey, Paul Theroux, *New World, Granta 29,* Winter, 1989.

The Man With No Name, John Pilger, *Distant Voices,* Vintage, 1992.

Beggars of Britain, Tony Parsons, *Arena,* September/October 1991, reprinted in *Dispatches From the Front Line of Popular Culture,* Virgin, 1994.

An African Feast for Flies and Other Parasites, Germaine Greer, *The Guardian,* 25th July 1994.

A Response to Germaine Greer, David Belton, *The Guardian,* 3rd August 1994.

Media Duty Begins When the Dying Stops, Germaine Greer, *The Guardian,* 8th August 1994.

Rwanda Press Photographs by Jean Marc Boujou and David Guttenfelder, *The Guardian,* April 27th 1995 and *The Sunday Times,* April 23rd 1995.

The Brutal Truth, Phil Redmond, *Brookside, The Magazine, Issue One,* 1994.

No Name Woman, Maxine Hong Kingston, from *The Woman Warrior,* Picador, 1981.

I Know Why the Caged Bird Sings, Maya Angelou, *I Know Why the Caged Bird Sings,* Virago,1993.

Black Boy, Richard Wright, from *Black Boy,* Longman Imprint Books, 1970.

An Evil Cradling, Brian Keenan, from *An Evil Cradling,* Vintage, 1992.

The Eruption of Vesuvius, Pliny the Younger, from *Letters,* translated by Betty Radice, reprinted in *The Faber Book of Reportage,* Ed. John Carey, 1987.

The Street Sellers of 1851, Henry Mayhew, from *Mayhew's Characters,* Henry Mayhew, Ed. Peter Quennel, Spring Books.

Baghdad Under Fire, Marie Colvin, *The Sunday Times,* reprinted as 'I Could See Its Little Fins' in *Despatches from the Gulf War,* Ed. Brian MacArthur, Bloomsbury, 1991.

When the Wolves Stopped Howling, John Edwards, *The Daily Mail,* reprinted in *Despatches from the Gulf War,* Ed. Brian MacArthur, Bloomsbury, 1991.

On the Bottom, Primo Levi, from *If This is A Man,* and *The Truce,* translated by Stuart Woolf, Abacus by Sphere Books, 1987.

Finding the Tollund Man, PV Glob, from *The Bog People,* Faber and Faber Ltd, 1969.

The Tollund Man, Seamus Heaney, *Wintering Out,* Faber and Faber Ltd, 1972.

Tantrums, Penelope Leach, from *Baby and Child,* Penelope Leach, Penguin, 1988.

The Facts About Drugs, Melissa Benn *The Education Guardian,* reprinted in *The Guardian's World of Learning Source Book,* 1992.

The Trial of Craig and Bentley, Transcripts from the trial by the Chief Clerk at the Old Bailey, reprinted in *Trial of Craig and Bentley,* Ed. Montgomery Hyde, William Hodge, 1954.

The Day of Execution, Montgomery Hyde, from *Trial of Craig and Bentley,* ibid.

The People's Charter - A Petition to Parliament 1842, from *A Radical Reader,* Ed. Christopher Hampton, Penguin, 1984.

The Criminal Justice and Public Order Act 1994, Chapter 33, HMSO, 1994.

How to write a Letter, Garrison Keillor, *We Are Still Married,* Garrison Keillor, Faber and Faber, 1989.

A Last Letter, Sir Walter Ralegh, from *The Faber Book of Letters,* Ed. Felix Pryor, Faber and Faber, 1990.

A Love Letter, Rupert Brooke, ibid.

A Sister to a Brother, Dorothy Wordsworth, from *Letters,* Penguin.

Mira's Letters Home, from *Between Ourselves, Letters between Mothers and Daughters,* Ed. Karen Payne, Virago, 1994.

Prison Policy: Letters to a Newspaper, *The Independent,* Saturday 3 June, 1995.